CHRISTIAN ETHICAL PRINCIPLES
and their application to the major issues
are subject of this treatise by one of
best-known contemporary teachers in
field of applied Christianity.

The starting point for any valid Chris-
ethic is the revelation of the nature
will of God that has come to men
through Christ. Recognizing that no hu-
mind can so fully enter into the di-
-human consciousness of Jesus to say
t decision he would make in every
crete case, the author yet shows that
Gospels provide us with an adequate,
endable, and indispensable guide to
christian action.

The first part of the book deals with
biblical foundations of Christian
cs and the latter half with specific
emporary problems—self and society,
riage, economic life, race, the state,
peace, and others—interpreting
n in the light of the gospel.

veryone concerned with the inevi-
e problems of Christian decision will
over in these pages new insight into
biblical foundations of a mature mo-
y and helpful suggestions toward solu-
s of major contemporary problems.

Georgia Harkness

Professor of applied theology at the
Pacific School of Religion, studied at
Cornell University, Harvard, Yale, Union
Theological Seminary, and received the
Ph.D. degree from Boston University.
Before going to her present position, she
taught at Garrett Biblical Institute and
at Elmira and Mount Holyoke colleges.

Dr. Harkness is an ordained Methodist
minister, and she has preached from many
of the most distinguished pulpits and college chapels in the United States. She has
also participated in a number of outstanding lectureships, including the Earl Lectures at the Pacific School of Religion.
She also gave the Rall Lectures at Garrett Biblical Institute.

Following completion of this present
volume, Dr. Harkness left for the International Christian University in Japan to
serve as visiting professor of Christianity
for one year.

CHRISTIAN ETHICS

GEORGIA HARKNESS

CHRISTIAN
ETHICS

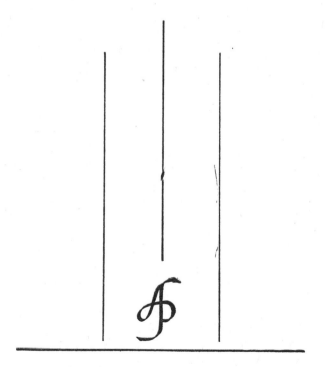

NEW YORK • ABINGDON PRESS • NASHVILLE

CHRISTIAN ETHICS

SET UP, PRINTED, AND BOUND BY THE
PARTHENON PRESS, AT NASHVILLE,
TENNESSEE, UNITED STATES OF AMERICA

TO

MY STUDENTS

at Garrett Biblical Institute
and
The Pacific School of Religion

*eager to serve the present age
in the name of Christ*

Foreword

WHY PRODUCE ANOTHER BOOK on Christian ethics when the library shelves are already full of them? This may be the reader's query upon seeing this title, and it merits an answer.

In the first place, Christian living is an imperative for our time. Whether in the immediate relations of the family, the job or other personal contacts, or in the larger social scene, "where there is no vision, the people perish" (K.J.V.). This has always been true, but the complex and precarious situation within which our lives are now set makes it evident in a startling and at some points tragic manner. Any light that can be thrown on the problems of human decision ought to be shed—and the light that shines from the Christian gospel is a source transcending all others.

Furthermore, in spite of the plethora of books on Christian ethics, there are not many which do what this one attempts. There are the classics of the past, and fortunately some of the present, which are great books for the serious student but which are not apt to be widely understood or read by the ordinary person seeking light on his daily task. Also, there are the overly simple books. There are shelves upon shelves of books that deal with this, that, or the other ethical problem, but without a comprehensive frame of reference. There are books on moral philosophy and books on biblical theology. Among these are various moral philosophies and equally varied biblical theologies. This book has been undertaken because I have not found any which says just what I think needs to be said!

A word is in order as to the point of view from which this book is written. Any Christian ethic to be valid must take its starting point from the revelation of the nature and will of God as this has come to us in Jesus Christ. This revelation we know through what is recorded in the Bible, corroborated through many centuries of Christian experience, and

7

witnessed to by the Holy Spirit in our own highest Christian insights. There is no fixed or inflexible code of Christian morality, no single-track way to the discovery of the will of God for each concrete decision. Nevertheless, we do have a dependable and adequate basis of judgment in what God has given us to know of Jesus. As the great truth of Christian redemption is expressed in the words "God was in Christ reconciling the world to himself," so comparably the foundation of Christian ethics is epitomized in "Have this mind among yourselves, which you have in Christ Jesus."

This means that the recorded words and deeds of Jesus must be taken seriously, with the best biblical scholarship available for their understanding but without dismissal or disparagement. There is a tendency in some quarters today to put the stress so completely on God's redemptive act in Christ as to underestimate the ethical teachings of Jesus. Yet redemption and revelation belong together. When too little heed is given to what is revealed of God through the life and ministry of Jesus, there is danger of constructing an ethical system out of something else, whether the "road to happiness" or the demands of justice in the contemporary world. Paul spoke truly when he wrote, "For no other foundation can anyone lay than that which is laid, which is Jesus Christ."

The first chapter of the book attempts to clear up some common ambiguities as to the meaning of the term "Christian ethics" and to state a frame of reference. The next three chapters present the basic biblical foundations. Two are then given to important meeting points of Christian ethics with Christian theology. The last half of the book deals with the major contemporary problems of social ethics and attempts to turn the searchlight of the Christian gospel upon them.

I have tried to write in a way that would be intelligible and helpful to college and seminary students and also to thoughtful laymen and ministers concerned with the inevitable problems of Christian decision. The difficulty of adapting one's presentation to so varied an audience is obvious. Yet I have been emboldened to attempt it by the fact that Christian ethics is everybody's business and not alone that of the professional moralist.

The reader will find that no attempt has been made to quote widely except from the Bible or to draw into the discussion all the wealth of material available in print. To do so would have been confusing rather than helpful to the reader, but I must acknowledge my debt to many more persons than those whose names appear in the footnotes. To Miss Verna Miller, my friend and housemate, I am grateful as always not only for her help in typing the manuscript but for the kind of understanding companionship that enriches a Christian home.

GEORGIA HARKNESS

Contents

I. What Is Christian Ethics?

THIS IS A BOOK on Christian ethics. Its main focus will be on Christian action and on the principles, derived from the Christian faith, by which to act. It is at the point of a multitude of decisions about what to do or what not to do—how to do right and how to avoid doing what a Christian ought not to do—that the daily strains of living are most acute. Though there can be no exact blueprint by which to settle all these dilemmas, there is light to be had from our gospel.

The foregoing reference to action assumes the importance of Christian experience and personality. It was said of old of an evil man, "For as he thinketh in his heart, so is he" (K.J.V.), and this may be said of the good man as well. The indispensable connection between Christian character and conduct will, I trust, soon become evident.

Can a book on Christian ethics, however firmly rooted in the gospel, do more than to elaborate some great, but completely familiar, generalities such as that we ought to love God and our neighbor and try always to do the will of God? The answer is both Yes and No. No book, unless it is a manual put out by an authoritarian church or a dictatorial political power, can attempt to give specific rules for the manifold decisions of life—and even there the complexities of living are such that "circumstances alter cases." Jesus did not undertake to provide his followers with any such manual of rules, and it would be presumptuous for a modern Christian to attempt what our Lord apparently was too wise to do.

Yet, on the other hand, some things can be said with a fair degree of certainty and assurance. Is adultery right or wrong? Are double-dealing and dishonesty to be condoned in business and politics? Ought children to be starved in body, mind, or soul? Christians have no doubt as to the answer, though how to carry out the implications of the answer may not be simple. Even on such moot matters as race relations and war, the

Christian conscience has spoken in our time with an amazing degree of unanimity as to principle. And if principles can be agreed upon, the groundwork is laid for action.

This book will attempt to fulfill two functions: to present this groundwork of Christian ethical principles and to discuss their application to the major issues of Christian ethical decision in today's society. It is hoped that the reader whose primary interest is in the one or the other of these two approaches will agree to the necessity of the other. Said the philosopher Immanuel Kant, "Form without content is empty; content without form is blind." This is equally true in Christian ethics. Principles can never be rightly declared in a vacuum, and to try to say what is right in concrete issues without grounding decision in principle is to exalt personal preference—if not whim—into the status of universal truth.

1. *Frames of reference*

But what is Christian ethics? Before any attempt is made to define its principles, an important prior question must be settled. What are we talking about?

There are at least six frames of reference within which the term has been used. These overlap and meet at the edges, but much confusion has come about from failure to see clearly that they are different frames of reference. Christian ethics may mean (1) the best in the moral philosophy of all ages and places, (2) the moral standards of Christendom, (3) the ethics of the Christian Church and its many churches, (4) the ethics of the Bible, (5) the ethics of the New Testament, and (6) the ethical insights of Jesus.

These are in a sense concentric circles, for nothing is apt to be called Christian unless it is in some way—whether tightly or loosely—linked with the revelation of God in Jesus Christ. Yet in another sense, depending much on the tightness or looseness of this connection, they may more accurately be regarded as intersecting circles. Both in current Western society and in the churches much is advocated that bears some relation to what the Bible records of the life and teachings of Jesus, yet does not center focally at this point. The focus may be in Greek philosophy, or traditional Christian thought, or the Old Testament prophets, or the writings of Paul, or simply the demands of foreign policy and democratic action in the twentieth century, and still it goes

14

by the name of Christian ethics. One has only to look at a cross section of the moral injunctions in the sermons, the popular religious writing, and the church pronouncements of the present to see this illustrated, and even the writers of important books on Christian ethical theory do not always define their standing ground.

The term "Christian ethics," as I shall use it, means a systematic study of the way of life exemplified and taught by Jesus, applied to the manifold problems and decisions of human existence. It therefore finds its base in the last of these frames of reference, and in the other five only as they are consistent with the sixth and exist as applications or implications of the moral insights of Jesus. This is not to claim that we have a perfect record of the life and teachings of Jesus, for historical scholarship has made it clear that the records we have in the Gospels reflect not only what Jesus was and did and said, but also what the early Church believed about him. Still less is it to claim that any fallible human mind can enter so fully into the divine-human consciousness of Jesus as to say without error what his judgment would be in every concrete case of contemporary decision. It is only to affirm that we have an adequate, a dependable, and an indispensable guide to Christian action in what we know of Jesus and in what through him we know of God. No other guide, however important and useful, is either adequate, or so dependable, or so indispensable.

To define more explicitly what is involved in the moral perspective of Jesus will require presently more extended treatment. But it will be a step toward it, and a step away from confusing it with something else, if we now briefly compare and contrast it with each of the other five frames of reference.

2. Christian ethics and moral philosophy

The keynote in the life and teaching of Jesus with regard to man's moral duty is found in "obedient love." [1] This means that with faith in God as the energizing center of one's being, one is required to seek to do the will of God by loving God supremely and one's neighbor as one's self. However, as the total impact of Jesus' teaching makes evident, to

[1] This phrase is taken from Paul Ramsey's *Basic Christian Ethics* (New York: Chas. Scribner's Sons, 1950), where the term is used repeatedly to indicate the central note in Christian ethics.

love one's neighbor as one's self is not to be understood as any precise balancing and equating of love for others with self-love. Still less does it mean loving others for the sake of receiving love or other benefits in return. *Agape* love means, rather, an uncalculating, outgoing spirit of loving concern which finds expression in deeds of service without limit.

Such "obedient love" is defined for us in the Gospels less by specific statements than by the whole tenor of Jesus' ministry, culminating in his own death upon the cross in fidelity to it. Yet it is implied throughout his recorded words from the Sermon on the Mount to the Last Supper discourse. It is basic to his central teaching, the obligation to "seek first his [God's] kingdom and his righteousness." Its supremacy over any ordinary love comes to clear expression in the words:

For if you love those who love you, what reward have you? Do not even the tax collectors do the same? And if you salute only your brethren, what more are you doing than others? Do not even the Gentiles do the same? You, therefore, must be perfect, as your heavenly Father is perfect. (Matt. 5:46-48.)

How does this differ from the focus of reference in the various systems of classical moral philosophy? Though this is not the place for an extended exposition of them, even a casual glance may suggest that there are both affinities and differences. Platonic thought makes much of *eros*, and *eros* means love. Yet *agape* love, and Bishop Nygren has shown this at length in his now classic *Agape and Eros*, is not the same thing as *eros*. *Eros* (which must not be confused with its modern derivative, "the erotic") means a quest for the highest values, the harmonious adjustment of personality in a well-rounded life, self-fulfillment through seeking the Good. This is achieved in the individual only through promoting the well-being of others. It therefore involves mutuality in love. Its modern correlate is the quest for "the good life" through self-realization.

But is not this what a Christian ought to desire? It has much to commend it, and no Christian ought to disparage it. But to the Christian is *eros* enough? That is our problem.

Aristotle's eudaemonism, with its emphasis on a life of moderation with every man fulfilling the function for which he is fitted by nature, and thereby ensuring happiness, is a practical and down-to-earth system which still has much modern relevance. The hedonistic, or pleasure-seeking, ethics of Epicurus was by no means the crass sensualism suggested by the oft-quoted "Eat, drink, and be merry; for tomorrow we die"; it centered in a refined enjoyment of congenial friends, simplicity of living, and freedom from tension in a cultured and unstrenuous life. Stoicism, on the other hand, with its appeal to courage in the face of life's vicissitudes and the pursuit of virtue solely for virtue's sake, was both a more serious and a more religiously grounded ethic. Its doctrine of an all-pervasive World-Reason, or Logos, and of a natural law of morality fundamental to all existence and embracing in its scope all men, had a note of universalism which made Stoicism particularly open to amalgamation with Christian thought.[2]

These, of course, are not the only classical systems of moral philosophy. There is the formal, duty ethics of Kant with its categorical imperative, or unconditional demand, to treat all persons as ends, never as means, and to act only in such a way that one's conduct could be universalized. There is the utilitarianism of Bentham and Mill, centered in the "greatest happiness of the greatest number" and the measurement of all courses of action by their usefulness toward this end. And there is the modern, but in its elements very old, "social adjustment" philosophy of John Dewey which measures right conduct by the ability to take one's place as a good citizen in an ordered, democratic society.

It is apparent that there are good elements in all of these systems. But are they Christian?

From the early days of Christianity to the present, various courses have been followed with regard to the relations of Christian ethics to moral philosophies stemming from other sources. One has been the process of *incorporation and amalgamation*. In practice, this has often meant the accommodation of Christian principles to what was incorporated. Starting from a laudable desire to propagate Christianity by finding points of contact with the non-Christian world, it has tended to de-emphasize what is distinctive in Christianity in order to stress common ground. At its worst, this has meant the complete subsuming of Christian ethics within philosophical ethics even to the point of disclaiming that anything to be called *Christian* ethics exists. At its best,

---

[2] The reader who desires a rapid survey of these types of ethical theory, but with more amplification than is possible here, will find it in my *The Sources of Western Morality* (New York: Chas. Scribner's Sons, 1954), chs. vii and viii.

it has bred a form of "coalition ethics" [3] in which natural law and the insights of Plato, Aristotle, and other great philosophers are drawn upon to supplement Christian ethics in areas where the gospel gives no specific directives. Examples of such incorporation and amalgamation, with varying levels of success, are seen in the incorporation by Clement of Alexandria of the best in Greek philosophy, the Thomistic assimilation of Aristotle, and the present-day tendency to adjust Christianity to a workable synthesis with the rationalistic, scientific, and humanitarian ideals of modern culture.

A second course follows as a reaction from the first. In alarm at the tendency to accommodate Christianity to the accepted standards of the secular world, there is a *repudiation* by Christian leaders of all sources of moral decision not specifically grounded in the Bible. This is seen in the familiar Barthian mood of the present. In general this movement in ethics has gone along with the rejection of philosophical theology in the attempt to base Christian theology solely on the Bible. It was illustrated in the early Church by Tertullian, who refused to give any credence to Greek philosophy, asking scornfully, "What has Athens to do with Jerusalem?" It is illustrated today by the neo-orthodox school in its suspicion of not only liberal theology but the liberal social gospel,[4] though the tendency is not uniform throughout neo-orthodoxy. Some of its exponents, notably Emil Brunner, have a large place for "middle axioms," or practical social directives, derived in part from the Christian ethic but less than a full expression of Christian *agape*.[5]

Christian ethics is on unsafe ground if it either sells its birthright by accommodation to secular standards or refuses to respect and learn from the moral wisdom of the ages. The third possible approach is less easy to define, for its center lies more in attitudes than in specific procedures. These attitudes may be characterized as those of *mutual understanding and critical appropriation.*

[3] The phrase again is Ramsey's, *op. cit.,* p. 344.

[4] American neo-orthodoxy, and to an increasing extent the European, has a place for Christian social action in the fashioning of "the responsible society," but this is seldom called the social gospel. In many minds the latter term is too closely associated with the liberal emphasis on "building the Kingdom," which is thought to savor too much of human presumption.

[5] For example, the use of coercion and physical force for the maintenance of justice in the social order.

18

What is involved is that Christian moralists must familiarize themselves as thoroughly as possible with the history of philosophy, seek to
understand other world views in their best forms as well as their worst,
give them sympathetic but critical evaluation—then appropriate what
is worth appropriating if it is not at variance with Christian faith. But
in this process, there must be no amalgamating of what is different, no
surrender of what is distinctive in Christianity. If this process is followed
faithfully, there can be some hope of mutuality, with some appropriation
of Christian insights into secular philosophy, as there is not apt to be
on any other basis.

To state in barest outline what can result if this procedure is followed,
there can be a partial acceptance by Christians of the insights of Plato
and the Stoics, but no identification of *eros* with *agape*, no substituting
of stoic fortitude for devoted submission to the will of God. From
Aristotle's ethics not a few elements of practical wisdom can be taken,
but not their humanistic foundations. The self-centered hedonism of
Epicurus must be rejected because it is squarely opposed to Christian
agape, while the duty ethics of Kant, the utilitarianism of Bentham and
Mill, and the contemporary emphasis on social adjustment may well be
used as *instruments* for carrying out some aspects of the Christian moral
imperative but ought never to be confused with its *goals*.

If this third position is accepted, we shall neither scorn moral
philosophy nor identify Christian ethics with it. We shall rejoice that
God has found many channels for the disclosure of truth to men and
that these channels include the best rational thought of the ages on
the nature and aims of the good life. Yet while we thus rejoice, we shall
not substitute them for what God has disclosed to us in Jesus Christ
or admit any to be true which stands clearly at variance with his gospel.

This third position, which I believe to be the only valid one, is what
we shall attempt to maintain in this study. For its wider philosophical
basis, the reader is referred to my earlier book in this series, *Foundations
of Christian Knowledge*,[6] and for its historical backgrounds insofar as
they relate to Greek and Roman thought to *The Sources of Western
Morality*.

[6] New York and Nashville: Abingdon Press, 1955.

3. Christian ethics and the ethics of Christendom

By Christendom we mean those geographical areas and those types of culture which have been largely influenced by Christian ideals. It is nearly, though not fully, synonymous with "the West." Two important elements prevent it from being synonymous. The first is the expansion of Christianity into the Orient, so that there is now a world Church and a large penetration of Christian influence into areas predominantly non-Christian. The second is the ambiguous situation in those areas under Communist domination, wherein a political regime officially atheistic includes within its scope millions of persons who are still Christians. Should Communism succeed in stamping out Christianity, these areas would no longer be a part of Christendom; fortunately, this appears not likely to occur.

The identification of Christian ethics with the ethics of Christendom is more subtle, and hence more dangerous, than its identification with the various schools of moral philosophy. As one element it includes the latter, as is illustrated by the wide permeation of the social and educational philosophy of John Dewey within current American culture. Yet it is something more diffuse and usually more binding than the thought of any single philosopher or school. It involves the whole "climate of opinion" within which one is reared, lives, and does his work. And because there is so much that is good about this climate of opinion and environing structure, it is easy to identify it with the best and hallow it with the name of Christian.

There is not space here to canvass in any detail the ways in which Christian ethics gets mixed up with the ethics of Christendom. This I have tried to do in *The Modern Rival of Christian Faith*,[7] particularly in Part II, where under the general caption of "Rival Secular Faiths" I have indicated elements of agreement and difference between Christianity and scientism, humanism, democracy, nationalism, racism, fascism, capitalism, and Communism. Further observations will be made on specific questions as we come to them later in this book. It may be noted in passing, however, that there is little danger of an identification of Christian ethics with humanism, racism, fascism, or Communism when these are recognized for what they are, since their foundations are

[7] New York and Nashville: Abingdon Press, 1952.

so clearly opposed to those of the Christian faith. Even racism, widely practiced by Christians, is repudiated in principle.

It is at the point of the other four—scientism, democracy, nationalism, and capitalism—and their diffusion into an exaltation of scientific and technological achievement, the American way of life, patriotism, and free enterprise, that the identification becomes most common. Add to these a sense of the dignity of man, humanitarian concern for the weak, the helpless, and the suffering, a wholesome respect for law, and in general, attitudes of kindness, generosity, and responsible citizenship— and one comes out with what most Americans regard as "acting like a Christian."

Is this judgment mistaken? It is, and it is not. All the achievements and virtues above mentioned have in them large elements of goodness. Some of them—particularly humanitarian concern for others and a sense of the worth of every person—can be traced directly to Christian roots. Yet taken as a whole, they do not add up to Christian agape. One can believe in every one of them and be a decent, respectable, even admirable citizen, and still not be a Christian. A major, and perhaps the most difficult, task of Christian leaders is to induce people who are virtuous in all these respects to see that such goodness is not good enough. As long as one identifies Christian ethics with the ethics of Christendom, one does not cry out, "God, be merciful to me a sinner!" or lay hold in humility upon divine grace, or seek in costly self-surrender to follow the path of obedient love.

4. Christian ethics and the churches

The ethics of the Church, and individually of the churches, stands midway between the ethics of Christendom and the ethics of the gospel as it comes to us in Jesus Christ. The Church, insofar as it is faithful to its mission as the carrier of the gospel and is a fellowship of persons sincerely trying to follow Jesus, sees more clearly what is right than does the surrounding society. It is for this reason that it is called to be the "conscience of the State" and is obligated without falling into a trite and secularistic moralism to proclaim and practice the principles of Christian morality. Its official pronouncements, whether in a papal encyclical or a statement of the World Council or National Council of Churches, or an action of a General Conference, are likely to be on a plane above that of current practice. This is not to say that any human document is flawless, but when the Church through its leaders tries to speak from a Christian frame of reference, it both indicts current practices and sets higher goals. This is as it should be if the Church is to be effective in applying the principles of its eternal gospel to the changing temporal scene.

Nevertheless, except in such authoritarian churches as the Roman Catholic and Eastern Orthodox, it is seldom contended that the voice of the Church is to be equated with the voice of God in Christ. Even in Roman Catholicism this claim is not made except when the Pope speaks ex cathedra. It is the genius of Protestantism to recognize that any Christian may grasp something of Christian moral truth, and comparably, that no Christian, or group of Christians, has a monopoly upon the gospel and its ethical demands.

The Church exists to be the carrier of the gospel in a fellowship of Christians. But the Church exists also as a human institution, a social group with a common center of professed loyalty to Christ, yet a social group made up of fallible human beings. These fallible human persons "who profess and call themselves Christians," who are of varying degrees of ethical insight and fidelity to Christ, are also enmeshed in a network of other human institutions, political, economic, domestic, recreational, cultural. It is only natural, therefore, that the standards current in these other social institutions should impinge upon their life as Christians and so find access into the structure of the churches. Hence, the churches are always in danger of themselves becoming secularized and conforming to the standards of the world instead of being agencies of Christian transformation.

A statement on *Christian Principles and Assumptions for Economic Life* adopted by the General Board of the National Council of the Churches of Christ in the U.S.A. puts this pointedly:

The churches themselves own property, invest funds, and employ labor. Often their policies have been no better than those which the Church condemns in the secular world. Its divisions often reflect and seem to give a religious sanction to the social divisions that are characteristic of society at large. In all these matters judgment should "begin at the house of God." [8]

[8] Adopted September 15, 1954.

This statement, unfortunately too true to give comfort to any discerning Christian, describes a state of affairs which can be countered only by a combination of clear Christian insight and courageous, patient Christian action. Both the individual Christian and those corporate groups that make up the churches need always to keep in mind the piercing injunction: "Do not be conformed to this world but be transformed by the renewal of your mind, that you may prove what is the will of God, what is good and acceptable and perfect" (Rom. 12:2).

It is apparent, therefore, that while churches are the natural media for Christian enlightenment, Christian ethics cannot be identified with the ethics of any of the existing churches.

But what of the past? Was not the Church once pure? And if we look to the early days of Christianity, or to the Reformation, or to the beginnings of our denomination, do we not find there norms for action?

There is always a tendency, when we do not find things as they ought to be around us, to take this backward look. The tendency is in part wholesome, but in other respects it is bound to cause distortion. It is true that there have been at intervals great creative outpourings of the Spirit of God, which have always had ethical accompaniments, and sometimes very significant ones. Among these, in addition to the supreme event of the life and death of our Lord, may be mentioned the era of the eighth-century prophets, the voices of Jeremiah and the Second Isaiah, the birth of the Church and the beginnings of missionary witness, the implanting of the gospel in Western Europe, the work and ministry of Francis of Assisi, the Protestant Reformation, the struggle for religious freedom, the Wesleyan revival, the emergence of the modern missionary and ecumenical movements. We do well to learn whatever lessons they have to teach us. Yet one of these lessons is that there has never been a forward movement without some mixture of human error and sin. The Church of today is further along the road toward a true Christian ethics than was Paul in his attitudes toward women, or Francis of Assisi in regard to the care of the body, or Luther in regard to the economic status of peasants, or Calvin in regard to infant damnation, or Wesley in regard to the requirements of world order and peace.[9]

---

[9] Wesley, of course, preferred peace to war, but he seems to have given no major concern to the issues involved. It will be recalled that he sided with the British in the Revolutionary War and protested the rebellious spirit of the colonies.

The Church through the centuries has been the carrier of the Christian evangel and of a basic structure of Christian faith. Out of this evangel and this faith the principles of Christian ethics are fashioned. We owe, then, to the Church of the past and to our fathers in the faith an incalculable debt. The past merits to be known and understood, to be viewed critically where necessary, but never to be treated lightly. We need to know what Augustine and Aquinas, Luther, Calvin, and Wesley believed about the Christian life, both to learn from them and to avoid their errors. Yet while we acknowledge our debt to the "faith of our fathers, living still," and to those fathers who valiantly proclaimed it, let us not suppose that the Church of the past can be our norm for the ethical decisions of today.

5. Christian ethics and the Bible

We come now to a frame of reference on which we are on firmer ground. The Bible is certainly indispensable to our knowledge of Christian truth and moral obligation. Without it, it is very possible that there would be today no churches, no Christendom, no knowledge of Christ. It is, of course, conceivable that God would have found a way to propagate the faith by word of mouth without a Book through all the centuries, and the fact that Roman Catholicism could exist so long without access to the Bible by the laity makes it impossible to say categorically that the Bible is the *sine qua non* of Christianity. Yet few would dispute the fact that without the Bible we should be infinitely poorer in our Christian experience and moral insight.

Furthermore, in today's world the Bible is the common possession of all Christians, and hence serves to unite Christians across deep divisions. This is not to say that all Christians agree on what the Bible says. There are differences in translation, and far more radical differences in interpretation. Acute controversies and sometimes schisms arise from this fact. Yet the Bible is still our common possession, and it is no accident that its sales continue year after year to exceed that of any other book, that it has been and continues to be translated into many hundreds of languages and dialects, that it has become so deeply embedded in our literature and culture that even those who have no personal familiarity with it daily use its phrases in ordinary speech.

The Bible is the fountainhead of Christian theology. It is not the sole source, for there is a natural theology, also called philosophical theology, which finds evidences of God throughout his total creation and in the moral and religious aspirations and experience of all peoples. There is a place for such natural theology and at points where both biblical and philosophical theology are true, they cannot contradict each other. Nevertheless, the Bible is our firmer base for what is distinctively Christian, and the movement away from the more generalized conclusions of philosophical thought about God and his world to a more Christ-centered, biblically based structure of theology is in the right direction.

If this is the case, is not the Bible all we need as the foundation of Christian ethics? The answer is Yes and No.

This question may be followed by another. Are Christian ethical principles to be derived from the whole Bible or only from selected parts of it? Once more it is necessary to say Yes and No.

Reviewing what has been said about the relations of Christian ethics to moral philosophy, to Christendom, and to the Church, we see that "no other foundation can any one lay than that which is laid, which is Jesus Christ." In the supreme duty of love to God and neighbor, rooted in faith, obedience, and humble acceptance of divine grace, we find "all the law and the prophets"—and enough to give a basis for centuries of ethical application. But this gives the basis; it does not give the applications. We are still left with a multitude of concrete moral decisions to make. For guidance in making them we must look—not to any ethical compendium above the Bible or beyond it in wisdom—but to other ranges of experience that may throw light on problems nonexistent in Bible times or not treated within its scope. What, for example, about slavery, birth control, juvenile delinquency, polio, speeding on highways, labor unions, stock-market manipulations, hydrogen bombs and war? The first and last existed in full force within the period covered by the Bible, but the Bible does not tell us what to do about them; the others are for the most part modern problems.

It is apparent, then, that the Bible *alone* does not give us all we need. The thinking and experience of the centuries, whether in philosophy or the Church, will help us at some points. But we cannot live by the past, and we must know our times and the causes and consequences of prevailing evils. We must be continually on the alert to see what a sensitive Christian conscience, responsive to the call of Christ, will hold to be right and wrong courses of action in the circumstances where we are.

Turning to the second question, we ask, "Shall we use the whole Bible, or only parts of it, as the basis of ethical decision?"

This question may mean either of two things. One angle it takes is the question as to whether we should use the Old Testament as well as the New. And if the answer is Yes, shall we equate them in value? The other angle of the question goes to the heart of biblical interpretation and separates into two camps—at times one could almost say, armed camps—the literalists and the liberals. This issue is, of course, the degree to which the historical method is to be used in discerning the ethical as well as the theological truth within the Bible. Let us look at these questions separately, though they impinge upon each other.

As to whether we should look to the Old Testament for our ethical foundations, the answer is "Yes, but with discernment." I have said, and shall repeatedly insist, that the basic foundation of Christian ethics is in the ministry and teachings of Jesus Christ, as these bring to us the supreme revelation of God's nature and will. Yet the Old Testament contains also much that is revelatory in its own structure, as well as preparatory for the coming of Christ. We could not dispense with the Ten Commandments or the great moral insights of the prophets or the matchless devotional poetry of the psalms. Even the ups and downs of Hebrew history, with their sordid spots as well as high moments, with moral weaklings as well as giants in the story, and much that reflects the lights and shadows of the times, teach us that

> God moves in a mysterious way
> His wonders to perform.

The discernment we need, if we are to see God's light in the midst of earthly shadows, is found in the measuring rod of Jesus Christ. Are the polygamy, the trickery, the vindictiveness, found on many pages of the Old Testament Christian? Unquestionably not. Are the twenty-third psalm, or Isaiah's vision in the Temple, or Micah's definition of true religion Christian? Unquestionably yes. They are not the whole of Christianity, but they are fully consistent with what Jesus taught and did. So, too, are a wealth of other passages in the Old Testament.

The Old Testament, we must remember, was Jesus' Bible. He did not repudiate it; he loved it and learned from it and often quoted it. But he did not slavishly feel bound to it. In the Sermon on the Mount the six-times-repeated "You have heard that it was said to the men of old. . . . But I say to you . . ." indicates how he used it. He took it as a foundation, but put deeper meaning into the issues involved. This we must do, drawing from his insights.

On the question of a historical versus a literalistic approach to the Bible I have stated my convictions elsewhere and need not here discuss the subject in detail.[10] It is not a question of *inspiration*, for one who sees in the Bible a progressive revelation of the living God as he moves in the events of Hebrew history, the coming of Christ and the birth of the Church, accepts the Bible as the Word of God as truly as does any literalist. What he attempts to do is to hear this Word more clearly as he discerns the Spirit of God moving in the midst of the human, historical situation, and thus aims to discover in the Bible the heavenly "treasure in earthen vessels." He is likely to be called an infidel by one who believes that the Bible must be taken "letter for letter" or not at all. But that does not matter if his studies lead him to clearer vision and deeper faith.

If we are to find in the Bible dependable guidance for our own time, such a historical approach is indispensable. No situation is an exact replica of the past, and words spoken in the past to other situations take on distorted meaning unless these situations are understood. This is not to say that the literalist discerns no moral truth in the Bible. He does, and often lives by it in his personal relations an admirable Christian life. Yet in matters of complexity and doubt as to the right thing to do, he tends to follow his own course of action and find a proof text in the Bible to support it. He usually defends a traditional point of view in which an attempt is made to preserve the *status quo*, not infrequently with harsh words and attitudes toward those who differ. For ethical sensitivity and responsiveness to the Christian thing to do in doubtful situations, one who sees the Bible in its total historical setting is on safer ground.

[10] In *Understanding the Christian Faith* (New York and Nashville: Abingdon Press, 1947), ch. ii; *Foundations of Christian Knowledge*, ch. v; and throughout my *Toward Understanding the Bible* (New York: Chas. Scribner's Sons, 1954).

6. Christian ethics and the New Testament

The final question for this chapter is a closely related but still a somewhat different one. What about the authority of the New Testament, not only in relation to the Old, but within it in the relations of its parts?

Most Christians, without rejecting the Old Testament or disparaging its many marvelous elements, find the New Testament more authoritative for their faith and living. This is as it should be, for while the Old Testament tells us much about God and foreshadows the coming of Christ, it is the New Testament that records for us the historical revelation of God in Christ. Their interrelatedness has thus been well expressed by a group of eminent scholars in the ecumenical movement:

It is agreed that in the case of an Old Testament passage, one must examine and expound it in relation to the revelation of God to Israel both before and after its own period. Then the interpreter should turn to the New Testament in order to view the passage in that perspective.

. . . .

It is agreed that in the case of a New Testament passage one should examine it in the light of its setting and context; then turn to the Old Testament to discover its background in God's former revelation. Returning again to the New Testament one is able to see and expound the passage in the light of the whole scope of *Heilsgeschichte*.[11]

Seeing the Bible as a whole, we make the revelation of God in Christ our norm for understanding and for judgment.

But within the New Testament, is one part any more authoritative than another? In order to answer this question, we must avoid two common courses, both of which have been responsible for error.

One of these courses is to take the New Testament as if it were all on the same level of Christian insight. Because the words are there, Paul's words enjoining women to keep silent in the churches and Jude's words contending "for the faith which was once for all delivered to the saints" have again and again been used as a bulwark against change. That these injunctions reflect particular situations in the early Church

[11] From *Biblical Authority for Today* by Richardson and Schweitzer, 1952, The Westminster Press. Used by permission. *Heilsgeschichte* (the history of salvation) refers to the dominant theme of the Bible as giving us knowledge of God's redemptive activity within human events.

instead of being universal principles, and stand squarely in opposition to Paul's other word, "Where the Spirit of the Lord is, there is freedom," is too frequently overlooked. Passages attributed to Jesus which seem to predict a speedy Second Coming and a catastrophic end of the world by divine intervention are equated in importance with the Sermon on the Mount—and seemingly ranked superior to it—by eminent theologians whose conception of Christ as the hope of the world is primarily eschatological rather than ethical.[12]

On the other hand, the recognition that the Gospels are the product of the experience of the Church in the first century, not firsthand accounts, and that Paul's early letters antedate by nearly a quarter-century even Mark, which is the earliest of the Gospels, has led some scholars to shift the focus of attention away from Jesus to Paul. There is wide latitude among New Testament scholars as to the historicity of the Gospels; there is general agreement that none is completely historical, with John the latest and least so of the four. That Paul has much to teach us both about redemption through the grace of God in Christ and about the requirements of the Christian life need not be disputed. Yet it may be asked whether it is not Jesus of Nazareth, seen clearly even though not photographically through the records we have in the Synoptic Gospels, that is our surest foundation of the Christian life. Paul was a great Christian, a great theologian, a great missionary and administrator, a great teacher, but it was not he in whom "the Word became flesh" to dwell among us. It will be a basic assumption of this book, as it is not of some contemporary treatments of Christian ethics,[13] that the picture we have of Jesus in the Synoptic Gospels is in essential outlines correct and that what we see there of his life and death, his ministry and teaching, is the one adequate foundation for Christian ethics.

Yet to take this as our base does not mean that we can indiscriminately take every word recorded as spoken by Jesus to be accurate or authorita-

[12] Note, for example, the First and Second Reports of the Advisory Commission on the Main Theme for the Evanston Assembly of the World Council of Churches and the address by Professor Edmund Schlink at the opening session of this assembly.

[13] Note, for example, Emil Brunner's classic *The Divine Imperative* (Philadelphia: Westminster Press, 1947). The index lists forty-six references to Luther, thirty-five to Calvin, twenty to Paul, and none to Jesus. By diligent search one finds an occasional mention, but they are few.

tive. At the end of Mark, in a passage now generally regarded by scholars as a later addition to the original text, Jesus is reported as saying:

And these signs will accompany those who believe: in my name they will cast out demons; they will speak in new tongues; they will pick up serpents, and if they drink any deadly thing, it will not hurt them; they will lay their hands on the sick; and they will recover. (16:17-18.)

Regardless of what we may today believe about the exorcism of demons, speaking in tongues, or healing by the laying on of hands, can we really believe that the Christian ethic requires snake handling and the drinking of poison as a proof of faith? Some of Jesus' more naïve followers have tried it in our own time, and they died. We should doubt that Jesus ever said it even if there were no textual evidence to the contrary.

To cite another example, there is a verse at the end of the parable of the pounds as it is given in Luke which is generally omitted when the story is read. In Luke 19:27 appear the words: "But as for these enemies of mine, who did not want me to reign over them, bring them here and slay them before me." Why do we omit it? Because it does not sound like Jesus! It simply does not seem like the words of one who could say on the cross, "Father, forgive them; for they know not what they do." And even though the textual accuracy of Luke 19:27 is less disputed than of Luke 23:34, we still believe it is the latter in which the real Jesus speaks.

These illustrations indicate what must be a basic procedure—a difficult but a very necessary procedure. This is to get to know Jesus from the total picture the New Testament gives of him—find our main point of reference in the first three Gospels, then interpret these Gospels and all the rest of the New Testament *in the light of what we believe he was and said and did.* This, of course, immediately opens the door to the charge that one is reading in what he wants to find there. But there is no other way. We cannot take the record as it stands, and we cannot discard it. Whatever interpretation we place upon it, we shall still be interpreting. And the best interpretation is that which is most faithful to the total picture of Jesus as our Lord, the Son of God, the supreme revelation of the Father and the supreme gift of God for our redemption.

What, then, is Christian ethics? It is the systematic study of the way

30

of life set forth by Jesus Christ, applied to the daily demands and decisions of our personal and social existence.

Since Christian ethics centers in the ethical insights of Jesus, a logical "next step" might be to move directly into an examination of these as they are to be discerned from his recorded words and deeds— thence to an application to the problems of our time. The reader who wishes to follow this sequence is free to do so, and the table of contents will direct him in it. Yet if we are to understand Jesus, or if we are to discern the centrality of his message in reference to the entire Bible, we cannot proceed so simply. Jesus had a past, and from his life and influence came the Church of which the beginnings are recorded for us in the New Testament. It is essential, therefore, to look first at the Old Testament, then at Jesus, then forward from his earthly life to the birth of Christianity. From this wider biblical perspective we shall be the better equipped to judge what is truly Christian.

II. The Covenant, the Law, and the Prophets

FOR A TRIPLE REASON, we turn now to certain basic ideas in the Old Testament. The first is the light that the Old Testament can throw upon Jesus as we note what he retained, consciously or unconsciously, from his heritage and what he set aside in response to higher insights. The second is the need to understand the Old Testament as a whole and to see it in perspective, since it too is the Christian's Bible and grave errors of ethical interpretation have often resulted from lack of such perspective. The third arises from the fact that the social teachings of the prophets supply a degree of concreteness and of social application to specific circumstances which appears only marginally in the teachings of Jesus. This is not to say we can substitute them for Jesus, but where they are not at variance with his view, they can throw valuable light on our present need for concrete directives within comparable historical circumstances.

It is obvious that within a single chapter it is impossible to canvass the total ethical structure of the Old Testament.[1] I shall attempt to deal only with three key concepts: the covenant, the law, and the message of the prophets.

1. The covenant

The idea of the covenant between Yahweh and his chosen people is the most basic and distinctive idea in the Old Testament, affecting as it does the total religious and moral outlook of Israel. In it are involved

[1] For a brief but still somewhat detailed summary, the reader is referred to my The Sources of Western Morality, chs. v, vi. For a more detailed study, J. M. Powis Smith, The Moral Life of the Hebrews (University of Chicago Press, 1923), though old is still the most useful single volume. For a penetrating survey, see Harry Emerson Fosdick, A Guide to Understanding the Bible (New York: Harper & Bros., 1938) in the chapter on "The Idea of Right and Wrong."

the nature of their God, his relation to them and to the stream of history, the framework within which they conceived their moral obligation, the grounds of divine judgment, and the hope of salvation which was to grow into the expectancy of the promised Messiah and the kingdom of God. This is not to say that in the initial establishment or acceptance of the covenant the people foresaw all this, but it laid the groundwork on which all the rest could be erected.

We need not here go into the moot question as to whether Yahweh was a Kenite deity taken over by Moses for his people or whether the Yahweh concept has earlier roots. What is vital to our study is that from the time of Moses onward the people felt themselves to be in a particular relationship to their God.[2] This relationship centers in a covenant voluntarily initiated by God, offering Yahweh's protection and support in return for obedience to his will and law.

The nature of this covenant can best be seen in terms of certain contrasts. There were blood covenants among many primitive peoples, ratified often by ritualistic sacrifices, but with the assumption that the deities must be appeased, or their vanity flattered, or at best that the honor of the gods depended on the faithfulness of the people. As Israel's God is different, so is the covenant different. There are elements of primitivism in Israel's faith, yet its primary note is the union in Yahweh of sovereign power with righteousness. Yahweh was not obligated for any extraneous reason to enter into covenant relations with Israel; he did it freely. Yahweh's chief pleasure was not in the blood of the rams or bullocks, though the ceremonial law might require them; it was in obedience to his holy will, which came in the insights of the prophets to mean "mercy and not sacrifice."

It is now commonly believed that Israel's faith was not fully monotheistic before the sixth century B.C. and that a watershed is marked by the great declaration of the Second Isaiah in Isa. 44:6 where Yahweh is represented as saying:

> I am the first and I am the last;
> besides me there is no god.

---

[2] The biblical narrative places the institution of the covenant in the time of Abraham (Gen. 17:1-8) with a still more general covenant in God's promise to Noah (Gen. 9:8-17). These, however, are doubtless proleptic statements of a later development.

However, the existence of monolatry before that time ought not to obscure the fact that apparently from the beginning of Israel's thought about God, he was more than the common run of tribal deities. Though other deities were believed to exist, Yahweh alone had any power or function. The making of a golden calf or the worship of the Baalim was apostate religion. He alone was the maker of heaven and earth, and the determiner not only of the total structure of nature but of the events of history. In his control of events he revealed both his righteous judgments and his saving power, and in spite of the attribution to him of bellicose and other anthropomorphic traits the God of Israel is singularly free from common primitive tendencies.

Its [Israel's] God stands quite alone. It is he who, even in the old creation story (Gen. 2:4 ff.), created all things without assistance or intermediary; his very name Yahweh claims for him this function. No pantheon surrounds him. He has no consort (the Hebrew does not even have a word for "goddess") and no progeny. Consequently the Hebrews, in sharpest contrast to their neighbors, developed no mythology.[3]

This is not to say that no myths are to be found in the Old Testament. They are there, but they do not constitute the nature of deity or form an integral part of ritualistic worship, as in so many pagan faiths. Rather, they serve to illustrate the nonmythological character of the Eternal.[4] Yahweh is a moral Being who controls all nature and all history. Hence, when he chooses to establish a covenant with Israel, he is not to be bargained with, but his sway and his will are to be gratefully accepted and flouted only at the people's peril.

But did the people in their acceptance of the covenant make a bargain with their Deity? The answer is both Yes and No. It was not in any case a bargain based on equality of status, such as might be made between the "party of the first part" and the "party of the second part." Still less was it a *social contract*—a voluntary surrender of power in order to delegate authority to a sovereign—as envisaged by Hobbes or

[3] John Bright, The Kingdom of God (New York and Nashville: Abingdon Press, 1953), p. 25. Used by permission of the publisher.
[4] For example, such important myths as those of the creation story, the fall, the tower of Babel, and the flood indicate Yahweh's sovereign control of nature and history, and his union of righteousness with power.

Rousseau.[5] The covenant was more of a command than a bargain, stemming from the inherent, undelegated authority of Yahweh over the total structure of existence. Yet it was not without its elements of give and take. What is involved on both sides is epitomized in the Hebrew word *hesed*, for which there is no single synonym. On God's part it signifies divine grace, a continuing requirement of obedience, but mercy and "lovingkindness" even in the midst of judgment. On man's part *hesed* denotes the response to divine grace, complete loyalty to Yahweh and obedience to his will. It was not their own obedience, all too often patently surrendered, which made the Hebrews sure that God would not go back on his part of the covenant; it was their faith in his faithfulness that gave them confidence in his righteous judgments even when adversity seemed to indicate denial of his protection.

The covenant was thought to have all the inviolability of the order of nature, not because of its impersonality, as we are prone to think of nature, but because both nature and history stemmed from a common personal source—the will of Yahweh. The doctrines of creation, judgment, redemption, and providence, never systematically formulated but always presupposed in Hebrew thought, had a single foundation— the sovereign rule of Yahweh over his people and his world. This is at the root of the common observation that Hebrew faith, as contrasted with Greek philosophy and religion, is historical. Both the events of Hebrew history and the interpretation the people placed upon them—notably but not exclusively the exodus from Egypt and the giving of the covenant on Sinai, then Israel's conquest of Canaan, her struggles with her foes, and finally the exile and return—are impregnated with the idea that the supreme Ruler of heaven and earth had in a special way chosen Israel as his people and was concerned in all their fortunes. It was not a covenant of merit, for it was never assumed that Israel deserved to be thus chosen; it was a covenant of grace.

A note of greater universality in regard to God's love was destined to emerge in the teachings of the prophets, to be reflected in Jonah and some of the Psalms, and to come to full expression in the teachings

[5] Paul Ramsey, *op. cit.*, ch. x, gives a significant comparison of the Hebrew covenant with the social contract views of Hobbes, Rousseau, Bodin, and Grotius.

of Jesus. But this does not alter the fact that the Old Testament as a whole has a note extremely important to Christian ethics today: namely, *that God alone is the final arbiter of human affairs and that in him power, righteousness, and grace are inseparably joined.* Apart from the conviction that God alone has absolute sovereignty, the nation or some other political, economic, or social structure becomes regulative. Apart from the conviction that the supreme Ruler is also good, the vicissitudes of history appear as the "trampling march of unconscious power" [6] or at most as stages in the spiral of evolutionary progress wherein the anticipated goal fails to redeem the loss along the way.

Israel's covenant relation foreshadows in a number of ways what was to become more explicit in Christianity. The most obvious connection is, of course, the "new covenant" and the establishment of the Church as the "new Israel" with Christ as its center and head. But this is not all. Both judgment and redemption on God's part rest on the foundation of the covenant idea; likewise the demand for obedience and hence for unremitting moral responsibility on man's side. So also does the hope of the coming of the Kingdom, not as something earned by man's good works nor yet as a state in which God can be indifferent to human effort, but rather as a consummation in which the conditions of the covenant would be fully met. The apocalyptists of later Judaism distorted the covenant idea into an expectancy of the salvation of God's elect solely by the direct intervention of God; those Jews who envisaged Israel as a holy commonwealth whose holiness was to be tested and proved by moral obedience came closer to its meaning.

Apart from the covenant idea, both the prophets' preaching of the doom to fall on a sinful and rebellious people and their hope for the future either would have been nonexistent or would have taken a very different turn. Here again there are modern counterparts and derivatives, for apart from foundations in a God of supreme power, righteousness, and grace who is implicated in the suffering of his people, who condemns their sin yet offers release, prophetic preaching today escapes from soporific optimism only to fall into moral diatribe.

[6] The closing words of Bertrand Russell's classic statement of atheistic faith, *A Free Man's Worship* in *Mysticism and Logic, and Other Essays* (New York: Barnes & Noble, Inc., 1954).

2. *The law*

In the previous section I have stressed mainly the kind of God who was believed by Israel to have entered into the covenant relation with his chosen people. We must now look at what the people believed commensurately was required of them in this crucial bilateral agreement.

There were two basic tests of being a Jew. One was circumcision; the other was the more general requirement of the keeping of the law. The first was clearly repudiated by Christianity, as became evident in the very important decision recorded in the fifteenth chapter of Acts. What Christianity did with the law is a much more complex question, and the answer depends on what aspect of the law is being considered and in what context it is understood.

As we shall note again in Chapter IV, it is both necessary and difficult to draw a line between the moral and the ceremonial law of Israel. Christian ethics must make this distinction, else we not only shall lose the Ten Commandments from Christianity but will be obliged to ascribe to Paul a disregard of the moral law at variance with the moral concern which appears on every page of his letters. Yet it is a distinction which is not easy to make, for in all of the great law codes of Israel—the Covenant Code (Exod. 20:23–23:33), the code embedded in the book of Deuteronomy, and the Holiness Code (Lev. 17–26)—specifications for ritualistic and ceremonial observance stand side by side with those indicating humaneness and moral insight.

A further distinction, important to make but not self-evident, is the extent to which Israel simply took over prevailing social regulations, and on the other hand, gave unique and distinctive meaning to the duties they believed laid upon them by their covenant with Yahweh. It is easy to err in either direction. There is ample evidence that Israel's morality did not simply emerge full-grown out of supernatural revelation. In some respects it follows the common pattern of primitive societies; in some it shows Canaanitic and through this channel Babylonian influences. In others, however, the morality of the covenant and hence its embodiment in reverence for the law of Yahweh is unique among all Israel's neighbors and contemporaries. Its uniqueness centers in the event, the condition, and the promise, which Israel in her worst apostasies never forgot:

You have seen what I did to the Egyptians, and how I bore you on eagles' wings and brought you to myself. Now therefore, if you will obey my voice and keep my covenant, you shall be my own possession among all peoples; for all the earth is mine, and you shall be to me a kingdom of priests and a holy nation. (Exod. 19:4-6.)

The moral implications of the covenant did not readily take on the character of universal obligation and were never so conceived by the rank and file of the people. Not until Jesus, and the "new covenant," was it fully universalized. Yet it was assumed throughout Israel's history that the law of the covenant must be observed as divine command within the covenant brotherhood, and this had a radical influence on Israel's attitude toward the law. In part, this limitation of obligation to the covenant brotherhood was an aspect of the common tendency, primitive but still persisting to our day, to draw a sharp distinction between the "in-group" and the "out-group." But in part also, it was uniquely related to Israel's God. This will become apparent if we note some stages of development in her history.

It is probable that the most primitive code in the Old Testament is the ceremonial code (the so-called J Decalogue) which is found in Exod. 34. Its content need not detain us except to observe that the codification of Hebrew law begins, not in a statement of general ethical principles such as the prohibitions of murder, adultery, theft, lying, and covetousness found in the Decalogue of Exod. 20, but in provisions for exclusive and imageless worship of Yahweh, feasts and sacrifices. The note of exclusive worship was vital to the keeping of Israel's faith pure; the ceremonialism, which it shared in kind with other primitive groups, was destined to be in tension with morality throughout Israel's history.

Though the dating of the Decalogue as it appears in Exod. 20:2-17 is in dispute, and it is doubtful that in its present form it is Mosaic, there is no adequate ground for doubting that under Moses both the religious and the social structure of Israel took shape.[7] What is more

[7] See W. F. Albright, *From the Stone Age to Christianity* (Baltimore: Johns Hopkins Press, 1946), for the most authoritative statement of evidence to this effect.

significant than its date is the unique convergence of duties owed to Yahweh with universal moral principles which it embodies. Without this convergence, it could neither have occupied the place it held in Israel nor lasted to be normative in Christianity up to our own time.[8]

The Covenant Code, which is affixed to the Exodus Decalogue, illustrates admirably the blending of moral with religious considerations, and within religion the mixture of adoration and gratitude with ceremonial observance, which characterizes Israel's faith as a whole. It begins with an injunction to imageless worship, provisions for altars and sacrifices, and assurance of the divine presence and blessing. Then follow nearly three chapters of very explicit provisions concerning slaves, punishment for deeds of violence and theft, restitution for injury to property, family relations, helpfulness to the stranger and to the poor, observance of the Sabbath as a day of rest for servants and even for the animals. They are not provisions for our day, but in the setting of agrarian society in the tenth century B.C. they show an admirable sense of justice, moral responsibility, and humane concern for the underprivileged. Interspersed are stern warnings against sacrifice to strange gods and firm injunctions as to the modes and times of sacrifice to Yahweh. The code proper ends with the strange injunction,[9] which sounds to modern ears neither moral nor religious, "You shall not boil a kid in its mother's milk," and is followed immediately by the renewal of the covenant.

Not only its preface and epilogue, but recurrent references to the Hebrews having been strangers in the land of Egypt, give the Covenant Code its setting. Without a sense of gratitude to Yahweh and of moral obligation derivative from his care a law code might have been developed in Israel at this time, as had occurred centuries earlier in Babylon in the Code of Hammurabi. But without the covenant it is doubtful that it would have been so humane; it is certain that it could not have had the powerful sanctions it possessed.

Yet it is not so clearly in the codes as in the voices of the prophets

[8] D. Elton Trueblood in *Foundations for Reconstruction* (New York: Harper & Bros., 1946) takes the principles of the Ten Commandments and applies them vitally to the problems of our time.
[9] Repeated from Exod. 34:26, as are provisions for the Sabbath, feasts three times a year, the use of unleavened bread in sacrifices, and the offering of the first fruits to Yahweh.

that we see the roots of Israel's attitude toward the law. In the next section we shall consider further what they say to us today. But we cannot read them correctly unless we see them in protest against perversions of the covenant, endeavoring to call Israel not only forward but back to what was deepest in her history. Many generations have thrilled to the story of Nathan finding the courage to say to the guilty David, "Thou art the man" (II Sam. 12:7 K.J.V.), and of Elijah rebuking Ahab for the theft of Naboth's vineyard (I Kings 21). It was not simply because murder and theft were forbidden by the law of the land, but because they were contrary to the law of a higher Sovereign, that these men could thus speak up to kings. The message of Amos is in no sense an abrogation of the doctrine of the chosen people, as is sometimes inferred from Amos 9:7; it is an attempt to jolt the people loose from a self-centered, complacent, mechanical conception of the covenant. Its true center, he saw, lay in obedience to God's law, not in feasts, solemn assemblies, and burnt offerings, and divine election meant election to moral responsibility. The stance from which Amos speaks, giving meaning to all he says about social justice and the coming "day of the Lord" in his call to repentance and prediction of doom, is epitomized in the words:

> You only have I known
> of all the families of the earth;
> therefore I will punish you
> for all your iniquities.

A similar note rings through the prophecies of Hosea, Micah, and the first Isaiah. The harshness of Amos is alleviated by the portrayal of God's tender love for his erring people, the promise that a remnant shall repent and be spared, the prevision of the coming of the Prince of Peace. But at no point in the writings of the eighth-century prophets is the law of the covenant abrogated or universalized. It is because the Hebrews are God's people that they are obligated to obey his law. Their disobedience cannot cancel out God's hesed, but neither will God's mercy save them from destruction if they persist in flouting his just demands.

With the appearance of the Deuteronomic Code and the great reformation under King Josiah in 621 B.C., the law becomes both more ritualistic and more humanitarian. The emergence of both notes, the one so clearly in keeping with the teaching of the prophets, the other apparently at variance with it, calls for explanation. We shall understand it best if we do not import into it modern notions of "narrowness" versus "breadth," but see both as aspects of Yahweh-centeredness. The political situation of Judah was becoming more precarious; the people had seen Samaria swallowed up by Assyria a century before, and now the new Babylonian octopus was extending its tentacles from the East. What more natural than that the combination of nationalism and fear should intensify the demand for the destruction of all foreign cults (Deut. 12:1-3), make idolatry a capital offense (Deut. 13), and center all worship in Jerusalem alone (Deut. 12:13-14; 16:5-6)? Again and again it was affirmed that the very existence of the nation depended on loyalty to the God of the covenant and obedience to his law. The prophets had said this repeatedly, and it was only natural that the law should be understood as entailing both ceremonial and moral obligation. The dual thrust of the book of Deuteronomy should not surprise us in view of the fact that in our own time political and social insecurity appears to be giving an impetus to a revival of religion which is in part marked by moral discernment while in other aspects it is perfunctory and external.

A few years after the great reformation, a fresh voice was heard, proclaiming persistently in opposition to the soothing optimism of the lying prophets of the time that this was no true reform (Jer. 6: 13-14; 8:10-11). We cannot at this point follow the tragic, challenging story of Jeremiah, but with reference to the law he saw, more clearly than any other man of his time, that its essence could not be fulfilled by cultic busyness at the temple. Only the clean heart could suffice. This the people were not rendering to Yahweh (cf. Jer. 4:3-4, 14; 7:21-23; 31:33), and without it neither flirtation nor warfare with Egypt or Babylon could save them. There is a stark hopelessness about Jeremiah's message which sets forth in bold silhouette the great hope of the new covenant. This complete despair of the inviolability of the national state, reinforced a little later by Ezekiel, paved the way for a new understanding of Israel's destiny.

With the Exile, as every student of the Bible knows, came the discovery that Israel could still be Yahweh's people, even without a

41

political state, far away from the Temple and in a strange land. It is significant that this period is marked not only by the emergence of the synagogue as a place of worship but by a fresh attempt to recover, codify, and study the law. From then on, Judaism was to be a religion of the Book, and no small part of it, along with the accounts of the great events of their past, was embodied in the law.

It was a natural development that postexilic Judaism should have become essentially a community of the law. From earliest times, Israel's primary obligations had been to worship Yahweh only and to obey his law. These obligations had not been set aside by the destruction of the state and of Solomon's Temple; in fact, the doom which had fallen through failure to observe them had but validated their binding character. The final chapters of Ezekiel, which give the constitution for a new messianic state centering in a purified Temple and its cult, foreshadow the emergence of a new legalism.

From the time of the Restoration onward, two strains characterize Judaic thought. They were prevalent in the time of Jesus, and as the Evanston discussions of "Christ—the Hope of the World" made evident, their counterparts were taken over into Christianity and persist to the present. One was the apocalyptic expectancy of the establishment of the kingdom of God by divine intervention. The other was the necessity to keep the law of the covenant within such remnants of the state as might remain and under any political regime that might temporarily hold sway. They stemmed from a common source, the rule of Yahweh over his people, and were expressions of a common hope, the "good time coming" when Yahweh would again restore his people to greatness. Yet both the nature of this consummation and the requirements for its fulfillment were different. "If the Apocalyptic longed for the establishment of the Kingdom by the direct activity of God, the law gave voice to the strong feeling that God would neither bless nor set up his Kingdom over a people which did not keep his law." [10] From the latter conviction stemmed the minutiae of oral tradition which constituted the Mishnah and the written commentary upon it which made up the Talmud. It produced both a "holy commonwealth" of the faithful and an artificial legalism against which Jesus had repeatedly to protest.

[10] Bright, op. cit., p. 171.

42

Let us see now what general observations can be gleaned from Israel's course with reference to the law.

The first is that the law was by no means the barren and external thing that the legalists of Jesus' time or the literalists of ours have too often made it. It was founded on bedrock—the righteous, sovereign rule of a protecting, gracious God who demanded its observance. It took on concreteness from the circumstances of the times—social, political, and economic—as ours inevitably must. Yet its basic frame of reference is timeless.

Second, as the God of the Hebrews was too small, so was their moral outlook. Reference has been made to the humaneness of the codes. This was there, but so also was the line between the Hebrew and the alien. Those "strangers" living within the community of Israel had some rights, those outside it none. This distinction appears again and again with regard to treatment of enemies, family relations, slavery, debt, and even to the selling of diseased meat! [11] The laws about sacred seasons, Sabbath observance, details of sacrifice, clean and unclean foods, bulk large in all the codes recorded in the Old Testament. And these were but the nucleus of the "sumptuary legislation" which had become so complex in Jesus' time that thirty-nine different types of labor were forbidden on the Sabbath, each type requiring further oral legislation to designate what did or did not constitute it.[12] Why? The basic reason is that the Hebrews believed Yahweh to be the kind of God who required these things, and not all the preaching of the prophets could dispel this view.

This, of course, is not the whole story. There were injunctions to justice, mercy, and faith both in the law and in the prophets before Jesus' time, and the Old Testament concept of God has in it grandeur as well as narrowness. Yet the codes could go no further than what the people believed their God to require, and in the concrete details of living their restricted vision of God left them limited.

The third deduction we must draw is in regard to what Jesus did with the law. Both of the foregoing elements must be taken into account to understand his attitude. He stood in a great tradition of law observance which he felt no desire or impulse to surrender. It was

[11] Note, for example, Deut. 1:16; 7:2; 14:21; 15:1-2; 23:3.
[12] See Ramsey, op. cit., pp. 49-50, for the list with illustrations of the finespun distinctions thus entailed.

embedded in all his past, and with good reason he could say that he came not to destroy but to fulfill the law. Yet such fulfillment could come only through obedience to the God whose moral demands had undergirded it at its best, not through the petty legalism into which it had fallen. And his God was not the God of Israel only, but the Father whose love with infinite concern for human need embraced all men within its scope. Thus, where the law served both to honor God and to serve human need, he could rejoice in it; where it was at variance, he could boldly set it aside.

It need not surprise us, though it did both surprise and anger his contemporaries, to hear Jesus say:

The sabbath was made for man, not man for the sabbath. (Mark 2:27.)

There is nothing outside a man which by going into him can defile him; but the things which come out of a man are what defile him. (Mark 7:15.)

If you are offering your gift at the altar, and there remember that your brother has something against you, leave your gift there before the altar and go; first be reconciled to your brother, and then come and offer your gift. (Matt. 5:23-24.)

Any other attitude toward the law would have been to forsake both the hesed of his fathers and the way of the God he came to serve and to reveal. It was obedience in love which actuated Jesus, and it is this which he sets before us today.

3. The prophets

Jesus brought together the universal love of God and universal moral obligation, and saw in both the true fulfillment of the law. The prophets before him had in a measure approximated this insight, and Jesus stood in the prophetic tradition. Though we have already had occasion to speak of them, we must now see what was distinctive in their approach to the problems of social morality.

It is the almost universal consensus of serious students of the Bible that in the message of the prophets is the high-water mark of the Old Testament. There are fascinating and meaningful stories in the J, E, D, and P documents and the postexilic short stories, great devotional passages in the Psalms, substantial wisdom literature, and as we have seen, significant structures in Israel's law. Yet the insights of the prophets from Amos through the Second Isaiah surpass them all. I shall attempt not to deal with the message of each one individually, for this has been done many times,[13] but to draw some deductions from their general structure of thought.

The first observation to make is that the prophets, like the compilers of the law, proceeded from the assumptions of the covenant. This made their messages both religious and ethical, with an intertwining which makes it impossible to withdraw either element without losing the heart of their message. They never doubted that Israel was the chosen people of God and that a righteous, gracious, but exacting God demanded obedience of his people. What they objected to, as the burden of their message, were the misunderstandings of God's will which substituted ceremonialism for justice, mercy, and faith, and the apostasies whereby the people persistently violated their side of the covenant.

Did the prophets reject the cultic side of Israel's religion? Their invectives against the substitution of ritualistic correctness for righteousness leave open this possibility, and of the greater prophets Ezekiel alone, standing on the threshold of the postexilic period, expressly calls for a purified ritual as an integral part of the worship of Yahweh. Opinions differ as to whether the others rejected outright the sacrificial cult. It seems more probable, however, that what they protested was not its existence, deeply embedded as it was in the covenant relation, but its perversion through exaltation to a place of primacy. Comparably, no Christian today need object to the ritual and traditional observances of the Church when these contribute to the worship of God, but every Christian ought to protest when "doing things right" in the Church becomes a substitute for righteousness.

Second, the prophets must be understood in both an individual and a social context. This is true whether what is being considered is the source or the object of their message. They were for the most part lone figures assailing the popular mores, and hence misunderstood. But to assume that they were solely individual religious geniuses is to miss the fact that they emerged out of a religious community and spoke to a religious community. They were *Hebrew* prophets, not Greek phi-

[13] The reader who desires a brief summary of the messages of Amos, Hosea, Micah, Isaiah, Jeremiah, Ezekiel, and the Second Isaiah will find it in my *Toward Understanding the Bible*, pp. 67-74, or *The Sources of Western Morality*, pp. 120-40.

losophers or Buddhist Bodhisattvas, and they never dreamed of stepping outside of this framework. Furthermore, though we are accustomed to think of a progressive growth in a sense of individual responsibility from Amos to Ezckicl, the difference at this point is probably overstated. The message of every prophet, Moses, Samuel, Nathan, and Elijah as well as those who came later, was to every individual within the community of Israel, and neither king nor humblest subject was exempt from the obligation to obey the will of Yahweh. The application of this fact to mistaken modern notions of an "individual" versus a "social" gospel is obvious.

Third, though explicit monotheism and universalism were a late development, their nucleus is implicit in all prophetic preaching. The ceremonialism of Israel, though understood by the people as the mark of Israel's particularity, had actually much in common with other primitive religious rites. This similarity was one reason why they found it so easy to take over Canaanitic worship. It was in the ethical insights of Israel, as these were seen most clearly by the prophets, that the greatest distinctiveness lay, and in their vision of the God of righteousness was the germ cell of monotheism. The gods of the nations were many because the nations were many; the God of righteousness was one, and in his hand lay the destinies of nations. As we noted earlier, no sharp distinction was drawn between nature and history; God was the Maker and sovereign Ruler in both spheres. From this conviction, implicit in the whole idea of the covenant but seen with fullest clarity by the prophets, it was a logical step to the conclusion that God had given to Israel special privileges in order to be the special servant of all mankind. This insight, glimpsed by Amos, was destined to come to full expression in the Second Isaiah.

Fourth, the prophets saw with utter clarity the persistent fact of sin, and saw it not as maladjustment or even as failure to "hit the mark" of some objective human standard, but as sin against God. It was rebellion against God and disloyalty to God that made the self-centered luxury of the rich, the exploitation of the poor, bribery, drunkenness, and harlotry such evils. This is not to depreciate the prophets' sense of social justice; they had it in splendid measure. But it was grounded in something more basic than human law or tribal standards. Micah said:

what does the Lord require of you
but to do justice, and to love kindness,
and to walk humbly with your God?

This conviction was the basis of both prophetic judgment and the message of hope. The God who could not countenance sin would not save from destruction even his chosen people who persisted in sin. But neither could the God of mercy abandon his people to their sins. A remnant would return; the Messiah would be sent; the Kingdom would come. Although one reads in the prophets page after page of denunciation and promised doom, it was never the prophets' last word, for it was not God's last word. Those prophets and theologians of today who, like the Old Testament prophets and Paul, from whom they draw much of their message, have a clear and powerful sense of sin would do well to accent as much the prophetic note of hope through the grace of God.

And fifth, in everything the prophets said, they spoke to the current situation. They spoke from a perspective that was more than "current," but they never spoke in abstractions. Where they enunciated general principles, as in Micah's definition of true religion just noted (6:8) or Isaiah-Micah's still unfulfilled vision of a warless world (Isa. 2:2-4; Mic. 4:1-4), they spoke to the people as they were, in terms of what ought to be. The prophets saw and set forth visions that still stir us, but they were not "visionaries." It is because of their utter realism as they spoke within the conditions of a social and political community—or to adopt a current term, a responsible society—that next to the teachings of Jesus we find in them our firmest basis of social ethics.

4. Jesus and the Old Testament

Let us now try to draw together what Jesus took from the Old Testament and what, therefore, Christians may hold to be of permanent validity.

First, Jesus shared with Old Testament thought the general structure of God-centered moral living. It apparently never occurred to him to give ethical injunctions derived from any other source. A great deal of our contemporary problem about "love perfectionism" centers in the attempt to ground ethics either in human nature or in the struc-

47

ture of social institutions. The biblical view—both Old Testament and New—makes obedience to the will of God the final criterion of the good life.

Did Jesus accept the idea of the covenant, and with it of Israel as God's chosen people? This question is crucial for the universality of his message. Apparently, at the beginning of his ministry he conceived his mission as to the "lost sheep of the house of Israel." It was to this group and not to the Gentiles that he commissioned the twelve (Matt. 10:5-6), and his encounter with the Canaanite woman (Matt. 15:21-28) is significant in the fact that he both at first demurred and then yielded to her entreaty for the healing of her daughter. This gives the key to Jesus' attitude. His own people were precious to him, and he never expressly repudiated the covenant relation. Yet to him so universal was the love of God, so compelling the need to serve every human being, that the covenant with its exclusive bounds was left behind. It remained for his followers in the early Church to make concrete the break which his acts and attitudes foreshadowed.

Second, his ethical principles were those of Judaism, yet with a difference in emphasis which makes their impact new. Point for point, there is nothing in the teaching of Jesus which cannot be found in the Old Testament or in the rabbinical teaching. Pharisaism, though it had its faults which called forth Jesus' rebuke, had also in it much that was great and good. Witness, for example, this passage from *The Testaments of the Twelve Patriarchs*, written toward the end of the second century B.C.:

Love ye one another from the heart; and if a man sin against thee, speak peaceably to him, and in thy soul hold not guile; and if he repent and confess, forgive him. But if he deny it, do not get into a passion with him, lest catching the poison from thee he take to swearing and so thou sin doubly. . . . [But] if he be shameless and persist in his wrong-doing, even so forgive him from the heart, and leave to God the avenging.[14]

Nevertheless, taken as a whole, the ethical teaching of Jesus leaves an impression which nothing in Judaism does. This is due in part to the conviction of Christians that Jesus fully exemplified his message, as no individual in prophetism or Pharisaism fully did. But it is due

---

[14] *The Testament of Gad*, tr. R. H. Charles, VII, 3-7.

also to the extent to which Jesus always made human need the criterion of acts of obedient love to God. If the law of the Sabbath stood in the way of human service, it was to be suspended; he ate with publicans and sinners to win them to the Kingdom even at the cost of ceremonial uncleanness. Love of neighbor becomes freely given, uncalculating, unrestricted service, such as is epitomized in the parable of the good Samaritan, and this flows from the nature of the love of God. The love of God, though it appears not infrequently in the Old Testament and in the rabbinical writings, there carries with it a connotation of God's love for the people Israel which was too small for Jesus. He took the moral framework of Israel and transformed it into something so universal, so compelling, that it became new.

And in the third place, as we shall see more fully in the next chapter, Jesus took the eschatology like the ethics of his time and made it into something different. His inheritance from the prophets moralized his expectancy of divine intervention; his own sense of relationship to God gave a new turn to both eschatology and ethics. Probably because of a conviction of the nature of his own messiahship, but certainly because of his conviction that the kingdom of God meant the righteous rule of God in a redeemed community for this world and the next, he made the kingdom of God and not the triumph of Israel the supreme note in his teaching. With all the ambiguities that surround the records of his teaching regarding the Kingdom, it is clear that it embodies the goal of God's reign over the hearts and lives of men, and thus sets forth the great hope of a better world both now and in the world to come. To make Jesus' conception of the Kingdom solely into a better society on earth is to lose its great overtones and foreshorten its vista; to deprive it of ethical content is to emasculate it into something Jesus himself would never have recognized.

Thus it comes about that Jesus, the greatest of the prophets, the fulfillment of the law, inaugurated a new covenant for the redemption of mankind. It is to him, and not to any other teaching or teacher, that we must look for our basic moral insights. It is with good reason that one is reported as saying of old, "Lord, to whom shall we go? You have the words of eternal life."

III. The Ethics of Jesus

IN THE FIRST CHAPTER, reasons were given as to why we cannot find our *primary* authority for the demands of Christian decision in the general field of moral philosophy, or in the moral standards of Christendom, past or present, or in the ethical pronouncements of the churches, corporately or through the words of any one of its leaders, though from all of these sources important insights may be gleaned which we cannot afford to overlook or to discard. It was also said that Christian ethics is rooted in the Bible, but not equally in all parts of it, the New Testament being our more definitive point of reference. It was said, furthermore, that within the New Testament no final authority is to be located in particular words or passages but rather in the total picture it gives of the person and work of our Lord, the life, teachings, ministry, and death of Jesus Christ as the revelation of God.

It would be an engaging task to devote a chapter now to this picture, as it shines through the pages of the Gospels in the records of this life and ministry. However, this has been done a thousand times. The prophecy in the last words of John's Gospel, that if the many other things which Jesus did were to be written, the world itself would not contain the books, comes close to fulfillment in the oft-repeated enterprise of writing a life of Christ or an interpretation of some aspect of his teaching. We shall have to assume that to one who will take the trouble to read this book, both the life and the teaching of Jesus are familiar enough so that references can be made without specific elaboration. Where this is not the case, it is hoped that the passages cited will be consulted as a basis for understanding.

Jesus did not "just happen." He came as the gift of God to all mankind, and his greatness consists both in the purpose of revelation and redemption which God laid upon him and in his own willing, obedient response. The universality of his message is attested by the fact that today, in a world far removed from the peasant simplicity of his life in an occupied province of the Roman Empire, he still wins men to God, transforms lives, and gives guidance for moral decisions. He is the "light of the world" to millions, in an expanding circle of followers that embraces persons in virtually every nation and within every race, class, culture, and economic situation.

So universal is Jesus that while everybody knows he was a Jew, this is not what we ordinarily think about when we look to him for moral guidance. The Sermon on the Mount is for the twentieth-century American as much as it was for the first-century Jew, and requires only a little transference out of its Palestinian context in order to "speak to our condition." This is not to say there are no problems in it. Yet its universal affirmations and imperatives so far transcend its problems that for centuries hosts of Christians, most of them not theologians or professional moralists, have been guided and nourished by it.

Nevertheless, Jesus was a Jew—an uncommonly good, discerning, and devout Jew—as well as the Son of God. When God chose to incarnate himself in human form and Jesus accepted his God-given mission, this incarnation occurred within the stream of a particular history, the history of the Jewish people. Indeed, there could have been no incarnation in an abstraction, for incarnation means concrete embodiment, and concrete embodiment is always historical. The incarnate Lord had to live within a particular time and place, and the time and place of Jesus, with all the past that was focused there, gave the framework for what Jesus was and what he taught.

What will be attempted in this chapter is a summary of what is universally relevant to our lives in the ethical teaching of Jesus. Only enough interpretation will be attempted to make clear the central importance of the elements noted. These moral insights of Jesus, however, will be basic to all that is attempted in the way of application to current problems in Part II of the book.

1. What did Jesus teach?

It is not difficult to summarize with a fair degree of conciseness the principal ethical teachings of Jesus. They are not stated systematically or in a developing logical sequence, as a philosopher might state them, but over and over again they appear—in aphorism, parable, simile, striking hyperbole, in words of commendation or rebuke or in Jesus' own recorded deeds. It is only when we try to balance them one against another and ask how they are to be applied that we run into serious difficulty as to what Jesus meant. Our confusion then may be caused, as the good Bishop Berkeley put it regarding another matter, that we "raise a dust and then complain we cannot see"; yet it is also due at points to a real lack of consistency in what the records tell us Jesus taught. Of this more will be said presently. What, now, is it clear that he did teach?

a) *Jesus taught an ethic completely integrated with his religion.* This is seen in its clearest expression in the two Great Commandments, where the duty of love of neighbor is not an addendum to the obligation to love God without reservation, but is an implicate of it. It appears repeatedly both in Jesus' words and in the total tenor of his life. It was his sense of calling by God that led him at the beginning of his ministry to read in the synagogue the words of Isaiah:

The Spirit of the Lord is upon me,
because he has anointed me to preach good news to the poor.
He has sent me to proclaim release to the captives
and recovering of sight to the blind,
to set at liberty those who are oppressed,
to proclaim the acceptable year of the Lord. (Luke 4:18-19; Isa. 61:1-2.)

These words doubtless state what he felt to be his mandate for action. Are they religion or ethics? The only answer is that they are both, and the passage loses its force if either is withdrawn. Whatever the historicity of the Fourth Gospel, it is fully consistent with his spirit for him to have said before Pilate at the end of his ministry, "For this I was born, and for this I have come into the world, to bear witness to the truth." Is this "truth" religious or moral? It is so clearly both that only a perverted Christianity can deny their relatedness.

To illustrate by a few examples from his precepts, note the reason given for the course of action that is enjoined, "Love your enemies and pray for those who persecute you, so that you may be sons of your Father who is in heaven" (Matt. 5:44-45), or "Blessed are the peacemakers, for they shall be called sons of God" (Matt. 5:9). The term "sons of" was a familiar Semitic expression to denote likeness of character. The same idea is borne out in the oft-debated last verse of the same chapter, "You, therefore, must be perfect, as your heavenly Father is perfect" (v. 48), and in the correlative passage in Luke, "Be merciful, even as your Father is merciful" (6:36). Omit the reference to God from these passages and they simply become counsels of perfection.

b) *Jesus laid primary stress on ethical and spiritual inwardness.* This is not to say that he was indifferent to outward acts, or to the way men conducted themselves toward one another. On the contrary, his most stinging words are directed toward those who "preach, but do not practice"; to those who "bind heavy burdens, hard to bear, and lay them on men's shoulders; but they themselves will not move them with their finger"; to those who "devour widows' houses and for a pretense . . . make long prayers"; to those who are "blind guides, straining out a gnat and swallowing a camel" (Matt. 23:3, 4, 14, 24).[1] Yet the same passage, as well as many others, indicates that his chief concern was with right attitudes from which right acts might proceed. Jesus was completely opposed to the substitution of either ceremonial acts or correct outward behavior for humble obedience to God and loving concern for one's neighbor. This is the main burden of his indictment of the scribes and Pharisees:

Woe to you, scribes and Pharisees, hypocrites! for you tithe mint and dill and cummin, and have neglected the weightier matters of the law, justice and mercy and faith; these you ought to have done, without neglecting the others.

. . . .

Woe to you, scribes and Pharisees, hypocrites! for you cleanse the outside of the cup and of the plate, but inside they are full of extortion and rapacity. You blind Pharisee! first cleanse the inside of the cup and of the plate, that the outside also may be clean. (Matt. 23:23, 25-26.)

Note that he does not condemn ceremonial tithing or making clean

[1] Matt. 23:14, familiar from the King James Version, is placed in a footnote in the R.S.V.

the "outside of the cup"; what he condemns is the substitution of these for something more basic. In gentler tones this is also the burden of the Sermon on the Mount where, without any abrogating of the Ten Commandments, the emphasis is shifted away from legalism to those inner attitudes that determine the nature of a man, and hence his acts.

c) *Jesus set forth a clear pattern of the demands of the God-centered life.* By clear pattern is not, of course, meant a blueprint or easily applicable set of rules. But that we can today speak of "Christian virtues" is due to the fact that one who reads the Gospels seriously is left in no doubt as to the general structure of what a life lived in obedient love would embody. We see it in Jesus himself; we find it on every page of the record; it is epitomized in the Beatitudes. Its primary qualities are a God-centered faith and love. Its derivative aspects are purity of heart, sincerity, humility, forgiveness, love toward enemies, mercy, charity in judgment, honesty in speech and action, sexual purity, renunciation of worldly aims with the preferring of spiritual to material treasure, compassion toward those in need. The good life is that of generous and self-giving service to all men and unbroken, unworried trust in the goodness of God.

It is significant that agape did not have before its use in the New Testament the richness of meaning that it came there to have. In classical Greek it carries "none of the magical power of eros and hardly any of the warmth of *philia*. . . . Its meaning is colourless and indefinite." [2] In fact, it was often used as a mere synonym for eros (passionate, though not necessarily sensual, desire) or for *philia* (liking or caring for another person in the ordinary sense). Jesus gave so clear a picture of what a life centered in the love of God and expressing itself in love for others would be that, when the New Testament was written in Greek, the meaning of agape was transformed. A glance at the list of virtues enumerated in the paragraph above makes it apparent that, taken as a list, they represent merely a set of admirable qualities. One's reaction to them may quite reasonably be that there is nothing unique about them, for they are to be found advocated in Judaism and certain of the non-Christian religions as well as in Greek

---

[2] The Kittel *Wörterbuch* article on agape by Gottfried Quell and Ethelbert Stauffer in *Bible Key Words*, tr. and ed. J. R. Coates (New York: Harper & Bros., 1951), p. 28.

philosophy and the modern secular world. Or one may dismiss them as admirable but unattainable, and of doubtful value even if they could be attained.

To take either of these courses, and let the matter rest there, is to miss what Jesus was concerned about. He did not set out to give a catalogue of virtues, and was apparently quite untroubled as to whether he was saying something new or expressing fully attainable goals of action. His concern was to proclaim the nature of a God-centered, love-filled life lived in obedience to the call of God, and to win men to it. And this he succeeded in doing, in unmistakable terms.

d) *Jesus had a realistic knowledge both of human sin and of the possibilities of the redeemed life.* It is significant that Jesus does not talk about sin nearly as much as Paul. A concordance shows that the word "sin" as a noun appears in his recorded sayings very few times in the Synoptic Gospels, though more in John, and with one exception (the sin against the Holy Spirit, Matt. 12:31; Mark 3:29), when he uses the term, it is in the plural. The Lord's Prayer in Luke contains the petition "Forgive us our sins" (11:4), and it is perhaps unfortunate that we do not commonly use this form instead of "debts" or "trespasses." To the paralytic (Matt. 9:2-6; Mark 2:5-10; Luke 5:20-24) and to the woman who brought the alabaster flask of ointment (Luke 7:47-49) he said, "Your sins are forgiven." Doubtless he said it on occasions that are not recorded, and equally to the discomfiture of those who heard him. Yet if the record in the Synoptic Gospels is to be trusted, he did not, like Paul, look upon sin as an enveloping state of evil resulting from Adam's fall and corrupting man's whole being. Fuller recognition of this fact might give a more constructive turn to much of contemporary theology.

Yet this is not to say that Jesus set forth a doctrine of the natural goodness of man, such as is characteristic of Greek thought and common in present-day humanism. In the records of what Jesus said there is no doctrine of total depravity, but neither is there a sentimental assumption that if a person is well nurtured and his intentions are good, his acts will be good enough. Because "he himself knew what was in man" (John 2:25), he pierced through the veneer of "good" people to their chicanery and self-deception, and saw that the keeping

55

of the commandments from one's youth up was no substitute for single-minded devotion to God (Mark 10:17-22). Yet, on the other hand, he never scaled downward man's possibilities, and the very virtues that have been enumerated as belonging to the life of faith and love are implicit witness to his confidence that man with the help of God could live as the "salt of the earth."

Jesus gives us no explicit doctrine of sin; what he does do is to show us what is wrong with our living and what the good life, centered in obedience to God's will, might be. But how is this to be brought about?

As with sin, Jesus gives no explicit *doctrine* of redemption. Yet there is not the least doubt that Jesus viewed the sins of men with utter seriousness and gave himself with his whole being—even to the Cross —to enable men to find forgiveness and release. The ethical and spiritual insights of Jesus inevitably judge us if we are sensitive to them, yet his primary approach was a positive setting forth of the way in which men's sins could be overcome. The author of the Fourth Gospel caught perfectly the dominant mood and method of Jesus when he wrote, "For God sent the Son into the world, not to condemn the world, but that the world might be saved through him" (3:17).

What are the requirements for sin's conquest? Although these must be gleaned from Jesus' total teaching and ministry and not from systematic analysis, the directives are clear enough. God forgives in infinite love and mercy the sinner who turns to him, as is epitomized in the parable of the prodigal son. The primary focus is on God's act. But the sinner himself must do something about it; it does not happen without cost on man's part as well as God's. These requirements are: *commitment of will* (seek first God's kingdom and his righteousness), *repentance* (repent, for the kingdom of heaven is at hand), *forgiveness of others* (for if you forgive men their trespasses, your heavenly Father also will forgive you; but if you do not forgive men their trespasses, neither will your Father forgive your trespasses), *faith* (your faith has saved you; go in peace) (Matt. 6:33; 4:17; 6:14-15; Luke 7:50). While most of the numerous occasions on which Jesus said, "Your faith has made you well," were in connection with miracles of physical healing and the casting out of demons rather than the conquest of sin, he seems to have drawn no sharp distinctions

56

at this point. To any soul in need the promise of faith was, "Ask, and it will be given you; seek, and you will find; knock, and it will be opened to you" (Matt. 7:7).

And this could happen! Repeatedly, it has happened. Although those contemporary theologies which stress the persistence of sin even in the best Christians have a note of truth which rightly challenges complacency about the redeemed life, it is also true that there are Christian saints who attain to a very high measure of the God-centered faith and love portrayed by Jesus. It is not unreasonable to suppose that most readers of these pages will have known at least one such by whom his life has been blest. But the Christian saint, in whom sin appears to be so nearly conquered, will be the last person to claim merit for himself. For any achievement he will give humble and grateful praise to God. This is what Jesus did when he said, "Why do you call me good? No one is good but God alone." (Mark 10:18; Luke 18:19.) And it is to this spirit that he calls his followers.

c) *Jesus declared the supreme worth of every person to God.* He did not use the phrase heard very commonly two decades ago, "the intrinsic worth of personality," or the one now in more common usage, "the dignity of man." His idea of man was not at variance with either of these concepts, but it is not the way in which he thought. Rather, every person was of supreme worth to him because every person was beloved of God. His total ministry was a ministry of the redemption of persons—whether it was redemption from physical illness, mental disturbance, error, or sin—because he shared the love of God for every person and so gave himself completely to a ministry of helpfulness to all.

The words of Jesus make clear that he valued personality above material things or institutions. "Of how much more value is a man than a sheep! So it is lawful to do good on the sabbath." (Matt. 12:12.) In another setting he declared of God's loving care, "You are of more value than many sparrows" (Matt. 10:31)—a graphic way of affirming the worth to God of man above the total subhuman world. Yet it is in his attitudes and acts, rather than in specific words, that we find the charter of human equality in God's equal concern for all. Whether he dealt with women, children, or slaves, whether the persons in need

57

were Jew, Roman, Syro-Phoenician, or Samaritan, whether he associated with "respectable" people or social outcasts, whether he was illustrating true neighborliness by the story of the good Samaritan or declaring the principle of divine judgment on the basis of "as you did it to one of the least of these my brethren"—all persons were of equal and supreme worth to him because he saw them through the eyes of God.

It is commonly, and correctly, affirmed that democracy has its chief root in Jesus' concern for the worth of persons, though it is not true that this is its sole root. There was democracy as the political ideal in the Greek city-states before Jesus' time, and there are democratic roots—always impinged upon by aristocratic tendencies—in Greek philosophy. Still, the message of Jesus is its chief fountainhead within Christendom. What is not so commonly realized is that the democracy of Jesus in manifold person-to-person relationships was rooted in his relationship to God. He did not set out simply to exalt the dignity of man; yet he lifted the status of men, women, and children wherever his message was heard because he saw all persons as precious to God and equally the recipients of God's love.

Thus it came about that in the early Church democracy and evangelism went hand in hand. The gospel of redemption through the love of God in Christ broke down earthly barriers, and people of every occupational status, degree of wealth, or social standing saw the "middle walls of partition" melt away. In him there was "neither Jew nor Greek, . . . neither slave nor free, . . . neither male nor female," for all were one in Christ Jesus. This grounding is important to any sound preservation or extension of democracy in our own time. But of this, more later.

 f) *The central teaching of Jesus was the kingdom of God.* I have thus far deferred discussion of this central theme, which was on Jesus' lips continually, because in large part its meaning is determined by the teachings already mentioned.

There are both great clarity and great ambiguity in the records as to the message of Jesus in regard to the Kingdom. Everybody agrees that it was his central message, yet there is nothing in New Testament interpretation and scarcely anything in Christian theology about which opinions differ more. The disputed elements center mainly in the bearing of the Kingdom on the ethical demands of the present life in relation to what lies beyond it in a realm that transcends human history—that is, in the relations of ethics to eschatology. Fortunately, the matters most directly related to the practical requirements of the Christian life are those most fully agreed upon, and we shall begin with these.

First, the Kingdom means the sovereign, righteous rule of God in a redeemed society—that is, in a society of persons who accept God's rule and endeavor to live in obedience to his will. The kingship, like the lordship, of God are terms drawn from a monarchical or feudal order, but ought not to suggest to us autocracy or dictatorship. Though Jesus had a realistic sense of divine judgment, as is evident from the parable of the last judgment in Matt. 25:31-46, he never divorced his conception of the Kingdom from the forgiving mercy of God and God's loving care of the individual person. This is evident throughout and conspicuously in this same parable, where one's place in the Kingdom is to be determined by one's responsiveness to human need. Yet it is God, not man, who rules the world, and for the coming of the Kingdom his rule must be accepted by all men.

By a redeemed society—a term which Jesus did not use, though we may—is meant a community of persons responsive to the call of God in faith and love. It does not mean *directly*, as far as we can read Jesus' thought, a set of reconstructed social institutions. He does not have a great deal to say about political or economic structures. But he has much to say about the attitudes and motives of men in their corporate life. He was vitally concerned about sin and the harm it did, both to the sinner and to others.

Jesus' concern about social iniquities always sprang from his indignant perception of their ill effect on individuals. The victim of the bandits on the Jerusalem-Jericho road, the widow mistreated by an unjust judge, the unfortunates on whom publicans like Zaccheus practised extortion, the destitute at a rich man's door, prisoners unvisited and hungry folk unfed—always it was wronged individuals who called out from Jesus a social message.[3]

Therefore, while the Kingdom cannot be directly equated with the

---

[3] Fosdick, *op. cit.*, p. 76. Used by permission of Harper & Bros. The biblical references cited are Luke 10:30-37; 18:2-6; 19:2-10; 16:19-31; Matt. 25:42-43.

social gospel, as American liberal theology has tended to do, the impulse to social action in order to help persons—whether individually or corporately—is in keeping with his spirit and is a legitimate derivative from his message.

Second, Jesus regarded the kingdom of God as the supreme good, worth any cost. It is God's gift, yet it must be sought with all that one has. This appears again and again in such passages as "Seek first his kingdom and his righteousness" (Matt. 6:33), the treasure hid in a field for which one sells all his possessions (Matt. 13:44), the pearl of great price (Matt. 13:45-46). It is a mistake to suppose that man by his own effort can "build the Kingdom," and it is well that this unbiblical metaphor is heard less often than formerly. Yet it is equally a mistake, if we are true to what Jesus tells us, to suppose that God will give the Kingdom without the assumption of responsibility on man's part. Although we are told, "Fear not, little flock, for it is your Father's good pleasure to give you the kingdom" (Luke 12:32), it will not do to forget that the verse before this one says "seek his kingdom" and the one after it enjoins selling all that one has for treasure in heaven.

Third, Jesus is clear as to the conditions of entrance into the Kingdom. All that was summarized as to the pattern of the God-centered life and the requirements for the conquest of sin is here involved. It is not the self-righteous moralist, trusting in his own virtue and his fidelity to the law, who enters the Kingdom; it is one who receives it with the humble trustfulness of a child (Mark 10:15). It is not everyone who is voluble about his religion who shall enter the Kingdom, but he who does the will of the Father (Matt. 7:21). The Kingdom is present among the poor in spirit (Matt. 5:3) and among repentant sinners (Matt. 21:3). The discerning scribe who saw the validity of the two Great Commandments was said to be "not far from the Kingdom of God." (Mark 12:34). The burden of Jesus' message as of John the Baptist's, though with greater gentleness and the strength born of love, was "Repent, for the kingdom of heaven is at hand."

2. Eschatology and ethics

We come now to some issues regarding Jesus' message of the Kingdom about which there is less agreement. We cannot in this brief survey go into every nuance of thought regarding them. But neither can we disregard them, for they are too central to the message of Jesus and hence to our faith.

Eschatology is the doctrine of the "last things." The *eschaton* means the end, and eschatology has to do with what happens at the end of human history and beyond it. There is an eschatology of the individual with reference to concepts of heaven, hell, final judgment, and in general of "eternal life." There are also eschatological beliefs about the future of society and the final destiny of the human race. It is in this second framework that disputes about the Kingdom mainly center, though the two cannot be sharply separated.

A basic question is with regard to the time of the coming of the Kingdom. Is it a present attainment or a hope for the future? And if it is both, is the full consummation of the Kingdom to be in the immediate future or at some indefinite time known only to God? Is the Kingdom to come on earth, or beyond all history? There are passages in the Gospels which seem to support all of these views.

The easiest of these questions is the first, for it is not impossible to suppose that Jesus believed the Kingdom to be in some measure already present while its final consummation was yet to come.

Being asked by the Pharisees when the kingdom of God was coming, he answered them, "The kingdom of God is not coming with signs, to be observed; nor will they say, 'Lo, here it is!' or 'There!' for behold, the kingdom of God is in the midst of you. (Luke 17:20-21.)

This may mean what through the influence of Professor C. H. Dodd has come to be called *realized eschatology*, the belief that Jesus had brought the Kingdom to fulfillment in his own person and he was thereby affirming his messiahship.[4] It seems to me more probable that Jesus meant primarily though perhaps not solely to declare the possibility of entrance into the Kingdom here and now by repentance, the acceptance of God's forgiveness, and the assumption of the obligations of discipleship. The parables of the leaven (Matt. 13:33; Luke 13:20-21), the mustard seed (Mark 4:30 ff.; Matt. 13:31-32; Luke 13:18-19), and the seed growing secretly until it becomes "first the blade,

---

[4] See his *Parables of the Kingdom* (New York: Chas. Scribner's Sons, 1936) for an elaboration of this view; also Bright, *op. cit.*, ch. vii, for a modified form of it.

then the ear, then the full grain in the ear" (Mark 4:26-29) not only are parables of growth; they are indexes that what the Kingdom will be is already present in what is. Yet the references of Jesus to the Kingdom again and again have a futuristic note, and if there were no other reason, the fact that he taught his followers to pray, "Thy kingdom come," would be sufficient evidence that he did not regard it as having fully come.

The issues of chief difficulty arise at the point of questions as to whether Jesus expected the Kingdom to come on earth or only in some realm beyond earthly history, and in the latter event, whether he expected earthly history to end very soon by a catastrophic divine intervention when he himself would return in glory to reign over a transfigured world. Thus, the whole question of the Second Coming is tied in with the issue. These problems all come to focus in the question as to whether Jesus' view of the Kingdom was primarily eschatological or ethical and spiritual. Anyone who followed in the slightest the discussions before and at the Evanston Assembly of the World Council of Churches on the main theme "Christ—the Hope of the World" will recognize the disparities of judgment among Christians today at this point.

There are some, though it is a minority position among New Testament scholars, who think that the apocalyptic passages attributed to Jesus were interpolations of early Christian thought. This would be a comfortable way out of the impasse if we could think so, for in view of the fact that the end of the world has not yet come, it is not easy to fit into the rest of his words such sayings as, "Truly, I say to you, there are some standing here who will not taste death before they see the Son of man coming in his kingdom" (Matt. 16:28; cf. Mark 9:1; Luke 9:27), or after a vivid description of the signs of the end, "Truly, I say to you, this generation will not pass away till all these things take place" (Matt. 24:34; Mark 13:30; Luke 21:32). Nevertheless, the passages are too deeply embedded to be thus discarded. Some may have been confused by the early Church with prophecies of the destruction of Jerusalem, for Jesus saw that his countrymen knew not the "things that make for peace" (Luke 19:42) and that their doom was approaching. Some of them may have been, as

Professor Dodd suggests,[5] mixtures of references to Jesus' resurrection and his second coming. But with due recognition of these possibilities, it still remains probable that Jesus shared the apocalyptic expectations common in Judaism in the first century and looked upon himself as God's chosen agent for bringing these things to pass. The incarnate Lord lived at a particular time and place in history, and in his apocalypticism Jesus was apparently a man of his time.

What does this do to his ethics? Does it destroy the validity of his teachings as universal principles? The answer is No.

It does not make his teachings an "interim ethic." In later Judaism it was believed that the precepts of the Torah were valid for the next world as well as this. Jesus apparently held this view with regard to what he proclaimed to be the will of God, for he never suggests that he is saying something of only temporary relevance. In fact, the contrary is clearly implied in the declaration, "Heaven and earth will pass away, but my words will not pass away" (Matt. 24:35; cf. Luke 16:17).

It does not make of his teachings counsels of perfection for the next life only. As was earlier remarked, Jesus was apparently not concerned over the exact degree of attainability of his precepts. He stated what he believed to be *right*—what a person would do if he loved, trusted, and obeyed God completely. It is unlikely either that he was so naïve as to suppose that men could be perfect as God is perfect or that the attempt to do so was inconsequential.

It does not submerge his ethics in eschatology. Eschatology was undoubtedly present in the thought of Jesus, as it should be in ours, an eschatology of both eternal life for the individual and the hope of a final consummation of the reign of God beyond earthly time and space. Both the corruption of earthly history by persistent sin and the grandeur of a vista that transcends it lend support to the view that the kingdom of God will fully come, not on earth, but beyond this world. In this final victory

> He shall reign forever and ever,
> King of kings! and Lord of lords!

and the only appropriate response of the Christian is "Hallelujah!" But

[5] *Ibid.*, pp. 97-101.

this does not mean that what Jesus has taught us of the good life here and now is set aside. Christ is our hope—now, in the earthly future, and for eternity.

The eschatology of Jesus was never the ethically barren thing that either the apocalyptists of his time or the premillennialists of ours have too often made it. Not only repentance, but sensitiveness to a brother's need, determined status in the Kingdom (Matt. 4:17; 25:31-46). There is a tension between this world and the world to come, but to Jesus its resolution lay in God's control over both realms and man's responsive, obedient acceptance of God's rule in faith and love and deeds of service. The God to whom Jesus prayed was the Lord of heaven and earth; his will must be done "on earth as it is in heaven." Jesus' outlook was too profoundly God-centered and ethical to permit him to fall prey to pessimism regarding this world's fate, or asceticism regarding God's gifts within it, or spectacularism regarding the grand finale, or moral indifference regarding the pedestrian steps God's servants must take along the way. In short, his total outlook without eliminating eschatology transformed it.

3. The ethics of compromise

A word must now be said on a matter on which Jesus did not say very much, and because he did not, Christians are left in great disagreement as to how to apply his principles. This is the question of compromise in the practical affairs of the social, political, and economic orders, where any course that can be followed leads to unideal results below the standards of the Kingdom. This is the familiar problem of "love perfectionism" and the absoluteness of Jesus' ethics in contrast with the necessary relativity of their application.

We shall best get a perspective on it by asking, first, where the problem centers and, second, what light we get from Jesus as to its solution.

It centers in two focuses: eschatological and mundane. By the eschatological focus, as we must continue to insist, we do not mean that Jesus proclaimed a completely otherworldly and transmundane ethic. Yet if we take eschatology in its broadest sense as equivalent to "heaven," and heaven again as equivalent to the "realm of God," Jesus announced an eschatological structure in his proclamation of

64

the Kingdom. It is significant that he used the terms "kingdom of God" and "kingdom of heaven" interchangeably. He did not place "heaven" wholly in a transmundane sphere, but he did proclaim the way men would be and would live if they were fully responsive to the rule of God in the realm of God. Apparently such social applications as he made were incidental to this primary purpose. It is well for us that he did so, for not only did he give us what we need most, but with radically changed social conditions the applications must change from age to age while his insights are eternal.

The other focus centers both in human sin and in the complexity of human social relations. Of sin, Jesus had ample awareness. It was for men's "hardness of heart" that Moses permitted divorce (Matt. 19:8; Mark 10:5); it is the "cares of the world and the delight in riches" that choke the word (Matt. 13:22; Mark 4:19). And for sin, repentance, forgiveness, faith, and obedience in love were the answer. It would never have occurred to Jesus to talk about the "lesser of two evils," for to him sin was the supreme evil which must be eradicated root and branch—or to use his own metaphor, eye, hand, and foot (Matt. 5:29-30; 18:8-9; Mark 9:43-48).

Of the complexity of human relations Jesus says little that is explicit. He makes some observations about the difficulty of a rich man's entering the kingdom of God (Matt. 19:24; Mark 10:25), about the futility of massive accumulations of goods as a source of security (Luke 12:16-21), about the inevitable doom awaiting those who were not following the ways that lead to peace (Luke 19:41-44). Yet, both because the making of changes in the institutional structure was not his chief concern and because his human vista was limited by the conditions of a simple peasant society east of the Mediterranean in the first century A.D., he obviously could not foresee or make pronouncements upon the vast complex of particular problems that confront Christians in today's world.

Nevertheless, he does not leave us in the dark. What, then, must we hold before us as we deal with the relativities of human existence in which some compromise seems inevitable?

First, Jesus never relaxed or scaled down the necessity of absolute, single-minded devotion to God, whatever the circumstances. There is no evidence that he believed the methods of love would always "work" in human society. In fact, he foresaw that they would not. Regarding his own fate, he "began to show his disciples that he must go to Jerusalem and suffer many things from the elders and chief priests and scribes, and be killed" (Matt. 16:21; Mark 8:31; Luke 9:22); regarding his followers, he promised them that fidelity to his gospel would bring upon them not peace but a sword and the severest of domestic tensions (Matt. 10:34-36; Mark 13:12; Luke 12:51-53). Yet there is no easing of the requirement of utter integrity and of complete fidelity to the call of God. Some, though not all, contemporary discussion of compromise presupposes that physical security or social adjustment are ends so important that recourse must be had to compromise in order to secure them. This was not Jesus' view.

Nevertheless, as if with tongue in cheek, Jesus tells his followers that the "sons of this world are wiser in their own generation than the sons of light" (Luke 16:8) and suggests that as they go out into a wolflike world, they be "wise as serpents and innocent as doves" (Matt. 10:16). Does this mean that they were to emulate worldly subtlety? Hardly, but to Jesus fidelity to God was no excuse for naïveté. The gospel requires of men their best, including the best of strategy. One must "beware of men," and there are occasions for flight rather than martyrdom (Matt. 10:17-23). But not at the cost of fidelity and faith. The Oxford Conference in its report on "The Universal Church and the World of Nations" caught perfectly the deduction to be drawn when it affirmed, "To do what appears as relatively best is an absolute duty before God, and to fail in this is to incur positive guilt." [6]

Taken as a whole, the message of Jesus does not tell us to choose the lesser of two evils. It does tell us, with a realistic awareness of the range of these evils, to choose the greater good. This is more than a verbal difference, for the one takes the world's evil as its base line, the other takes God's goodness as it has been made manifest in Jesus. The greater good is that course of action which, in a given circumstance, is relatively the fullest embodiment of faith and love with God at the center in the act of decision.

Circumstances change, and with them courses of action. God does

[6] The Oxford Conference (Official Report), Section V, 7.

not change, nor the type of obedient, faith-filled love which Jesus embodied and proclaimed. He does not, therefore, leave us unguided at the point of the concrete decisions of life. How his principles give guidance among the relativities of our present world will be the main theme of the second half of this book.

IV. Ethical Perspectives of the Early Church

BEFORE SURVEYING the principal elements in the ethics of Jesus, we looked at the underlying notes in the Old Testament. These are important both for the permanent wisdom they yield, as part of our Christian Scriptures, and for the light they throw on the framework of Jewish life and thought in the midst of which Jesus lived and did the work of his earthly ministry. Comparably, there is a forward movement from Jesus, of which the New Testament tells us much if we read it with discernment. It is recorded by implication in the epistles, the Gospels, and Revelation, and explicitly in the book of Acts. This period also we must examine, both for its permanent contributions to Christian morals and for light as to what the Church in its earliest beginnings did with the Good News that had come to men in Jesus.

As before, no attempt shall be made to cover the entire field. The most crucial issues are those of the relations of the law and the gospel, the relations of the Christian community to its concept of the Kingdom, and the attitudes of these first Christians to social institutions. These problems, though in very different circumstances, are still our problems. The answers then accepted need not in every respect be our answers, but neither can they be disregarded, for these issues are deeply embedded both in the Bible and in the demands of Christian moral decision.

These three issues, as will presently become evident, are closely interrelated. Yet we must attempt to look at them in sequence.

1. The law and the gospel

The problem of the relations of the law and the gospel is essentially that of two kinds of authority: code morality or externally given or authoritarian morality versus the loving, faith-filled response of the Christian to the grace of God in Christ. To see more clearly what this means, we must look at two major issues: the relation of Christianity to the moral obligations resting upon Israel, and the more difficult and important problem of the relation of the gospel of salvation through Christ to the law of love.

On the first of these issues enough has already been said to note the attitude of Jesus, and thus to get directives for ourselves. The moral law of Israel, as obedience to the will of the God who required of men justice, mercy, and faith, Jesus never set aside, though by his acts and his words he put deeper and wider content into these terms than any before him had done. The ceremonial law, as a good Jew, he apparently retained except where it conflicted with service to human need, and this was often. Then he did not hesitate to disregard it.

When Paul speaks as he does at length about "the law," he does not draw the distinction made in the previous paragraph between the moral and the ceremonial law. It would have saved much confusion for later generations of Christians if he had, but he had no idea that he was writing for later generations. As a Jew trained in the Pharisaic tradition, the law meant to Paul simply the law of his fathers. A basic question of the early Church was what to do about it.

With regard to the ceremonial law, the answer was clear enough, and it is familiar. It came to Peter in the vision of common and unclean animals let down from heaven, and the voice which said to him, "What God has cleansed you must not call common" (Acts 11:9). It came in the dispute in the Jerusalem church over whether to require circumcision of Gentile Christians and the compromise proposed by James— a compromise in which one of four prohibited elements is a moral issue still relevant to Christians while the other three have ceased to have significance (Acts 15:1-21). It came to Paul in the conviction that the law was our schoolmaster (R.S.V. custodian) until Christ came, but that being justified by faith we are no longer under it (Gal. 3:23-26).

Was Paul antinomian? That is, did he reject the law as binding upon Christians? It depends on what aspect of the law is meant. When Paul illustrates the law, he usually cites circumcision, and thereby typifies

69

the basic structure of Jewish ceremonialism.[1] He is as clear in his repudiation of this as the source of salvation as he is in his repeated assertions that it is through faith in Jesus Christ, and not through works of the law, that a man is justified. Yet if the moral law means moral obligation ordained of God, Paul did not repudiate it as binding upon Christians or regard it as irrelevant. Unmistakable pointers in the opposite direction are found not only in his repeated moral injunctions, epitomized in Rom. 12 and Gal. 5, but in the express statements that "love is the fulfilling of the law" (Rom. 13:10) and "the whole law is fulfilled in one word, 'You shall love your neighbor as yourself'" (Gal. 5:14).

But is love a command? And how is it related to the good news of justification by faith? And how are both related to the person and work of Christ? And if "love is the fulfilling of the law," does this establish or abrogate a moral legalism? The mere posing of these questions indicates that the problem of what Paul and the early Church did with the law is by no means settled by the fact that they set aside the ceremonial requirements of Judaism and retained a sense of God-given moral obligation.

To begin with the first of these questions, it must be recalled that in the Bible it is agape, not philia or eros, that is a divine demand. Agape is unmotivated love—in the human setting, concern for a neighbor's need regardless of whether the neighbor is likable, or worthy of it, or likely to reciprocate it. Philia is the emotional response of one personality to another; eros is the recognition of and quest for value, whether in another person or the total situation, and hence it is always "motivated" love. Agape is the word most often used for love in Paul's letters as well as in the Gospels. It is agape which is "patient and kind; . . . not jealous or boastful; . . . not arrogant or rude . . . does not insist on its own way; . . . is not irritable or resentful; . . . does not rejoice at wrong, but rejoices in the right" (I Cor. 13:4-6). Such love is for the Christian an unconditional demand.

Yet this demand does not rest on any "natural," that is, ordinary human, basis. Agape is required of us because agape has been given to us by the free, uncalculating, unmotivated love of God. This agape of God has come to men through God acting in Christ, and is mediated through the Holy Spirit. The heart of Paul's understanding of the gospel

[1] Rom. 2:25-29; 3:27-31; 4:9-12; I Cor. 7:18-19; Gal. 5:6; Phil. 3:3; Col. 2:11; 3:11.

is found in the words, "God shows his love for us in that while we were yet sinners Christ died for us" (Rom. 5:8), and "God's love has been poured into our hearts through the Holy Spirit which has been given to us" (Rom. 5:5). As to Paul the Holy Spirit and the Spirit of Christ are terms used interchangeably, so for most purposes and in most contexts the *agape* and the *charis* (grace) of God are identical, and both represent the love of God coming to us in Christ. It is this which is the ground of the Christian's faith and hope, and the source of his obligation to love his neighbor.

Thus it appears that *pistis* (faith) is very intimately connected with love, and it is "faith working through love" (Gal. 5:6) that sums up the Christian's moral obligation. The follower of Christ surrenders himself in gratitude and faith to Christ, lives in Christ, finds himself released from bondage to sin, and affirms with utter confidence, "There is therefore now no condemnation for those who are in Christ Jesus. For the law of the Spirit of life in Christ Jesus has set me free from the law of sin and death."

As a result, Paul is the great exponent of the "liberty of the Christian man." The letter to the Galatians makes this its main theme; it is implied throughout Paul's writing. There is arresting tautology—but more than that—in the exclamation, "For freedom Christ has set us free" (Gal. 5:1), for Paul repeatedly stresses the need to be free from the bondage of sin in order to live freely as the bond servant of Christ. In the new freedom thus won there are obligations to be met; liberty does not mean license. Yet the man who has "put on Christ" is no longer chained to the law.

So far, the message of deliverance from sin through the grace of God in Christ, with the consequent duty of the Christian to live in faith and love, is unequivocal. It does not attempt to analyze the infinite mystery of God's grace, on the one hand, or on the other, to tell Christians precisely and legalistically what to do in all the events of life. Yet its focus and base are self-consistent, and set forth the union of faith and love in obedience to Christ which are primary and indispensable notes in Christian living. We owe Paul an incalculable debt for thus formulating the foundations of Christian life and thought.

But what about post-conversion sin? Here Paul is much less clear and less helpful. It is a question we cannot avoid, for it is an empirical fact that Christians continue to sin after being converted by the grace of God in Christ. The problems of Christian ethical decision would be greatly simplified if the sole requirement were to accept the gift of salvation through Christ, and then feel full assurance that all we did after that was approved of God! Christians have again and again tried to maintain this view but the fruits of such a doctrine of "entire sanctification" have not been such as to convince others of its validity. The Roman Catholic confessional is built upon the realization of continuing sin, and the Protestant emphasis on justification by faith, though rightly stressing the lifting of the burden of sin by God's act, still is forced to recognize the sinning of the redeemed.

There is no doubt that Paul himself upon his conversion experienced an "about-face" that gave him not only a new center of loyalty in Christ, but a moral dedication which was broader in its range, more sensitive in its insights into the nature of the "fruit of the Spirit," than before. Yet this does not mean that Paul never sinned thereafter. In fact, he expressly disclaims the notion that he is "already perfect" (Phil. 3:12-16). Yet elsewhere, in his eagerness to declare the difference Christ makes, he seems to say that it is impossible for the Christian who is under grace and not under the law to sin. At the beginning of Rom. 6, where the question is raised as to whether we are to continue in sin that grace may abound, he answers emphatically, "How can we who died to sin still live in it?" and that this means not only that we *ought not*, but *cannot*, continue to sin is implied throughout the rest of the chapter. In fact, this is expressly stated in the words, "For sin will have no dominion over you, since you are not under law but under grace" (Rom. 6:14).

In practice, Paul assumed that Christians though under grace still sinned; yet he gave no theoretical basis for this assumption. This was a serious omission. What is needed and not stated is a doctrine of the need of continuing repentance correlative with God's continuing grace and forgiveness. The Church, both Roman Catholic and Protestant, found it necessary to supply it; but as any good concordance will indicate, the word "repentance" appears scarcely at all in Paul's writings.

That this omission had consequences in the life of the Church is apparent from the diversity of doctrines—not all of which can possibly be true—that have been drawn from Paul's words. At one extreme is the doctrine of the entire sanctification of the redeemed. At the other, in protest against the self-righteous "perfectionism" thus implied, is the current neo-orthodox tendency to stress the continuance of sin in the most saintly Christians, with reluctance to grant any significant moral achievement as the result of redemption lest it savor of human presumption. Yet both of these are mistaken views, for no Christian is sinless and no real Christian fails to find some moral victory over sin. A Christian ought to—and manifestly often does—"grow in the grace and knowledge of our Lord and Savior Jesus Christ" (II Pet. 3:18), and to grow in grace is also to grow in the works of love.

Both these perversions stem from a common source, which has haunted the history of the Church. This is the tendency to think of being "in sin" and "under grace" as states of existence, not as moral attitudes directed to particular moral choices. Jesus, we saw, stressed continually the necessity of right inner attitudes but never in dissociation from the concrete decisions men must make in daily life. Paul did this also, when he was giving moral advice to the churches. But when he was writing theology, he seemed to assume that sin could be "put off" and Christ "put on" with one cataclysmic change. As a result, he failed to give guidance to the point of the need of continuing, repeated acts of repentance, and opened the door to an "unmoralizing" of Christian conversion which is the antithesis of what Jesus taught and Paul doubtless intended.

That this did not have more serious consequences in the early Church is due to the fact that, in general, its moral insights were not greatly at variance with those of Jesus. Paul did not know Jesus personally, but the memory of Jesus' words and deeds was still fresh in Christian circles. The ethical content of "faith working through love" must thus have been considerably influenced. In spite of a certain parochialism in the primitive Church, the general trend of its moral standards shows far more agreement with the spirit of Jesus than departure from it. This makes it possible, unless one is so slavishly literalistic as to overlook all the situation-conditioned elements, to find a common pattern of Christian morality in the New Testament. This has long been a part of the Christian message and ought still to be.

To return to the positive notes in the message of Paul, it is of prime significance that in both Jesus and Paul it is the love of God that calls forth the human response of faith, of hope for this life and the life to come, and the requirement and possibility of agape love for one's neighbor in need. It cannot be too strongly stressed, in contrast to a secular moralism which finds its base in social adjustment, or a balancing of human values, or a natural law of morality, that the center of New Testament ethics lies in the love requirement which in turn stems from the free gift of God's love to the undeserving. It is because "a man is not justified by works of the law but through faith in Jesus Christ" (Gal. 2:16) that faith working through love becomes not only a source of emancipation from the law, but the supreme moral obligation.

But is there no goodness outside the circle of those redeemed by Christ? The sharpness of Paul's condemnation of those who try to save themselves by the works of the law, and the vividness of his description of "this body of death" before the power of sin is broken by Christ, have traditionally been made to bear the weight of a doctrine of total depravity in the natural man. It is possible that Paul never fully faced or resolved this question, but he seems nevertheless to have recognized some measure of moral discernment outside of both Judaism and Christianity:

When Gentiles who have not the law do by nature what the law requires, they are a law to themselves, even though they do not have the law. They show that what the law requires is written on their hearts, while their conscience also bears witness and their conflicting thoughts accuse or perhaps excuse them on that day when, according to my gospel, God judges the secrets of men by Christ Jesus. (Rom. 2:14-16.)

The significance of this passage is great for a secular world which tries to "do by nature" what social expectation, or civil law, or conscientious impulses dictate, with resulting accusations and excuses. The trouble with such morality is not its immorality; it is its inadequacy. And its inadequacy stems from its failure to be rooted in a God-centered faith and love which are the fruit of a Christ-filled life. Paul makes it abundantly clear that for this, there is no substitute.

In short, for Paul no legalism, Judaic or Gentile, would suffice. Nor should it for us. This is not to say that the Christian is entitled to cast aside the moral law of Israel, or the law "written on the hearts" of men through a long moral heritage in which God has been endeavoring to educate the human race. Yet in the conflict of opinions which daily confronts us, only one law is either adequate or mandatory. This is to trust, obey, and love supremely the God who has loved us enough to give us Christ, and living in Christ to love our neighbor as the fulfilling of the law.

2. The Kingdom and the Christian community

This absolute demand of the gospel, when stated as a generalization, is seldom questioned by Christians, though no Christian if he is honest with himself will claim that he has met it. But one must attempt to meet it within a particular time and place. And in this attempt, prevailing patterns of thought are bound to affect one's outlook. So it was in the early Church. The early Christian community, partly from prevalent Jewish apocalyptic ideas and partly from the words of Jesus, was eschatological in its frame of reference. Hence, problems of eschatology and ethics are basic to much of the record.

In the preceding chapters it was insisted that Jesus had an eschatological outlook, though not so otherworldly and nonethical an outlook as some premillenarians, adventists, and contemporary dialectical theologians have ascribed to him, and that he probably anticipated an end of the existing regime in the not distant future. In any case, the early Church unmistakably held to this view, as is evident not only from the writings of Paul (Rom. 13:11; I Cor. 7:29; 15:51; I Thess. 4:17) but from other passages as well (cf. Heb. 10:25; I Pet. 1:5; 4:7; Rev. 1:3; 22:6-7, 20). This did not give the Church an "interim ethic" for the relatively short remaining time in the sense made famous by Schweitzer in *The Quest of the Historical Jesus*, though it did lead to counsels of celibacy by Paul, and still more to injunctions to readiness in view of the sudden, unknown hour of the coming of the day of the Lord (I Thess. 5:1-11).

More influential, however, than the thought of the early Church about the time of the coming of the Kingdom was the way in which the Kingdom itself was conceived. For this we must look at the total setting of the New Testament kerygma, or witness to the faith, for while references to the Kingdom were constantly on the lips of Jesus, they become noticeably fewer in the rest of the New Testament. They are found occasionally in Paul's writings and recur in the Apocalypse, but outside of the Gospels the main theme of the New Testament becomes, not the Kingdom, but Christ and redemption through his Cross.

The implicit eschatology of the Kingdom in the New Testament centers in the transformation of the old covenant into the new; in fact, the very words "New Testament" mean "New Covenant." The old covenant, so vital to the faith and life of Israel, was now transformed into something having no national boundaries. Already this had been anticipated by Jesus in his freely given healing and service to all and at least indirectly in his words (Matt. 8:11; 21:43); now the break becomes clear and explicit. The Church is the "Israel of God" (Gal. 6:16); to belong to Christ is to be "Abraham's offspring, heirs according to promise" (Gal. 3:29). In words strongly reminiscent of the Mosaic covenant (Exod. 19:6) the fellowship in Christ is declared to be a "chosen race, a royal priesthood, a holy nation, God's own people" (I Pet. 2:9). This conviction is stated repeatedly, and the words immediately following the last quotation give the reason—"that you may declare the wonderful deeds of him who called you out of darkness into his marvelous light." The words of institution of the Lord's Supper, still heard around the world in the most sacred of Christian rites, bear witness to this conviction, "This cup is the new covenant in my blood" (I Cor. 11:25; Luke 22:20).

But not only had the old covenant been set aside; its promise and hope had been fulfilled in the coming of Christ. In Jesus as the Messiah, the hope had been vindicated; God's victory over sin was manifest; his final victory over the world and the powers of evil was assured. With the coming of the Son of God the Kingdom was already at hand; with his death and resurrection the power of sin and of death was broken, and Satan vanquished. Henceforth, the followers of Christ could live as citizens of the new age—heirs of a Kingdom already established though in its fullness it was a Kingdom yet to be consummated.

There is an important difference between the eschatology of the Old Testament and that of the New. While the faith of Israel presupposed God's continuous control over nature and history, the hope of the Kingdom was always projected into the future. In the New Testament, the Kingdom of the future is already a *present possession.*

Not only is this duality to be found in the recorded words of Jesus, as we have noted, but with or without the use of the term "Kingdom," its presuppositions appear throughout the literature of the early Church. The Christian has been delivered by the new Adam from the legacy of the old Adam into a new kingdom of the spirit (I Cor. 15:22, 45-49); he has been delivered from the kingdom of darkness and transferred to the kingdom of the Son of God (Col. 1:13); he has "tasted . . . the powers of the age to come" (Heb. 6:5) and his commonwealth is in heaven (Phil. 3:20). Nevertheless, he still awaits "the time for establishing all that God spoke by the mouth of his holy prophets from of old" (Acts 3:21) and the coming of the glorious consummation.[2]

This idea of the Kingdom as already present, and as yet to come, was bound to have important ethical consequences. To observe them it is necessary to note that it was not simply a telescoping of two incompatible ideas; it was an assertion of two basic truths, both so indispensable that neither one could be surrendered then, or ought to be surrendered now.

The positive moral value that emerged from this conviction was a sense of joyous confidence, that transformed the little community from a mood of passive waiting to urgency in witness, fidelity in mutual service, and at least relative steadfastness in the Christian virtues. The Church of the first century never identified its own visible structure with the kingdom of God, and both the accounts of unbrotherly strife in the churches that give realism to the records and Paul's continuous moral injunctions give evidence that the citizens of the commonwealth of heaven still retained plenty of earthly qualities. Yet the picture as a whole shows not only remarkable courage in the spread of the evangel, but great mutual concern as they shared their daily bread and ministered to those in need (Acts 2:44-46; 6:1-6). As earlier noted, the witness to the evangel had a great democratizing influence, and before it human distinctions melted, walls of partition were broken down.

It is, of course, possible to say that this would have happened anyway through the love commandment of Jesus, regardless of eschatology.

---

[2] This interpretation of New Testament eschatology, which follows closely that of John Bright in *The Kingdom of God*, differs from "realized eschatology" in that the latter stresses the Kingdom as a present fact inaugurated by Jesus without the counterbalancing futuristic element. Cf. Bright, p. 237.

This could theoretically be true, but in actuality the obligation to love one another, to have faith in the "God and Father of our Lord Jesus Christ," to rejoice in membership in his Kingdom, and to await in steadfastness its coming were blended into one. This is illustrated not only by the references to the future in the thirteenth chapter of First Corinthians, but by the fact that in the most "moralistic" book of the New Testament, the epistle of James, there are warnings as to the futility of riches and the fate of exploiters in the last days (5:1-6), and injunctions to steadfastness as the brethren wait in patience for the coming of the Lord (5:7-9).

A second effect, less true to the spirit and teaching of Jesus, was the tendency to substitute the new community of the faithful for the old community of Israel, and except for the obligation to spread the gospel, to have relatively slight concern for those outside the Christian fellowship. Limited as were the opportunities for general social service in the little Christian minority, they can scarcely be charged with failure to undertake large projects of relief or reform in the world about them. At this point the Pauline injunction, "So then, as we have opportunity, let us do good to all men, and especially to those who are of the household of faith" (Gal. 6:10), probably represents the best that could be done under the circumstances. More serious, however, was the drawing of sharp lines about the Christian group as the recipients of God's love and favor. This was in part the result of the eschatological concept of salvation that pervaded the early Church, in part the result of a too limited idea of the scope of *agape*.

As Israel had looked for the coming of the Messiah to establish God's kingdom and reign in glory over the people of God, so the Christian community was convinced that the Messiah *had come*, and that they, the followers of Christ, were now God's elect. Participants here and now in the Kingdom, destined to share Christ's victory in the world to come, they could witness to this faith and live or die with joyous abandon. Yet out of this conviction of the "apartness" of the Christian community came a parochialism which in the New Testament letters and the book of Revelation contrasts sharply with the universalism of the vista of Jesus, and which has pursued the Church to the present day. If we do not feel the force of this contrast upon casual reading, this may be because we tend to read the rest of the New Testament in the light of the Synoptic Gospels. For example, it is the opinion of not a few biblical scholars that the love commandments in the Fourth Gospel and the epistles of John, so often quoted to stress the universality of the Christian ethic, were originally understood as applying only within the Christian community, and as in the Old Testament "Love your neighbor" meant "Love your fellow Israelite," so the corresponding "new commandment" was taken to mean, "Love your fellow Christian." [3]

The effect of this restriction appears today if we ask the question, "Who is a son of God?" To some Christians the answer is self-evident —all men are. To others this appears as a "liberal" perversion of biblical truth, for it is contended that according to the Bible only the followers of Christ are sons of God and hence with Christ heirs of salvation. We shall in all probability align ourselves on one side or the other according to what part of the Bible we regard as definitive.

Eschatology and ethics meet in this basic issue, for it involves not only the scope of God's love and favor and of our responsibility but the question of eternal destiny. When Jesus said, "Love your enemies and pray for those who persecute you, so that you may be sons of your Father who is in heaven," he immediately followed these words with a statement of the universality of God's love and care (Matt. 5:44-45). Though he did not explicitly use the words so familiar in our time, the "fatherhood of God" and the "brotherhood of man," these implications are clear in what we know of his words and deeds. There is no suggestion in the Sermon on the Mount that in the prayer to "our Father," God is to be regarded as the Father of Christians only. The phrases "your Father" and "your brother" were often on his lips.[4] Paul by stressing the acquisition of sonship by acceptance of Christ, and circumscribing this still further by a doctrine of divine election (Rom. 8), introduced a note which has had far-reaching consequences. It marks today a line of division between those Christians who are committed to a social gospel because of the many-sided obligation to love and serve all men as sons of God, and those others who see the primary, if not

[3] Cf. Kittel, Wörterbuch, op. cit., p. 58.
[4] Note the words of Jesus in Matt. 5:16, 22-24, 48; 6:1, 4, 6, 8, 9, 14, 15, 18, 26, 32; also his reference to "my brethren" in Matt. 25:40. It requires much straining of the context to suppose that these words were intended by Jesus to apply only to Christians.

the sole, Christian obligation as winning others to *become* sons of God and hence heirs of eternal life.

To grasp the full significance of this distinction, it is necessary to recapture something of the eschatological mood of the first century. Who were to be "heirs of the promise" (Heb. 6:17; Gal. 3:29) sharing the glories of Christ's victory in the Kingdom that was to come? Obviously, God's elect, those "faithful unto death" to whom "the crown of life" was promised (Rev. 2:10). Fidelity in witness, steadfastness in faith, were constantly enjoined, but the moral requirement of service to "the least of these my brethren" so vividly set forth by Jesus as the criterion of a place in the Kingdom was largely overlooked if not forgotten. The fruits of this too limited view of the divine fatherhood, of our sonship, and of what it means to "accept Christ" are with us still.

3. *The gospel and social institutions*

We must conclude this chapter with a look at what changes came upon the early Church, through its conviction of salvation through the Cross of Christ, in relation to the social environment. Though citizens of heaven, free from the Jewish law, these Christians were still subjects of the Roman state living for the most part in families and supporting themselves by mundane labor. What, then, of the relation of the gospel to the "orders" of earthly society?

For several reasons this question is important. In the first place, we who are Christians today, like those of the early Church, must live in two worlds at once. These worlds, traditionally referred to as the "order of creation" and the "order of redemption," converge at the point of trying to be a Christian within the daily demands of the family, the job, the community around us, and the larger community of the state and the world of nations. Even the Church, as an ecclesiastical institution, is itself an "order" subject to the corruptions which impregnate other social institutions. If we cannot within these structures find moral guidance from the law of love and moral stability from faith in God as he comes to us in Christ, not even the most rapturous experience of joy and peace through the lifting of the burden of sin will be sufficient. Neither in one's own inner experience nor as a persuasive witness to others will the gospel be effective if its fruits are not manifest in social relations.

A second reason for looking at the fruits of the gospel in New Testament society has both a positive and a negative side. Was the world then like ours or different? The more obvious answer is, of course, that life in Eastern Mediterranean occupied territory, in a simple, leisurely, prescientific age, among a small minority having no political power, was very different from the conditions of today. Both modern conveniences and modern responsibilities were for the most part unknown. Yet from another angle, there were responsibilities to be met, temptations to sexual indulgence, acquisitiveness, factionalism, and the will to power to be overcome, rights to be defended, and duties to be undertaken in the name of Christ, which are perennial in character.

A third factor, both as asset and liability, stems from the preceding. There is much that is of permanent validity, not only in the words of Jesus but in the rest of the New Testatment, as to how a Christian should act in relation to other men. Though the words "environment" and "social institution" appear nowhere in the Bible, what the words stand for as the surrounding social structure is presupposed, and often referred to as "the world." On the other hand, it becomes fatal to the discernment of the deeper notes in Christian ethics to take literally every word, such as Rom. 13:1 or I Cor. 14:34-35 or Col. 3:18, 22, or I Tim. 2:11-12, and make it mandatory for all time and all circumstances.

In general, it may be said that the fruits of the gospel in first-century society were conservative but not reactionary, revolutionary but not iconoclastic or fanatical. A few illustrations, without attempting to cover the whole ground, will make this clear.

With regard to the State, there is no evidence of insurrection against Rome. It apparently did not occur to the first Christians either to foment political dissatisfaction or to take up arms against the governing authorities, even as it did not occur to them within the compass of the New Testament to declare the unchristian character of war. Yet indirectly, the stand they took in placing the authority of God above all human powers was to bring upon them the persecutions under Nero and Domitian, and precipitate the mood of spiritual confidence in defiance of earthly "principalities and powers" that is reflected in the book of Revelation and elsewhere. Furthermore, it is a well-known fact that the early Christians were pacifists, partly because military duty was not required of them by the Roman state but also because of an implicit sense of the incompatibility of war with the gospel of love.[5]

It is at the point of conflict with the ruling ecclesiastical authorities who tried to silence the witness of Christians to their faith that the question of fidelity to the higher authority of God became most overt. It is in this setting that we find Peter saying unequivocally, "We must obey God rather than men" (Acts 5:29). Yet whether it was the ecclesiastical or the civil authorities that opposed them by imprisonment, ejection, scourging, or death, or as often happened, a conjunction of the two when the crowd stirred up trouble, the book of Acts gives a remarkable picture of their steadfastness under opposition and attack.[6] The gospel of salvation through Christ put iron in their souls, and nothing could daunt them in their witness to it.

The picture is less clear with regard to work and the economic order, but again the gospel, moving within the established order without radical challenge, was destined to be a revolutionary force. Apparently most of the early Christians continued to work at their normal occupations, as Paul with Aquila and Priscilla, his fellow tentmakers, did for a time at Corinth (Acts 18:3). The members of the church at Thessalonica were urged to live quietly, to mind their own affairs, and to work with their hands, so that they might command the respect of outsiders and be dependent on nobody (I Thess. 4:11). Paul, reminding the same congregation of how he followed this advice himself while among them so that he might not be a burden to them, cites the stringent but sensible advice, "If any one will not work, let him not eat" (II Thess. 3:10). Whether freeman or slave, one was expected to have an occupation and to perform faithfully its duties.

So far, there is nothing revolutionary. The note of radical change in the mores appears, however, at two points. The first is the willingness of the Christian community to surrender their goods and to have "all things in common" (Acts 2:43-45). There is no evidence that this primitive communism became a general practice, but it is clear that the relief of brothers in need was felt as a Christian obligation. Faith

---

[5] See C. J. Cadoux, *The Early Christian Attitude to War* (London: Geo. Allen & Unwin Ltd., 1940); also *The Early Church and the World* (New York: Chas. Scribner's Sons, 1925), Part IV, ch. vi.
[6] Cf. 5:17-18, 40; 6:12; 7:58; 8:1-3, 25; 12:1-5; 16:19, 24; 17:5-8; 19:23-29; 21:27-36; 24:23, 27; 25:6-12.

working through love, even within the restricted limits of the Christian community, challenged forcefully the natural impulse to possess and to retain possession of worldly goods. The second major challenge was not to slavery as an institution, but to slavery and all other forms of occupational cleavage as barriers to brotherhood. One of the most beautiful passages in the New Testament is that in which Paul sends Onesimus back to Philemon—not emancipated in the legal sense, but "no longer as a slave but more than a slave, as a beloved brother, . . . both in the flesh and in the Lord" (v. 16). This spirit of Christian brotherhood, joined with Jesus' insight into the worth of every person as a child of God, was bound to create a ferment which led eventually to the abolition of overt slavery throughout the Christian world.

Regarding family life, the picture that is presented has both lights and shadows. Sexual looseness is repeatedly condemned; husbands are urged to love their wives; marital fidelity even when "unequally yoked together with unbelievers" (K.J.V.) is counseled though warnings are given against assuming voluntarily such a relationship (I Cor. 7:10-15; II Cor. 6:14). Women as lay members apparently occupied a place of considerable importance in the church, and Phoebe is referred to as a "deaconess of the church at Cenchreae" (Rom. 16:1). It is significant that among the "saints" listed in the greetings which comprise the last chapter of Romans, mention is made of twenty men, nine women, and two families. This is a higher proportion of women than would be representative of either Israel or Rome in a comparable group during the first century A.D., and gives evidence that the equalitarian spirit of Jesus was already at work in the Christian community.

On the other side of the ledger, however, there is no evidence of full equality of the sexes either in the home or in the leadership of the churches. There could be no more forthright declaration of male superiority than is found in the words, "Wives, be subject to your husbands, as to the Lord. For the husband is the head of the wife as Christ is the head of the church" (Eph. 5:22-23), and the injunction to women to keep silent in the churches, though it may have had some legitimacy under the conditions of the time, could hardly have been given in such unqualified form if the attitudes of Jesus had been more clearly grasped. At this point, as with reference to war, a note had been introduced by the gospel which was to germinate within the Christian conscience, but which has not yet fully borne its fruit.

What shall we deduce from these observations, in which for the most part we see both conservatism and revolutionary challenge being sanctioned by the gospel?

The first point to note is that the gospel never works in a vacuum, and because of the surrounding environment with its traditionalism, emotional ties, and social pressures, neither an individual nor a group is ever completely transformed. This is not to deny the transforming power of the gospel, to which Paul gave such eloquent witness, for by the workings of divine grace radical changes do take place in individuals, and through individuals in social institutions. Insofar as these manifest wider and deeper expressions of love, we can rejoice in them, and seek as we may to further them. Yet there need be no discouragement if the changes desired do not happen all at once, or if vestiges of the "old Adam" still survive. God has patience, and we must try to have it.

The second observation is that the slowness of men to respond to Christ is no excuse for lethargy, or vacillation, or inactivity on our part. Not all of those to whom the apostles preached were won to Christ, and among those who were, not all were saints. Yet by such witness and out of such human material the Church was formed, of which we today are the inheritors. By the grace of God and by persistent, devoted effort in faith and love, miracles of spiritual, moral, and social transformation still are wrought.

The third is the commonplace but essential observation that there can be no legitimate cleavage between an individual and a social gospel. There is one gospel, applicable to the whole of life, and to truncate it at any point is to make it into something less than the good news of salvation for which the world waits. Not only did Christ die for all men; he gave his life for the whole of every man. To love and serve him faithfully with a total witness is our total moral task.

What we have been surveying was Christianity in its beginnings. What has happened within the past nineteen centuries is a large story— but a story outside the compass of this study. Yet what was germinative was bound to bear fruit, and it is bearing it today. What, then, does it mean to us now?

V. God, Sin, and Christian Character

THE THREE PRECEDING CHAPTERS have attempted to outline the biblical basis of Christian ethics. We focused attention upon the ethical insights of Jesus because these are definitive for the Christian point of view. There are Christians who lay greater stress upon the messages of the prophets and the theology of Paul than upon the recorded words and acts of Jesus, and some who believe that it is impossible to recover any dependable view of the Jesus of history. However, we must continue to insist that Christian ethics stem from Jesus and his revelation of God as the source transcending all others, and even with some uncertainty as to the detailed accuracy of the historical record, the picture is clear.

It is the purpose of this chapter to look at the foundations and some of the problems of personal Christian living in terms of what we learn from Jesus, and secondarily, from the Bible as a whole. Mindful of the fact that neither Jesus nor his first great interpreter was a legalist, I shall try not to be. Yet Christian theology, far from being the barren and abstract thing many erroneously suppose it to be, yields at every turn directives that relate to life.

1. God and Christian character

As the primary note in the ethical outlook of Jesus, we noted the inseparable union of faith in God and obedient love for God with his attitudes toward men. The Old Testament is God-centered in its moral perspectives, though in a more limited sense in terms of the covenant with Israel, and so also was the early Church, though in identification of God with Christ himself as redeeming love. At the very threshold of Christian character stands belief in God as that faith comes to us through Jesus Christ.

85

But does it make a person a Christian to believe in God? Certainly not, in the sense of intellectual assent to the existence of a Supreme Being. Though statistics are not available and not very dependable where gathered, the polls taken from time to time indicate that the great majority of Americans—probably well over 90 per cent—would say Yes if asked if they believed in God. But this is not to say that so many are Christians. About 60 per cent are members of churches, but though only God knows how many of these are real Christians, it seems certain that Christian character in any thoroughgoing sense is a much greater rarity.

Yet belief in God, even as assent of the mind, is not irrelevant to Christian character. The postulates of naturalism and humanism may be held by good men, but to be a "good man" does not make a person a Christian. To see why, let us look briefly at these assumptions. In general, they are:

1. The universe is self-existent and self-contained, within which man has evolved to the position of the highest form of animal life.

2. Man has intelligence and the capacity for social adjustment and control, but is essentially a part of nature.

3. There is no purpose in the universe except that which man gives it.

4. Right and wrong have no objective validation beyond group standards.

5. The good life is that which is expedient for happiness and the satisfaction of man's desires.

6. Evil and maladjustment exist, but sin is an outmoded concept.

7. All improvement comes through education and the application of various forms of social pressure, psychological, economic, or political.

8. Man has no source of support, for either the good life or the conquest of suffering, except the resources in himself and his group.

9. Each man's personal existence ends with his biological death.

10. Jesus has no special significance except as an influential historical figure around whom the church, as a social institution and phase of culture, has been organized.

These postulates, so widely held that they might be regarded as the new Ten Commandments of our time, are radically at variance with the

Christian view of God and of man. One who holds them as his basic convictions may be a respectable, law-abiding, and even altruistic person, but he is not a Christian.

Yet so familiar are they that one may be inclined at first glance to ask, "What is wrong with them?" Doubtless some readers of these pages will immediately suspect the writer of being ultraconservative for saying that a person cannot hold these as his basic convictions and still be a Christian. So let us look at them one by one.

1. It is the Christian's faith that God is the Creator and Ruler of the universe, the "Father Almighty, Maker of heaven and earth." In the creation of the world through long evolutionary processes, God has made man "in his own image"—that is, with spiritual qualities akin to those of God. Christian ethics presupposes a God-centered view both of the physical world and of the worth of human personality.

2. Man's biological life is embedded in nature, and in a more complex form he shares many attributes with the animal world. He is, however, essentially a "living spirit," with a soul that is capable of worship, faith in God, and outgoing, uncalculating love for one's fellow man. Through these endowments of the Creator man is free to make moral choices. Christian ethics, therefore, cannot be deterministic in its view of man's moral life.

3. The Christian doctrine of creation implies neither a static perfection nor automatic progress. Yet it is the Christian's faith that both the goodness and the power of God are dependable and that a divine purpose underlies all existence. In this faith he can work with courage and hope as the servant of God for the conquest of evil. Life as a whole therefore becomes meaningful.

4. Man's ideas of right and wrong are greatly influenced by group standards. Yet it is the will of God as this is revealed in Jesus Christ that, for the Christian, is the ultimate point of reference. To the degree that this is discerned and lived by, social standards are transcended by agape love.

5. The good life is neither determined by, nor is it indifferent to, human happiness. The good life is the "blessed" life portrayed in the Beatitudes, the "abundant" life Jesus said he came to bring. It is the

life of obedient love toward God and selfless service to men disclosed in the words and deeds of Jesus.

6. Sin, as self-centeredness with regard to both God and other persons, is man's most persistent evil. It is expressed both in moral dullness to the love commandment of God and in positive acts of rebellion against God and injury to one's fellow men. It is "original" in the sense that human nature, if undirected or unchanged, is always self-centered.

7. Self-discipline and social forces contribute to the achievement of maturity, and these are important elements in the development of Christian character through Christian nurture. However, to be brought up in a good home or a good society does not automatically make one a Christian. The process of becoming a Christian occurs only through personal decision and the acceptance of divine help. The will then becomes unified, motivated, and consciously directed toward the effort to be a follower of Christ.

8. Neither sin nor suffering can be fully eliminated from human existence. Yet through the power of God in Christ, moral victories over temptation are won, often to an amazing degree, and suffering can be borne with courage and inner enrichment through trust in God's providential care.

9. The Christian lives in the hope and in the vista of eternal life as the gift of God. This enormously transforms his perspective upon the present life, less through hope of future reward or fear of punishment than through a sense of the enhanced worthfulness of the present as preparatory to eternal life in the presence of God.

10. To the Christian, Jesus is more than a great, good man who has exerted an influence upon the course of Western civilization. He is the supreme revealer of God, through whom God is known, personal salvation comes to men, and society is changed in the direction of a fuller embodiment of the principle of love. The Church, as the community of his followers united by his living presence as Holy Spirit, is more than a social institution; it is a divinely grounded fellowship.

Even so brief a survey of the affirmations of Christian faith in contrast with the assumptions of naturalism should make it apparent that the viewpoint from which the Christian looks at life is different. The Bible, as the framework from which this faith is derived, becomes a primary source of insight, and the structure of life to which it points has an orientation and a quality not to be derived from naturalistic or humanistic assumptions.

2. *The Christian virtues*

But is not the naturalist, or the humanist, or the person who does not have a label but makes no claim to being a Christian, as "good" as one who does? The crux of personal Christian character is at this point, for if believing what a Christian ought to believe and calling oneself a Christian makes no difference in one's personality or behavior, Christianity as a whole is bound to be discredited. The stock charge against the Church is that it is full of hypocrites, less sensitive to human need than many outside it. While this is doubtless an overstatement based on too hasty generalization, every "bad" Christian who can be set over against a "good" non-Christian is a barrier to the gospel.

At this point we must proceed with caution, avoiding either of two erroneous positions. One is to draw up a list of Christian virtues—honesty, generosity, courtesy, veracity, and the like—and define a Christian by their possession. The other is to define being a Christian in terms extraneous to moral qualities, as by right beliefs or church membership or faithful observance of the sacraments or some metaphysical change assumed to be wrought by conversion. The first of these procedures is moralism, against which the exponents of neo-orthodoxy continually inveigh. The second has no such neat label to designate it. It might perhaps be called fractionalism, from its tendency to take a fraction or aspect of Christian experience and make it the whole.

The truth lies between these positions. There are Christian virtues. Yet making a list of them and adding them together does not add up to being a Christian. These virtues, in greater or less degree, are found among those who are not Christians, and no Christian possesses them in unlimited degree. These virtues are not traits of character that can be put on point by point, as Benjamin Franklin in his *Autobiography* tells that he tried to do as he systematically cultivated one virtue after another. They cannot even be dissociated enough to analyze them atomistically, as Aristotle attempts to do in his *Nicomachean Ethics* and the Stoic philosophers were fond of doing. Every list one can draw up leaves one with the feeling that there is something more. Nevertheless, I repeat, there are Christian virtues, and in their possession Christian character bears distinctive marks.

The Christian virtues are the qualities of a God-centered life as one seeks, in the totality of his being, to follow the pattern of faith and love set forth by Jesus. The Bible presents them again and again, always vitally and not schematically, but with a consistency that makes the picture clear. Let us look at some of the greatest of these portrayals.

To glance again, as we did in Chapter III, at the Sermon on the Mount, what did Jesus do with Jewish legalism? Paraphrasing a bit we find him saying, "You have heard that it was said, 'You shall not kill, commit adultery, divorce your wife illegally, swear falsely, exact more than even-handed justice, hate your neighbor, though you may your enemy.'" The Christian virtues that he substituted, as the righteousness of the kingdom of heaven, are the mood and spirit to refrain from anger and lustfulness and the severing of the marriage bond, positive injunctions to straightforward speech, outgoing and uncalculating service, love of all men including one's enemies as befitting sons of the God whose love is limitless.

Again, the Christian virtues are epitomized in the Beatitudes. Who are the blessed ones—not simply the happy ones who have satisfied their desires, but those who have found their supreme happiness in God? They are those who are humble in spirit; comforted by God in their mourning; unpossessive, yet possessing God's richest gifts; eager and persistent in the quest for righteousness; merciful; pure in heart; peacemakers, as the sons of God ought to be; faithful to duty even under persecution; able to endure misunderstanding and scorn for the Kingdom's sake. In the immortal words of Matt. 5:3-11 there are nine affirmations which cannot be run into a list of virtues, if virtues are conceived abstractly, yet no clearer picture of Christian character was ever drawn.

Turning to the words of Paul, we have the Christian virtues again stated, not this time in nine sentences, but in nine words. The fruit of the Spirit, says Paul in Gal. 5:22, is "love, joy, peace, patience, kindness, goodness, faithfulness, gentleness, self-control." Several points beyond the words themselves must be noted. First, these virtues are not the product simply of human cultivation; they are the "fruit of the Spirit," the result of the indwelling presence of God as he comes to us in

90

Christ. Second, the verb is "is" and not "are"; they make a constellation of personality, not a collection of nine traits joined at random. And third, Paul disclaims legalism, as we must, when he adds after this inclusive picture of the Christian life, "against such there is no law."

There are other portrayals of the Christian virtues in the New Testament. Rom. 12, as a whole, is devoted to this portrayal, as is I Cor. 13. Doubtless the reason why the twenty-third psalm and the Corinthian ode to love, with the Lord's Prayer, are the most familiar passages in the Bible is that they gather up so perfectly the faith and love which lie at the base of Christian character. I shall not attempt to analyze or restate them, for they make their own case.

To return to the question raised at the beginning of this section, is this type of character, which means this total structure of personality, just as evident among those who are not Christians as among those who are? After one has finished citing cases of "fine people" who are not Christians and some who "profess Christ" but are not very attractive, the answer is clear. Christian character, though not flawless in any person, is a self-validating witness to the power of Christ to transform human nature. To the degree that a person is genuinely—not merely nominally or institutionally but actually—a Christian, his total life bears witness to the fact that Christian character is a reality.

3. The nature of sin

Look in any concordance of the Bible, and it becomes apparent that one of the words which appears most frequently is "sin." From first to last, sin is the story of man's behavior, even as salvation from sin is the great theme of the Bible. Christianity is through and through a religion of redemption, and while the whole gamut of salvation is not expressed in redemption from sin, this is its central core.

Although, as we noted, naturalism and humanism tend to think of sin as an outmoded concept and talk instead about maladjustment, insecurity, neurosis, or antisocial conduct, the term remains in the diction of Christians. But what does it mean? There is no clear agreement as to its meaning, and the ambiguity with which sin is regarded is responsible for much ineffectiveness in Christian preaching and in Christian living.

To some persons, and probably to the majority of ordinary Christian laymen, sin means transgression of those standards of conduct usually accepted by the people around them. A Christian is expected not to kill, steal, lie, commit adultery or other sexual infractions, or get drunk. How far he can move in these directions, as in exploiting others to one's own gain, driving a shrewd deal or pursuing an advantage, stretching the truth, "having a little affair," or drinking in moderation, depends for most persons less on the will of God or the revelation of God in Jesus Christ than on what is and what is not done in one's community.

The community, though it embraces the geographical area in which one lives, is a far more pervasive thing than this, for a community is in a large part defined by the social standards of like-minded people. For this reason conflicts as to what constitutes sin often arise between the younger and older generations, or between ministers and their laymen, or between the people of one church and another.

Take, for example, the matter of drinking a glass of wine or beer. To some Christians this is a sin. To others, if it is done in moderation, it has no more significance than to drink a cup of coffee. Some regard it as sinful for a minister to drink, but not for a layman—and still more is this disparity in evidence with regard to smoking. A Roman Catholic or an Anglican or a German Lutheran Christian is likely to take a much freer view of such indulgences than is an American Methodist. I am not at this point trying to say who is right. What this illustrates is the ambiguity that emerges when the attempt is made to define sin, or "a sin," by accepted social practice. A large part of the message of Jesus was the challenging of both Pharisaic and Gentile ideas of sin by a higher law.

The chief danger in defining sin by accepted social practice is not its ambiguity. This, if recognized, can be made the basis of mutual tolerance while holding to one's own convictions. The danger lies, rather, in taking social standards as the voice of God, "absolutizing the relative," and condemning all whose opinion differs in moot matters. Thus, Christians may sincerely differ as to the duty of the Christian to be, or not to be, a pacifist; but if one forms his opinion only by the standards of his group and then calls it the will of God for all, God has actually been left out of the picture. This procedure constantly happens, from the most insignificant matters to the greatest, and is a major source of the perversion of Christian ethics.

Identification with accepted social standards is a moralistic view of sin. To reject moralism is not to repudiate morality, but to declare the inadequacy of such a man-centered form of morality. Moralism has legalistic implications, for it is based on a set of socially determined "dos" and "don'ts." Its appeal is not wholly that of external compulsion, for social conditioning affects conscience until there may be not only fear of consequences but strong inner compulsions at the thought of infractions of the standards of society. What is distinctive about it is not the degree of legalism involved, or the amount of conscientious scruples invoked, or even the degree to which God is talked about as the professed sanction for a given opinion. Its primary note is the limiting of sin to certain acts that must not be done because they are socially disapproved.

At the opposite extreme is a view of sin which regards it as *state of being*, rather than as a set of concrete acts, and as a state of being in rebellion against God. It is in this context that Paul says much about the natural man being "in sin," until its burden is lifted and victory is won through justification by faith in Jesus Christ. Luther, in the Pauline tradition but with more realism as to postconversion sin, speaks of the Christian as being *simul justus et peccator* (at the same time justified and a sinner). It is this view of sin that lies at the base of the Reformation doctrine of total depravity. It is to misunderstand the latter to suppose that the Reformers thought an unconverted man could perform no moral act, such as being a good citizen or a kind father; what they meant was that man's nature was corrupted by a pervasive self-will and self-centeredness which made even his good acts sinful. Such sin is "original" in the sense of being born in us. Calvin thus states it:

Original sin, therefore, appears to be an hereditary depravity and corruption of our nature, diffused through all the parts of the soul. . . . And therefore infants themselves, . . . though they have not yet produced the fruits of their iniquity, yet they have the seed of it within them; even their whole nature is as it were a seed of sin, and therefore cannot but be odious and abominable to God. . . . Wherefore I have asserted that sin has possessed all the powers of the soul. . . . Man has not only been ensnared by the inferior appetites, but

93

abominable impiety has seized the very citadel of his mind, and pride has penetrated into the innermost recesses of his heart.[1]

Contemporary Reformation theology modifies this view at the point of rejecting the biological inheritance of sin as the result of the fall of Adam, yet holds essentially to this idea of sin as a pervasive state of sinfulness. It is a universal human tendency to try to be, as the Garden of Eden story puts it, "like God" (Gen. 3:5), exalting one's self into the state of supremacy which belongs rightly to God alone. Thus pride is the basic sin. Some would add also that sin roots in anxiety and the frustration of human finitude as the ego attempts to rebel against the limits set by our existence.[2] Redemption is granted when one becomes aware of his presumption and self-righteousness, repents in humility and turns to Christ in faith. Yet sin continues, for while its burden is lifted, its hold is never loosed. Outwardly one may live a highly moral life; inwardly he continues to rebel against God and seek to magnify himself. This rebellious and disobedient self-exaltation is the essence of sin.

Moralism stresses the need of avoiding particular wrong acts, but gets its frame of reference from social standards and conventions. The second view I have outlined meets this defect, and is more authentically Christian. Yet in stressing man's permeating sinfulness it often seems to give a too pessimistic view of human nature, with too little recognition of the God-given capacity of some persons to live victorious and highly virtuous Christian lives. Furthermore, in its stress on pride and rebellion against God as basic to the meaning of sin, it does not always give sufficiently concrete moral guidance as to how a Christian should conduct himself with relation to his fellow men.

Is it not possible to understand the nature of sin in a way that avoids these pitfalls? We can, if we draw our perspective from what is to be learned from Jesus. There, as love for God and one's neighbor is the supreme virtue, so sin is its opposite. Sin is an attitude of the soul, and

[1] *Institutes of the Christian Religion* II, 1. 8-9. A Compend of the Institutes of the Christian Religion, ed. Hugh Thomson Kerr, Jr. (Philadelphia: Westminster Press, 1939), pp. 43-44.
[2] Cf. Reinhold Niebuhr, *The Nature and Destiny of Man* (New York: Chas. Scribner's Sons, 1943), Vol. I, ch. vii, for an elaboration of this view; also John L. Casteel, *Rediscovering Prayer* (New York: Association Press, 1955), ch. 3, for an interesting application to the personal devotional life.

the prime essential for the elimination of sinful acts is that "ethical inwardness" which Jesus proclaimed so vitally in the Sermon on the Mount. Yet there are sinful acts, which are to be defined not by Pharisaic or Gentile or twentieth-century social standards but by the eternal will of God. *Any attitude or act in which one rebels against, or fails to be adequately responsive to, the love commandment of Jesus is sin.*

In this view of sin, as in the corresponding picture which Jesus gives us of the good life, relation to God and to one's fellow man are in inseparable union. No works of love are Christian unless they are God-centered, but no God-centeredness is truly Christian unless one is impelled by it to attitudes and to works of love toward one's fellow men. This is why any moralistic substitution of human good and evil, and on the other hand, any legalistic or ceremonial view of the demands of God, fails to do justice to the full seriousness of sin.

Sin, then, is self-love and self-centeredness with regard to both God and other persons—all persons with whom our lives either have or ought to have connection. With reference to God it may be called rebellion, or alienation, or estrangement, or simply "unbelief," but these attitudes all center in not caring enough to desire to render to God obedient love. Regarding man's relation to man, it means the negation of what Jesus taught, and the opposite of what was outlined in the previous section as the Christian virtues. This total structure of life which sin negates centers in the obligation to love and to serve to the uttermost of one's powers.

But can every person love in this manner? Is not this to ask the impossible? What of the immature, the untaught, the mentally defective or ill, the underprivileged, the frustrated and warped soul to whom life has given too little love—can these be asked to love without limit? And can even those of us who might not be included in these categories love everybody? The mere putting of these queries indicates the importance of human freedom and its bearing on Christian moral responsibility.

To be a sinner in the eyes of men, and presumably also in God's eyes, requires enough maturity, knowledge, and freedom to enable one to make moral choices. This is why a little child, even though self-centered by nature, is not a sinner, and sin is "original" only in the sense that the natural self-centeredness of childhood, if uncurbed, becomes sinful as the individual matures to the point of responsible decision. To the degree that any physical, psychological, or social restriction makes it impossible either to know what is right or to act responsibly in Christian love, our best impulses tell us that understanding and sympathy rather than condemnation are in order. Modern psychology and psychotherapy have done much to soften the sting of what formerly without qualification was called sin. This is good, if it is not carried beyond rightful limits, and much more work needs yet to be done before the relations of neurosis to sin can be clearly defined.

Yet this must not be allowed to vitiate the reality of sin. Granted that there are limits to human freedom, what of the person who can know, and feel, and do otherwise than he does? Though it is not humanly possible to draw absolute lines at the point where our "cannot" ends and "can" begins, sin is a persistent reality. To sin is not simply to be maladjusted, or mentally ill, or socially conditioned in a certain way, or otherwise to be a victim of bad circumstances. Nobody is responsible for what he could not know, or be, or do: yet to sin is to continue in self-will and self-love at those many points of decision in which, for a normal person, one's outlook and action ought to reach far beyond himself.

Can we love *everybody*? Here the distinction between *philia* and *agape* needs again to be drawn. One cannot feel a strong personal attraction toward everybody he knows, to say nothing of the unknown—and there are limits to the channels of service open to us. But love in the Christian sense of outgoing concern need have no limits: to set such limits either willfully or carelessly is to sin.

Sin, then, presupposes knowledge and freedom adequate to those attitudes and acts required by love, and without taking a "soft" view of divine judgment we may believe that God does not require of us the impossible.

> As a father pities his children,
>   so the Lord pities those who fear him.
> For he knows our frame;
>   he remembers that we are dust. (Ps. 103:13-14.)

Yet both sin and judgment are stark realities, and the most pervasive type of sin lies in the complacency, lethargy, and moral dullness of self-

96

love at those points where both knowledge and freedom are available. We all know what it is right to do far better than we do it; we all, in our dispositions and overt acts, place premature limits around our love and our service to others. Every man, if he is honest with himself, must echo the word of Paul, "None is righteous, no, not one" (Rom. 3:11).

Thus it appears that in the debate between the customary liberal view[3] that stresses man's freedom in the willful breaking of known moral laws and the neo-orthodox emphasis on unconscious sin as derivative from man's basic pride, anxiety, and rebellion against God, the truth may lie between. Without freedom and willful choice there is no sin; yet such freedom and willfulness can be exercised negatively as well as positively, becoming moral insensitiveness of the most devastating and unchristian nature. The effects of this we shall note repeatedly as we look more precisely at social sin and hence at the need of enlightened and loving social action.

4. Some illustrations

It may add concreteness to the foregoing, and move us a step closer toward practical applications, if we look at a number of questions that commonly confront Christians in daily life. As a handle for operation, let us go back to the list of things a moralistic view of sin prohibits, recognizing of course that the list given was only illustrative and not complete.

a) *Is it right ever for a Christian to kill his fellow men?* The depths of anguish involved in this question come to full focus in reference to personal participation in war, which is but one angle of the larger issue of the ethics of war, to be discussed later when we look at international relations. In anticipation it may be said that if it is right to do in war what would be murder in time of peace, this must find its Christian justification—not in the supremacy of the call of the state, or in the impersonality of group action, but in love for those persons believed to be protected thereby, without hatred toward any, and with due concern for what war does to persons. It is unequivocally wrong for

[3] Cf. A. C. Knudson, *The Principles of Christian Ethics* (New York and Nashville: Abingdon Press, 1943), ch. iv.

a Christian to kill wantonly, or without deep soul-searching leading to the conclusion that love requires it as the will of God. Some Christians do sincerely arrive at this decision while others do not, and it is not to be expected that all will reach the same answer. As the Methodist Church has put it:

Faced by the dilemma of participation in war, he [the Christian] must decide prayerfully before God what is to be his course of action in relation thereto. What the Christian citizen may not do is to obey men rather than God, or overlook the degree of compromise in our best acts, or gloss over the sinfulness of war. The Church must hold within its fellowship persons who sincerely differ at this point of critical decision, call all to repentance, mediate to all God's mercy, minister to all in Christ's name.[4]

There are other aspects of this question which confront us daily. Every careless automobile driver is a potential murderer, and Christians like others are too often insensitive to their obligations at this point. Taking unnecessary chances is "tempting fate," and hence is sin against the God who desires all his children to live out their normal span of years in health and well-being. The person who drinks, or who condones drinking, encourages reckless driving, and hence becomes a participant in the guilt of killing. He does not, of course, intend this consequence, but the fact that his love does not stretch far enough to give him a sense of moral responsibility makes him responsible. That this is no idle bit of moralizing is substantiated by the fact that traffic accidents take an appalling toll of about 36,000 lives each year, and in this killing, intoxication is a factor in over 25 per cent of the instances.

There are other more subtle angles of the question. One who would directly poison or set fire to another person would be subject to condemnation and the severest penalty the law can inflict.[5] Yet even Christians own and derive income from unhealthy slums—firetraps and breeders of disease. Most people are reasonably careful not to spread infection to their families or friends; there is less care with regard to

---

[4] Resolution on World Order and International Peace, *Discipline,* 1956, ¶ 2024.

[5] Capital punishment is itself of very questionable Christian justification. Though ostensibly based on the need to protect society against murder, it too often rests on the application of the *lex talionis.*

strangers in public places. The known laws of health are persistently violated, not alone by the careless who injure themselves or infect others, but even by conscientious Christians who in stubborn self-will wear out their energy, acquire nervous breakdowns or stomach ulcers or heart trouble, and collapse before their time. Or one can be so concerned with his own comfort and prosperity and the demands of his business, family, or other immediate circle that he can be quite obtuse to the fact that in half of the world's population, there are chronic hunger and malnutrition, high infant mortality, and a much shorter life span than in opulent America. It is, of course, not the Christian conscience alone that should have a sense of social responsibility about such matters. Yet if a Christian takes seriously the love commandment, he is obligated to have a quickened conscience. The words of Jesus, "What more are you doing than others? Do not even the Gentiles do the same?" ought to be to the Christian a persistent challenge.

b) *Ought a Christian ever to lie, or steal, or cheat?* Put thus baldly, almost everybody knows that the answer should be No. Yet it is when "extenuating circumstances" arise that exceptions are made, and Christians like others, if they are not sensitive to the call of God, will excuse themselves and succumb to temptation. One will not rob a bank, but he will conveniently forget to report some things when he pays his income tax, if he thinks he will not be caught. For an appalling number of people, younger and older, in current society there are two principal criteria governing conduct: (1) one does "what other people do" and (2) one does "what you can get away with" and escape detection or penalty. Consequently, one will not sell automobiles or stocks or bonds or jackknives in ways that are directly illegal, but one will "keep his mouth shut" on the assumption that it is the buyer's business to watch out or take the consequencs. Small lies, told to keep a social situation smooth or to help one's self out of a predicament, have a way of growing into extensive structures of deception. And rationalizations are ever available. Cheating on examinations may be condemned in general, but there is always a reason for doing it "this time." One's grade is too crucial to risk, or a friend needs help, so why not give it to him? And if a lie will help one out of a tight spot, why be so fussy as to think one must always tell the truth?

And so it goes. Any reader of these pages can give his own set of examples. The fabric of modern society is honeycombed with instances of lack of veracity, of basic honesty, and of that virtue so fundamental both to Christian character and to an ordered society which perhaps had best be called integrity. This ramifies through domestic, economic, political, and every sort of social relation, and is at the same time a major consequence and a major cause of the relaxing of Christian standards in a largely secular world.

There is no blueprint in the New Testament to tell us precisely what to do in every one of the manifold instances in which the temptation to deceive others, or to possess or to manipulate or to control what is not ours, confronts us. Admittedly, life comes to us with its issues mixed, and to contend, as some do, that one must always tell the truth, even if in time of war or tyrannical oppression it costs another person his life, is "straining out a gnat and swallowing a camel." Yet both Jesus and the prophets are clear in their convictions that any exploiting and callous dishonesty, by whatever name it may be called, is wrong in the eyes of God. Because it is rooted in self-love, every violation of personal integrity must be eradicated, root and branch. So strong is the impulse to acquisitiveness and to self-love that most of us, if we are honest with ourselves, will admit that only by the grace of God can we be honest with other men in those areas of life where only God's eyes see us.

c) *What of the sins of the flesh?* The medieval Church had a sound (even though an incomplete) insight into the nature of human temptation when it announced as the seven deadly sins pride, anger, envy, avarice, sloth, gluttony, and lust. If sloth is understood as moral indifference rather than lack of action, it is these which to the present day most persistently assail the soul. It is significant that the first five are sins of disposition, while only the last two are sins of the flesh.

Gluttony is not simply overeating, though even in this form of it, many Americans sin by setting up false standards of value, overburdening their bodies and consuming fine fare in indifference to the hunger of the world. Its most serious expression, however, is in the drinking of alcoholic beverages, with all the train of consequences ensuing therefrom.

Is it ever right for a Christian to drink? The mores have made social drinking a widely accepted contemporary practice, and not all Christians hold it to be wrong. In a book on Christian ethics two Anglican leaders after stating certain limits remark:

> However, after saying all this, one must add that alcohol, properly used, is one of the good gifts that God has given to His children. A group of friends drinking in moderation and experiencing the relaxation and warm fellowship that ensue, may be sacramentally rejoicing in the goodness of God's creation.[6]

Without reflecting on the motives or the moral integrity of these authors, one must differ radically with their judgment. Why?

First, because nobody ever sets out to be a drunkard. Yet all the tragedies resulting from alcoholism—death on highways, broken homes, shattered vocations, derelict bodies and souls—are the result of immoderate drinking by those who thought they were going to drink "in moderation." Although not every moderate drinker turns into a drunkard, many do, and there is no guarantee against it. About few practices is Paul's word so relevant, "Let any one who thinks that he stands take heed lest he fall" (I Cor. 10:12), for there is an abundance of evidence, cited in any meeting of Alcoholics Anonymous, that it can happen to one who least expects it. The *only* safeguard is to leave liquor entirely alone.

Second, the Christian with a conscience must think of effects beyond himself. Not a few of those who do succeed in keeping their drinking within bounds have been influential in encouraging others to drink beyond these bounds. Paul again was right when he said, "Then let us no more pass judgment on one another, but rather decide never to put a stumbling-block or hindrance in the way of a brother. . . . It is right not to eat meat or drink wine or do anything that makes your brother stumble." (Rom. 14:13, 21.)

And third, the way of love is to put the emphasis on a positive respect for one's body as the temple of God's spirit, on one's money as held in stewardship from God for constructive uses, on one's mind as needing to

---

[6] Chad Walsh and Eric Montizambert, *Faith and Behavior* (New York: Morehouse-Gorham Co., 1954), p. 33.

be kept clear and vigorous for God's service, on one's spirit and all one's social contacts as best finding active expression with "relaxation and warm fellowship" through channels that require no artificial stimulation. The way of Christian love is not self-righteously to condemn another for holding a different view, but neither is it to surrender conviction at a point of grave concern.

On the second sin of the flesh to which reference has been made— lust in the form of overt transgression or, as Jesus saw it, the lustful look and the impure thought—I shall not say more at this point. A later chapter will deal with family relations, and there is the place to discuss it. It is enough to say here that sex, unlike alcohol, *is* God's good gift and in relations of pure and holy love can be used sacramentally. Lust becomes, therefore, the more debasing and the more sinful when what is intended for good is perverted to selfish and sensual indulgence. Only a neurotic and pleasure-mad society could commercialize and pervert it as ours does.

5. Victory over sin

It will be best to end this chapter on the note, not of man's sinfulness, but of God's victory over sin. Sin and judgment are never God's last words, for "God so loved the world" that he gave his Son for our redemption. That is the message of Good Friday and of Easter, and of our total Christian faith.

It was said earlier that sin is a persistent state of the soul. This is true in the sense that self-love and self-centeredness are never fully conquered even in the most saintly Christian. Yet decisive moral victory over sin by the grace of God is real, with fruits manifest in the way one treats his neighbor as well as in reorientation of the soul toward God. We shall do better to speak of this with regard to others than ourselves, lest we think of ourselves "more highly than [we] ought to think," but the fact of it is basic to Christian character.

How does this victory take place? Here again Jesus tells what we need to know. The experience of Paul and of the New Testament community and the total history of the Church gives helpful amplification if we do not distort it into supposing that the change involved in becoming a Christian must always come about in just the same way. We noted in Chapter III what Jesus made the main requirements: com-

102

mitment of will, repentance, the willingness to forgive others if we would be forgiven, faith in God. Love and the doing of the works of love then become both the evidence and the obligation of a God-centered life.

Such conversion may be gradual or sudden. In the moral decisions of a lifetime that are involved in it, one of them may or may not over-shadow all the rest to become the kind of dramatic reorientation that Paul had on the Damascus road. Personal decision there must be, and background as well as foreground, and in the total experience, Christian nurture, Christian worship, and the acceptance of opportunities for Christian service play an essential part. I shall not attempt here to describe in detail what happens in conversion to the Christian life, for I have done this previously in a number of writings.[7]

Much is being said and written of late as to man's basic anxiety before the precariousness of existence as the source of all his other aberrations. While not much has been said about it in this chapter, since I believe that self-love rather than anxiety lies at the root of sin, faith and love must go hand in hand in the conquest of sin. "'There is no fear in love, but perfect love casts out fear." (I John 4:18.) It is the perfect love of God as this has come to us in God's Son that conquers both fear and sin; it is our faith and love that lead us to him. Victorious living comes through the conjunction of God's act with our humble, obedient, trust-ful acceptance of his proffered gift.

Thus it comes about that no man needs helplessly to struggle under the burden of his sin, and no man ought to assume that without per-sonal commitment to Christ he is good enough. Both courses lead to frustration and defeat. To the degree that personal Christian experience becomes a reality—whether it is called redemption through justification by faith or in more popular language simply "becoming a Christian"—it makes a profound difference in personality. It touches life at its center. By it the whole of life takes on a new orientation, vitality, and power. To enter into this heritage of Christian faith at first hand, and to become a "new creation" in Christ, is the most important step that can be taken by any soul.

[7] See my *Religious Living* (New York: Association Press, 1937; republished in *The Religious Life*, 1953); *Understanding the Christian Faith*, ch. viii; *Prayer and the Common Life* (New York and Nashville: Abingdon Press, 1948), ch. 12; *The Modern Rival of Christian Faith*, ch. xi.

VI. Duties to Self and Society

THE PREVIOUS CHAPTER dealt with personal character, from the standpoint of both what it means to be a Christian and the thwarting of what God requires by sin. We move now to a very basic issue. Granted the validity of the love commandment, how does a Christian put it into effect?

It is an evident fact that modern life is not simple. It was not wholly simple in the Galilee or Jerusalem of Jesus' day, or in the medieval era, or in the time of our Puritan fathers. Nor is it possible to escape entanglements by withdrawing to a cloister, for problems of the soul are there as well. It is an illusion to suppose that in some other time and place, being a Christian would be easy! Nevertheless, in terms of things and activities, with competing demands and possibilities, our lives are more complex than in any previous day, and this remains so in spite of our most earnest efforts at "the simplification of life." [1] And when duties to self, to those near at hand, and to the larger community conflict, how is one to know what to do? The more sensitive the Christian, the more he feels the impossibility of doing all that he ought in the service of human need.

The remainder of the book will deal with the issues involved in particular forms of social relationship, such as the family, economic life, the state, and the world of nations. Each has its own moral dilemmas. Yet certain principles are common to them all. With these we are concerned in this chapter.

1. Duty to self

Has Christian ethics any place for self-love? The question is not

---

[1] Thomas R. Kelly's *Testament of Devotion* (New York: Harper & Bros., 1941) has a remarkable essay by this title.

whether self-love is primary, for we have seen repeatedly that agape love is primary in the message of Jesus; it is whether self-love has any place at all in the Christian's moral outlook. This is a question on which Christians both learned and sincere have often disagreed.

The primary arguments in the negative are, on the one hand, biblical and theological, and on the other psychological and pragmatic. The first type centers in the fact that there is no specific defense of self-love in the New Testament, and many warnings against it. The second is that if a justification for self-love is granted in any degree, consciences are too readily soothed and convenient rationalizations found.

Bishop Anders Nygren in his *Agape and Eros* has become the accepted and oft-quoted champion of this view. He holds that Augustine was wrong in admitting eros into the Christian's outlook even at the point of man's desiring and seeking after God. New Testament love, according to Nygren, is always *giving* love, never seeking, and Augustine's distinction of *caritas* (man's love of God) from *cupiditas* (the love of the world) he holds to be invalid. He maintains that Luther did a great service, as significant as that of his doctrine of justification by faith alone, to which it is related, in removing the *eros*, or self-seeking, motive from Christian love and leaving *agape* as the only legitimate type.[2] Nygren is followed in this view by Paul Ramsey in *Basic Christian Ethics*, who regards the Augustinian position as essentially neo-Platonic, and the only right attitude of men toward God to be purely responsive love.[3] Albert C. Knudson, on the other hand, not only defends the position of Augustine as to man's duty to seek after God, but views the disjunction of *agape* and *eros* in general as a false abstraction.[4] Says he:

To reject the *eros* idea, to exclude self-love and duties to self as non-Christian, and to limit Christian love to an "unmotivated" love to others is to create an abstract Christian ethic and to fall into a sentimental immoralism. . . . The Christian ideal is self-realization through self-sacrifice.[5]

The objection to self-love from a practical standpoint is less subtle, and perhaps more persuasive. Certain it is that Christian ethics can never

[2] Part II, Vol. II, p. 232.
[3] Pp. 117-32.
[4] *Op. cit.*, pp. 124-32.
[5] *Ibid.*, p. 132.

be stepped down to a policy of "look out for Number One," or "blow your horn, for nobody else will," without encouraging an egocentricity and arrogance that are the antithesis of Christian love and humility. Against this attitude such words of Jesus as, "Seek first his [God's] kingdom and his righteousness," and, "Whoever would save his life will lose it," stand as a perpetual challenge (Matt. 6:33; 16:25). The danger of self-love, even in "spiritual" things, becomes apparent when God is used as a tool or instrument for curing neuroses and releasing tensions in order to have "peace of mind." [6] The temptation to make of one's faith a pleasant emotional luxury ever besets the path of the Christian. When this happens, religion becomes the "opiate" that Karl Marx claimed it is.

Yet it is by no means certain that either theological or practical considerations rule out wholly the place of self-love in Christian ethics. What can be said on the other side?

There is, first, the evident fact that Jesus said, quoting Lev. 19:18, "You shall love your neighbor as yourself." There is no suggestion, in either its Old or New Testament context, that such love of neighbor excludes all love of self. Indeed, that men will love themselves—and that such love suggests a standard of generous love for others—seems taken for granted. This is also the implication of the Golden Rule, "Whatever you wish that men would do to you, do so to them" (Matt. 7:12). But did Jesus mean by this that whatever I like, I must see that my neighbor gets? If so, there might be a duty to give him what is evil, for not all of our "likes" are good. "The Golden Rule, for instance, might be fully observed among sots and gluttons." [7] Manifestly, Jesus did not mean this. We naturally and rightly assume it is *what we ought to want* that should in love be given to our neighbor. But if there is that which, as Christians, we ought to want for ourselves, then self-love cannot wholly be ruled out.

I said above that Jesus took it for granted that men will love themselves. Does this mean that he simply regarded all men as sinners? This is one interpretation, easily defended because all men are sinners. But it is not the only interpretation. When Jesus said, "Love your neighbor

[6] See Paul Hutchinson, "Have We a 'New' Religion?" in *Life* Magazine, April 11, 1955, p. 138, for a well-balanced appraisal of the current tendency to a "cult of reassurance."
[7] Knudson, *op. cit.*, p. 39.

as yourself," he probably did not anticipate all the theological web spinning that was later to center around these words! But it is at least credible to suppose that in taking self-love as a base line for love of neighbor he was not condemning it as wholly evil.

A second approach to the problem is by way of a "natural law" of morality, which though Stoic in its origin has been to a considerable extent taken over into Christianity. It appears in a familiar form in the "unalienable Rights" [8] of "Life, Liberty and the pursuit of Happiness" as stated in the Declaration of Independence, in the Bill of Rights guaranteed by the Constitution, and more recently in the Universal Declaration of Human Rights adopted by the United Nations. Such statements are, of course, not distinctively Christian. Yet they stand for precious values which Christians have usually felt impelled both to defend for themselves and to seek for others. And there is at least a suggestion of a natural law of morality in Paul's words when he speaks of the Gentiles "who have not the law [but] do by nature what the law requires," and thereby "they show that what the law requires is written on their hearts" (Rom. 2:14, 15). Unless an absolute line is to be drawn between the law and the gospel, there is no need to abrogate as unchristian all those personal rights that the "conscientious feelings of mankind" have declared to be good.

A third type of argument is that which is basic to Knudson's position —the making of self-realization the Christian's ethical ideal. This is eros doctrine, and while I cannot go with him in the emphasis he gives it,[9] it may well be that the Christian's agape obligation carries with it the duty of the fullest possible self-development for the sake of service. We are bidden "to grow up in every way into him who is the head, into Christ" (Eph. 4:16), and "every way" need not be limited to the specifically Christian graces.

Where, then, do we come out? The truth in my judgment lies in between the Nygren and the Knudson positions. I do not find in the New Testament any justification for the identification of Christian

---

[8] The word ought to be "inalienable," but it is not in this historic document.

[9] Knudson says, "From the practical religious point of view the emphasis naturally falls on the agape idea; from the theoretical and ethical standpoint the eros idea is properly stressed." Op. cit., p. 132. Though he says immediately, "But both have a place in the Christian ethic," he seems to me to make too sharp a disjunction between the religious and the ethical.

ethics with the ethics of self-realization. The latter centers in a blending of the Platonic theory of the Good with a sense of the worth and dignity of the human person, which has its roots partly in Christianity but also in Stoicism, the Renaissance, and the Enlightenment. Among the great classical ethical systems it is the best, and bears much truth. But it is not the ethics of Jesus and the New Testament.

On the other hand, the Nygren position, as Knudson rightly says, sets up a false abstraction by drawing too sharp a line between "motivated" and "unmotivated" love. Granted that *agape* love is the only type to which we are expressly called by the New Testament, to say that this does not permit us to seek after God, lest we fall into *eros*, is to contradict much that the New Testament clearly says. Every one of the Beatitudes is "motivated"; we are to seek God's kingdom as we would a treasure hidden in a field or a pearl of great price; we are told without qualification, "Ask, and it will be given you; seek, and you will find; knock, and it will be opened to you." Every such injunction carries with it the implication that a Christian not only may, but *must*, desire for himself that which is of greatest worth.

What does this mean in daily Christian living? First, that we must not only wait receptively before God for his proffered grace, but desire it enough to seek it in repentance and humble obedience. Daily we must seek the divine presence, and endeavor to find light and strength from God for the duties before us. Daily we must cultivate self-discipline and self-control, in small matters as in great, and do this in order to be not only "better persons" but better servants and sons of God. The orientation is toward God in true Christian character. Yet honest self-examination and self-correction by God's help are a duty which we neglect at our peril, and without which we cannot go far in the service of society.

But are there duties to self beyond the quest of these "spiritual blessings"? Yes, if they are kept within the structure of *agape* love, with this as the central motivation. Since every person is precious to God, one may well consider that one's self is too! This means respect for one's own personality, as God wants us to respect those of others, and the avoidance of anything injurious to body, mind, or spirit. Positively, it involves the duty of care for one's health, the pursuit of as much education as is possible without the neglect of other responsibilities, careful preparation for the best doing of one's work, the finding of work that is both serviceable and congenial, fruitful and enjoyable use of leisure, wholesome family life, and the acquiring of enough material goods to make possible these other values. While it is a mistake to equate the "abundant life" with either material abundance or cultural advantages, it is a mistake also to limit it wholly to spiritual blessings.

The list of "good things" just enumerated may not, at first glance, look very different from those prized in a humane and cultured secular society. It is well that there are points of contact, for the Christian must often work with "men of good will" who are not Christians in order to secure these values for himself and others. Yet for the Christian, the perspective and the motive are different. Not because he loves himself on a hedonistic, pleasure-seeking basis, but because he knows God loves and prizes him and calls him to service, he must make the most worthy response he can. In short, he must be the best and most fully developed person he can be—not in moral excellence only but in every aspect of his nature—if he would seek to attain "to mature manhood, to the measure of the stature of the fullness of Christ" (Eph. 4:13).

A particular problem is involved in what is a familiar term on the lips of psychologists and psychiatrists, the need of *self-acceptance*. Often it is asserted that the Christian view of sin and guilt accents the lack of self-acceptance, induces feelings of inferiority, and therefore stands in the way of achieving personal maturity. Should not one be encouraged, then, to believe in himself, prize himself highly, come out of his shell of timidity and self-depreciation, and boldly take his place in society?

The issues are complex, and can here be only suggested. The major point in question is the total framework of meaning from which these charges are made and alternatives suggested. If it is contended that man has only the resources of himself and other persons to rely on, with a good social adjustment as the only criterion of excellence, the viewpoint is too narrow and by its narrowness becomes false. To the Christian, God is the ultimate source of strength, as his will is the final standard of what is good. But if the need of self-acceptance is acknowledged in a Christian frame of reference, it becomes a very important matter. One certainly cannot render his best service to God or neighbor when weighed down by timidity, self-depreciation, or excessive self-excoriation. A sense of sin in due humility we must have; this does not mean we must be torn apart by the tortures of remorse or rendered impotent by a crushing weight of inferiority which induces unhappiness and inhibits action. It is a Christian duty to try to find release, and in this process both repentance and respect for one's own personality are important. We are bidden to "rekindle the gift of God" that is within us, "for God did not give us a spirit of timidity but a spirit of power and love and self-control" (II Tim. 1:6, 7).

The duties to self which I have been suggesting had probably better not be called self-love without qualification, for the term too readily suggests a self-centeredness which is not what Jesus taught. Agape is still the basic and covering category of Christian ethics. Yet within agape, there are certainly very important, God-given duties to one's self. These ought not to be pursued either selfishly or in a morbid and unhealthy self-concern, but neither ought they to be depreciated. Without serious and resolute attention to them, we shall be but feebly equipped to serve God or our neighbor.

2. *Duties in interpersonal relations*

We shall look in this section at what has ordinarily been termed "individual ethics," or sometimes "personal ethics." Both terms are ambiguous, and have tended to draw too sharp a contrast with "social ethics." Every duty to another person is "social" in the sense that the obligation exists within a society of persons, in which there are greater or less degrees of intimacy of connection. Yet the setting within which Christian decision must be made and the obligations of Christian love must be met differs as between persons with a face-and-name relationship in the family, school, church, or other group of personal acquaintances and the vast complexities of society as a whole. No human being can be personally acquainted with more than a few thousand other persons, while there are many millions of other human beings who are beloved of God and toward whom some obligation of Christian love is presumably owed. It is within the circle of life touching life in direct relationship that our opportunities for the fullest expression of agape are found, yet with some of the greatest perils of perversion.

Ever since the publication of Reinhold Niebuhr's epochal book *Moral Man and Immoral Society* in 1932, there has been a general recognition of the difference between the way Christians respond to the love commandment in personal relations and the large-scale indifference or "immorality" of Christians in the complex structures of political and economic life. It is clearly more possible, even though still difficult, for one to "love his brother whom he has seen" than one whom he has not seen, may never see, and is related to only in terms of political or economic subjection or dominance, if he feels related at all. This fact has led some writers on Christian ethics, notably Emil Brunner, to maintain that the scope of Christian love is necessarily limited to individual relations, and to substitute justice as the norm elsewhere. This dualism I must reject, for reasons to be stated in the next section. Yet Christians, as well as other men, may well believe that love evokes particular obligations to those nearest.

Unless a Christian is to go to the length of saying that he has no more obligation to provide food for his own children than for the hungry in Korea—and not many Christians in practice, at least, would go this far—this appears to be indisputable. Yet this does not settle for us the many problems that emerge in daily life as to whom to serve and how best to serve them when human need is overwhelming and time, strength, and money are limited. If we can draw some directives from our gospel, we must find them, even though to find ready-made answers to all these impinging dilemmas is a vain hope.

It is a significant fact, suggestive of the outgoing character of Christian agape even among those who have never given serious thought to its meaning, that the Christian tends naturally to universalize it even when he fails to live by such an implication. What is "brotherly love"? Even a churlish and parochial Christian hesitates to say in principle that it means only an obligation to one's own family, or next-door neighbor, or fellow member of one's own local church! The brotherhood of man is assumed to include everybody; the problems begin at the point of acting in a brotherly fashion toward one of another race, or nation, or politics. Therefore, there is a common tendency to read into the recorded words of Jesus more than he says, while at the same time their application is far too constricted.

An unbiased reading of the Gospels—or at least, as objective a reading as possible, since every reading is an interpretation—leads to the conclusion that most if not all of the sayings of Jesus preserved in the records were spoken to individuals about their relations to God and to other individuals. There is a conspicuous lack not only of large-scale social programs but of corresponding social directives. For example, "Love your enemies, do good to those who hate you, bless those who curse you, pray for those who abuse you" (Luke 6:27), may well enough by us be taken to mean an attitude required toward the enemies of one's nation, but it is doubtful that Jesus had this context specifically in mind. One who is bringing a gift to the altar and remembers that his brother has something against him is enjoined, "First be reconciled to your brother, and then come and offer your gift" (Matt. 5:24).[10] In all probability this meant to Jesus and to those who heard him speak these words neither a blood brother nor a fellow Christian, but another personally known individual. Even the immortal parable of the good Samaritan fails to define for us precisely who "my neighbor" is; it makes clear the quality of neighbor love and leaves it to our Christian imagination to supply the answer to the lawyer's question (Luke 10:29-37).

From this fact, two cautions are in order, for Christians have often gone to one extreme or the other. The more serious error has been to restrict the meaning of Christian duty wholly to individual, or more correctly, to "small group" relations. This has been the traditional impact of Christian ethics through the centuries, cultivating the virtues of almsgiving, ministry to the sick and helpless, chastity, personal honesty, and in general a responsive conscience in the presence of immediate need, but with little sensitivity to those caught in the grip of an evil social system. To broaden the scope of the Christian moral imperative, and with it the scope of "brotherhood" and "neighborliness," the social gospel emerged. This was—and is—right in much of its emphasis on the need of applying the principles of Christian love to all men, but often wrong in its assumption that to Jesus, the kingdom of God and such a liberated and alleviated society were equivalent terms.

What we have to do is to begin from both the explicit words of Jesus and the implicit meaning of agape, and in times and conditions very different from those of first-century Palestine, attempt to discover how to be Christian in both immediate and large-scale relations with our fellows. There are no fixed rules but some basic necessities, in disre-

[10] See Ramsey, op. cit., pp. 92-93.

gard of which we fall into error and what is more serious, into sin. In every case we need to find, not a middle ground in the neatly balanced Aristotelian sense of the mean between extremes, but the truth within a paradoxical relation in which to state one obligation without its counterpart is to miss the full meaning of the obligation.

The first fact to be noted is that within the immediacy of interpersonal relations lies man's *greatest capacity for self-giving love and his worst temptations to self-love*. Not only within the natural biological unit of the family, but in the relations of pastor and people, teacher and student, employer and servant, doctor and patient, counselor and counseled, and many other relations of friend to friend, one sees at times very moving demonstrations of sacrificial love. Only the cynic can say that it is the desire for personal approbation or for mutual benefits that prompts every act of patient, forgiving, unrewarded, and possibly even to others unknown service. There are too many examples, not only of outstanding personal service to humanity in ways exemplified by such men as Francis of Assisi, David Livingstone, Wilfred Grenfell, Albert Schweitzer, and Frank Laubach but among thousands of unsung Christian saints, to say that all human acts are egoistic. "If I give away all I have, and if I deliver my body to be burned, but have not love, I gain nothing." The counterpart of this is the fact that without thought of personal gain Christians have again and again given all they had, even to the giving of their health or bodily life to be burned away, in sacrificial love.

Yet this is not the whole story. Where do tempers most readily flare up, and where are caustic, stinging words most often spoken? In the home, among those we know so well that our inhibitions are down. Where do we most eagerly covet prestige and recognition? Among those who know us. There is slight comfort in being heralded by the world if among those near us we feel we are "not appreciated!" Where is self-pity most rampant? Exactly at this point. Where is the temptation to manipulate and dominate other personalities strongest? Where it is possible—and this possibility is usually greatest in interpersonal relations. Where are the most subtle rationalizations of self-will? Precisely at the point where they can most readily be concealed under cover of friendship, of parental duty, of "doing the Lord's work," or some other plausible-sounding excuse for following our own desires.

As was earlier noted, the medieval Church showed keen discernment in focusing attention on the seven deadly sins of pride, envy, anger, sloth, avarice, gluttony, and lust. While these are not limited to the relations of individual persons to one another, their most frequent expressions (with the possible exception of avarice) are at this point.[11] It is in the impingement of one life upon another, multiplied throughout human existence by both overt and covert forms of sinful self-will, that the most deadly damage is done.

The deduction is clear. On the one hand, we must recognize and be grateful to God for genuine expressions of Christian *agape* as we see them in others, and be challenged by them to fuller self-giving. On the other, as we look at ourselves, the warning is always in order, "Therefore let any one who thinks that he stands take heed lest he fall" (I Cor. 10:12).

A second paradoxical situation with regard to Christian duty follows from what has been said. A person's *first duty is to those for whom he has most direct responsibility*. Yet it is this primacy of duty *which most often narrows his vision and curtails his wider service*.

To illustrate, it is the Christian's duty, as well as that of every other man, to provide for his (or her) family not only the material foundations of life but the conditions of happy and creative existence. One has a responsibility to one's own family that one does not have to any other. Not only by civil law and custom but by the obligations of Christian love it is wrong to sacrifice one's wife or husband or children to a diffused idea of "serving humanity." This does not mean that in the intimate relations of the home sacrifices may not be shared; it is obvious that in most forms of devoted Christian service they must be. Still less does it mean that one party in this relation is justified in imposing his or her will upon the other under a selfish plea of being neglected. This is a too common form of self-love, and many an act of Christian service is inhibited by the partner's whim or by a self-pitying assumption of martyrdom. Nevertheless, it *does* mean that it is not Christian to neglect or injure one's own family in the service of others to whom no such direct obligation is owed. To serve the Lord is our supreme duty,

[11] The sin of *superbia*, pride, centers in man's relation to God rather than his fellow men. Yet in its effects, it still remains true it is in interpersonal relations that its most serious moral consequences are visible. It is significant that Gregory the Great, who drew up this list and ranked their seriousness in this order, made pride the source of the other six with sins of the flesh at the bottom of the list.

but it may be doubted that God is well served in forgetfulness of immediate human duties or the immolation of those who ought to be loved and cherished. This applies to time, energy, and companionship as well as money, and many a "busy person" continually away from home at church meetings might well take heed.

A similar observation can be made regarding one's work. When one has "a job to do," whether in the form of a definitely assumed voluntary responsibility or paid employment, it is his duty to get it done to the best of his ability, and not to let his time and energy be frittered away by a multitude of competing, and quite possibly more attractive, forms of work.

If, as often happens, duty to family and work conflict, he must decide as best he can—if possible by mutual agreement—what is the prior duty in the particular situation. John Calvin felt impelled by a rigorous sense of duty to keep an engagement at the church while his wife was dying; one may well doubt that it was his duty. On the other hand, there are many occasions when major public responsibilities must be met at the cost of minor inconveniences at home—and this with no diminution of the fact that one is never entitled to disregard or trample upon the personalities of those to whom one is bound by special ties of love and obligation.

But what of the other side of the paradox? Granted that there is a primacy of duty to those for whom one has most direct responsibility, what of its dangers? For dangers it certainly has! To protect one's family and enhance their status, whether in regard to material comforts, social prestige, or in general the securing of "advantages," many a Christian will violate known principles of Christian behavior. In order to make one's own work prosper, in a situation where motives of self-love and service to one's group are mixed, one will do what he would sharply criticize another for doing. In such situations restraints of conscience are often less powerful deterrents than fear of the law or of social disapproval.

Furthermore, it is not in direct violation of known Christian principles that the most serious consequences occur. Where these are clearly confronted, there is a chance for the Christian conscience to operate in terms of *repentance after* if not *prevention before* the event. For this reason, Christian leaders without becoming moralistic must continue to give moral instruction with the hope that some of it will modify consciences and hence affect decisions. But the more serious situation lies in moral dullness, which in turn may be the result either of ignorance, or of willful moral blindness, or of unconscious self-deception, or a mixture of all of these factors.

This moral dullness, insofar as it is preventable, is sin. This is true, whether the moral dullness is with regard to the unconscious hurts one gives one's wife or husband or child or the large-scale complacency before the evils of the world that makes an "immoral society" out of "moral men." It is willingness to enjoy advantages in one's own situation with indifference to "my neighbor" in the broader context that both necessitates and imposes barriers to Christian social action. There is a legitimate primacy of love and Christian service in interpersonal relations; there is also an ever-present and often-yielded-to temptation to make of such relations a subtle cloak for self-aggrandizement and self-love.

There is a place for compromise. The absolute demands of love must be lived out within the relativities of human existence in which duties come mixed, and a perfect course of action is seldom open to us. This is true in interpersonal relations, as it more obviously is true in more impersonal social structures. The right course is the *best possible* course, not an impossible perfection. But compromise can be along the line of either the fulfillment of Christian love or its surrender. "To do what appears as relatively best is an absolute duty before God, and to fail in this is to incur positive guilt." All too often such guilt is incurred.

One further problem in this connection must be noted before passing on to look at the wider framework of society—a moral dilemma which seldom fails to confront the sensitive Christian. What of conflicting duties, not only among legitimate and needed services to others, but between one's duty to one's self and to others? There are times for noble self-forgetfulness, but the Christian owes some important duties to himself. What if he cannot pursue these ends and serve others at the same time?

To illustrate, virtually every Protestant Christian leader, and in particularly acute form nearly every married theological student, faces the dilemma of study versus family versus church to be served. Shall one neglect one's reading, thinking, and in general his intellectual maturation under the pressing claims which come from the other two sources?

The temptation is strong, and there is no single, all-time answer.

The answer must be found in terms of the largest possible service to God and to other persons within the total life span. This calls for careful and prayerful planning of the use of time. If Protestant ministers are to have homes, these ought to be good ones, and firm long-lasting foundations are not built by giving the family in the early years of married life the casually snatched fragments of one's time and attention. If ministers are to preach and be Christian leaders for the next fifty years, they must have something to say. This means that, save for the most pressing instances of immediate need, nothing should be allowed to interfere with preparation for a lifetime of Christian service. Not willfully or selfishly, but in sober and calculated Christian dedication, it is necessary to keep one's mind and soul fixed on the main objective. This entails that, not obstinately but firmly, one must sometimes refuse to serve for the sake of a larger service.

3. The larger society

We come now to the sphere in which most discussion of "social service" and "social action" centers—the larger society of individuals not personally known, who are related to us indirectly through large-scale and often very complex social institutions but not directly as persons with a face and name. Most relations in politics and economics, except in the immediate local community or small business unit, are of this type, and as schools and hospitals and churches increase in size to the point of including several thousands within one system, these traditional centers of personal ministry become more and more impersonal. There is a flexible line of division, varying with both situations and the capacities of individuals, between interpersonal and impersonal social relations, but somewhere the line must be drawn. What, then, is the Christian's duty to those on the other side of it?

This is an enormous problem, some of the more specific issues of which will be dealt with in subsequent chapters. All that will be attempted here is to outline the meaning of social sin, and to indicate somewhat the possibilities of Christian love within these impersonal social structures.

Social sin, like any other sin, is compounded of attitudes and acts contrary to the will of God. It is social rather than individual sin when

117

it is directed by groups of persons toward other groups. War is the major example of such collective sin. It appears, however, in peace times as in war on many fronts. Economic exploitation, waste of natural resources, acquiescence in or encouragement to preventable hunger, illness, disease, or delinquency, political tyranny or irresponsibility, racial discrimination, or any other voluntary curtailment by one group of the "abundant life" for another group is social sin.

It is hardly debatable that the world is full of it. But this is not to say that every form of social evil is sin. The presence of cancer and polio, for example, which to date the best medical research has not been able to eliminate, is an evil fact to be combated; it is not something to repent of. Any decision made by an individual *responsibly and in the light of the fullest knowledge it is possible to get* is not sinful if it turns out badly, and the same may be said of group decisions. To the degree that the German people under Nazi control and the Japanese under Japanese militarism were kept in ignorance of the true situation, they ought not to be judged sinful for supporting evil systems, and the same is true to a large degree of the people now living under Communist propaganda and censorship. Under varying aspects, it is true of every people who have not had the opportunity to have their minds informed or consciences stirred as to the evil in their accepted patterns of thought and action.

Though this must be said in the interest of both clear definition and tolerance in judgment, social sin nevertheless is rampant. No individual or group acts as fully or as well *as could be done* to bring about the "good society" or the "abundant life." Motives usually come mixed, and in such matters as defense of racial segregation, or the economic *status quo*, or autocratic political power, or ecclesiastical domination, or the curtailment of civil liberties, who but God is to say how much is due to sin? In such disputed matters there is usually a combination of knowledge with ignorance, of heavy-handed tradition with the confrontation of new and untried situations, of self-interest with concern for the status of one's group. A sincere defense of conviction often merges with a stubborn and willful resistance to what others regard as the Christian way. In short, in every major social issue *sin is present,* but seldom *sin only*. To attack such a situation as if sin were the only factor involved is to breed the counter-sin of arrogance and unkind

118

judgment; to overlook the fact of sin is to bypass evil with smooth words and by acquiescence, to become a participant in it.

What we have to do in such situations is easy to state but hard to do. We must attempt by God's grace to "hate the sin but love the sinner," meanwhile endeavoring by such ways as are open to us to increase our knowledge of the situation and to support the best modes of changing it. Courage, resoluteness, patience, sympathy, are required—virtues not always easy to acquire in combination. But to the Christian, he does not have to acquire them save by fidelity, for they are the gift of God.

It is certainly more difficult to carry out the principles of Christian love in large-scale group decisions and in matters of social policy than in interpersonal relations.[12] Some degree of compromise is always necessary. Neverthless, as Edward LeRoy Long has shown in his very discerning book *Conscience and Compromise*, it makes a great difference whether one compromises at the point of having done all that he can within the particular situation in which social evil must be challenged, or simply conforms to the existing situation and accepts it as inevitable. Paul put the principle with tremendous potency when he wrote, "Do not be conformed to this world but be transformed by the renewal of your mind, that you may prove what is the will of God, what is good and acceptable and perfect" (Rom. 12:2).

This conjunction of adjectives is significant. What is the "good and acceptable" will of God? Not that which is ideally or abstractly "perfect," but that which is the best we can do—provided it is *really* the best we can do, and not some premature substitute. In every case of social decision there is *an ideally right course, a best possible course,* and *the course we are tempted to take* because it is easy or alluring or in conformity to the standards of our culture. Our guilt lies in choosing the third rather than the second of these alternatives.

With this in mind, what can a Christian do to challenge and change the gigantic structure of social evil and social sin that infests our world?

Though situations vary, there are in general three types of Christian

---

[12] See John C. Bennett, *Christian Ethics and Social Policy* (New York: Chas. Scribner's Sons, 1946), chs. ii and iv, for an admirable statement of both why this is so and what can be done in spite of it.

action open to us. The first of these is generally termed *social service*. It consists of such matters as the relief of hunger and want, and the support of hospitals, homes, settlement houses, recreation centers, medical research foundations, and many other forms of "social welfare" and "charitable institutions" (as the income-tax blank designates them). It calls for the projection of Christian love through sympathy as well as through financial support into a multitude of situations of human need. Discernment must be exercised to know where to give preferentially, whether of time, effort, or money. Yet that through such channels we can give, and ought to give, in Christian love is hardly debatable.

A second type of duty to society is *social education*. It was noted above that in most evil situations, there is a mixture of willful sin with ignorance, provincialism, and narrowness of outlook, the blindness induced by the pull of the past through entrenched emotional attitudes, and in general a very complex set of social forces that thwart change under cover of identifying the will of God with things as they are. For example, one need look no further than the stubborn resistance that has arisen over the Supreme Court's decision on racial segregation in the public schools, or the persistent unwillingness of many draft boards to respect the religious convictions of the conscientious objector, or the hysterical curtailing of civil liberties through fear of Communism. Christians who will take the trouble to understand such issues, even though opinions differ, and to spread general understanding by "speaking the truth in love" can serve enormously in laying the foundations for social action.

The third form of social action is *political and economic*. It is here that the knottiest problems lie, for such action requires not only the peaceful casting of a vote on election day or the decision to buy or sell certain goods, but the exercise by our representatives if not by ourselves of coercive force. It is the difficulty of combining coercion with love, particularly in the clashing relations of nation with nation and of powerful labor unions with great capital-holding corporations, that leads some to say that in such matters it is not love but justice that is the Christian's norm of action.

If what has been said to this point is true, the way out lies neither in a sentimental reliance on love as the sole solvent of social tension nor in its repudiation. Love is relevant to every human situation; love is always our ultimate norm. It is political and economic realism, as well as Christian ethics, to believe in the rightness of reconciliation and to use every available channel to put this spirit into action. Justice that is not derived from love of persons becomes vindictive retribution. Yet coercion must be used that order, security, and the conditions of justice in a free society may be maintained. It is not the will of God that either anarchy or tyranny should prevail in the earthly relations of his sons. How best to use coercive force to secure justice without canceling out the claims of love is the Christian's eternal problem. That it has no perfect solution is no excuse for failing to confront it squarely, and as far as possible, to meet it in every situation with the spirit of obedient love.

Love does not always "work" in the sense of securing the desired results. Yet without it, nothing else is more than a temporary palliative for the checking of evil. Giant structures of power in conflict with one another breed other conflicts, until man's status upon earth grows more and more precarious. Justice we must have, but justice directed by good will and concern for persons. The only effective road to a good society was described centuries ago in the words, "Do not be overcome by evil, but overcome evil with good." If an earnest effort is made in faith and devotion to follow this route, God can be trusted to give us light and direction along the way.

What this means more concretely, in both personal relations and the larger social whole, it will be our task to examine in the remainder of the book.

VII. Marriage and the Family

WE BEGIN NOW our study of the problems of what has usually been termed "social ethics," although for reasons given earlier it is impossible to draw a sharp line between individual and social ethics. What we are about to consider has long been termed in America, particularly under the influence of liberal theology, the "social gospel." In European thought it has more often gone under the nomenclature of obligation in the "orders of creation." This term with one made popular through its use in studies under the World Council of Churches, the "responsible society," is in process of replacing reference to the social gospel. Any of these terms may well enough be used if its meaning is understood. All refer to the application of the principles of Christian ethics within social institutions.

1. *The primacy of the family*

There are several reasons for beginning our study of the ethics of social institutions at this point. In whichever direction we look for a frame of reference, the family is a "first."

From the standpoint of the "orders of creation," both the Bible and anthropology agree in asserting the primacy of the family among all social relations. The Genesis story of creation comes to a great climax in the words: "So God created man in his own image, in the image of God he created him; male and female he created them. And God blessed them, and God said to them, 'Be fruitful and multiply, and fill the earth and subdue it.'" (1:27-28.)

In the study of primitive origins, the family is universally found to be the basic unit of society. This is not, to be sure, always a father-mother-and-child, monogamous family in the modern sense, but with varying degrees of blood relationship and with the family varying in size

122

from the small unit to the clan. Yet everywhere the family is that social structure within which economic, political, and cultural patterns have come into being and are perpetuated.

So it is today. Every family in today's society is, of course, the inheritor of many centuries of social change within which not only morals, manners, and mores have been developed but also a vastly complex set of economic, political, and cultural institutions. Much, therefore, is "given," to which both the child and his parents must conform. So dominant are these pressures that the status of the individual family, while sustained by them, is at the same time imperiled. Yet it is still true that within the family is a nucleus of growth, action, and character development which determines largely the course each individual will take, and through the aggregate of many individuals the course of society as a whole.

In the Christian view, man is a composite of nature and spirit. Man, like the animals, is a biological creature subject to natural necessity, while unlike the subhuman animals he is a living spirit with freedom to choose his ideals and fashion his life by them. At no point is this more clear than with reference to the family relationship. The sex impulse is a biological impulse, designed for procreation and essential to it, without which neither animal nor human life would be perpetuated. The death of older organisms requires that the young should be born and take their places, and the sex instinct is biologically the instrument of this ongoing life. Yet sex in the human part of God's creation is much more than an instinct designed for reproduction of the species; it is a high expression of spiritual devotion, fidelity, and love. So likewise is the family more than a temporary expression of the maternal (and possibly paternal) instincts for the feeding and protection of the young; it is also the matrix within which the highest human qualities of love and tenderness are experienced and nourished.

This fact has a direct bearing on the longer period of infancy and of parental care in the case of human offspring more than in any other biological group. To the obvious fact that no individual could be born without parents must be added the fact that without parents, or at least without parent substitutes, no person could grow to maturity or learn to care for himself in the multitude of ways that human life requires. The home is the *natural*, and by general consensus under normal conditions the *best*, medium for such maturation and growth. While society must provide substitutes in foster homes and institutions where there is no parental home, this is never more than a palliative and is not, we may believe, either nature's way or God's. This fact stands as a constant answer to the various proposals, appearing at intervals from the time of Plato's writing of *The Republic* to the present, to place the general care and rearing of children in institutions.

The obverse of this is the fact, unfortunately too evident in the contemporary world, that when a totalitarian system sets out to destroy an existing social structure, it begins by attacking the home. Children are taught to spy upon and report their parents; counter-indoctrination is given to contradict and ridicule the influence of parents; parents are psychologically and sometimes physically separated from their children, and all are forced into abnormal relationships and activities. If this is not to happen in a democracy as it has under Nazi and Communist tyranny, the freedom and sanctity of the home must be safeguarded as a basic foundation.

The primacy of the family finds its chief support, furthermore, in the words and attitudes of Jesus. These over the centuries have been incorporated into Christian thinking and at least partially into the social structure of the Western world. That Jesus exalted family relations has sometimes been challenged, as we shall note presently. Yet it remains true not only that he sanctified the family by drawing from it his primary symbol of the nature of God as Father and of men as God's sons, but that he had a new and fresh insight into the personalities that constitute a home. As a consequence, wherever Christianity has gone with any vitality, it has lifted the position of women and children and brought about the enhancement of family life as a whole.

2. *Jesus and the family*

We must now look more explicitly at the way in which the Christian outlook upon family life is rooted in the ethics of Jesus. We shall do this by examining both his explicit teachings and the implications to be drawn from his general structure of life and thought.

First, some negative criticisms must be looked at for what they may be worth. It is apparent from the record that Jesus never married. We do not know whether he ever had a love affair or considered marriage.

The astonished outburst of his neighbors, "Is not this the carpenter's son? Is not his mother called Mary? And are not his brothers James and Joseph and Simon and Judas? And are not all his sisters with us?" (Matt. 13:55) would seem to indicate that he was a dutiful son in the Nazareth home until the beginning of his ministry.[1] But after that time, there is no evidence that he had much contact with his family. Although it is recorded that from the cross he commended his mother to the care of the beloved disciple (John 19:26-27), it is difficult to escape the feeling that there is harshness not quite "Christian" in his rebuff of his mother and brothers when they came desiring to speak with him (Matt. 12:46-50; Mark 3:31-35; Luke 8:19-21). In his thought single-minded devotion to the Kingdom took preference over attending one's father's funeral (Matt. 8:21-22; Luke 9:59-62); the rigorous cost of discipleship was to hate one's own father and mother and wife and children (Luke 14:26). Such passages as these have been quoted by Christians to justify an ascetic view of family life, and by those not Christians to disparage the wholesomeness of Jesus' outlook upon this most intimate of human relationships.

To these negative reactions two observations are in order. The first is that Jesus did not, like Paul, advocate celibacy as a higher state than marriage. In fairness to Paul it should be said that it was probably his eschatological expectation of a speedy end of things, rather than an aversion to women, that made him put a premium on the single state and advocate marriage only as a somewhat grudging concession to sexual desire (I Cor. 7:6-9). Less is recorded from the lips of Jesus than the pen of Paul about sex relations, but it is unlikely that our Lord ever expected celibacy to be exalted as the pattern of life for the "religious," as is the practice of the Roman Catholic Church. The second observation to be made is that the stringent and costing requirements of the Kingdom do sometimes take precedence over family ties. Jesus was enough of a realist to foresee the temptations that family love presents, the more so because it is a great good that is not the highest good.

For an affirmative estimate of how Jesus regarded the family, it is necessary to see him against the setting of contemporary Jewish life. Family ties were highly regarded, and it is this structure of family loyalty

[1] Cf. also Luke 2:51; Mark 6:2-3.

in Judaism that has enabled it to persist through the vicissitudes of twenty homeless centuries. "Honor thy father and thy mother" was embedded not only in the Mosaic law but in Jewish custom. An incidental reference at the end of the story of the child Jesus in the Temple is typical of the times, "And he went down with them [his parents] and came to Nazareth, and was obedient to them" (Luke 2:51). The self-willed disobedience of the modern child would then have received short shrift in a Jewish home!

Yet while women were honored as mothers and sons were desired to carry on the family name,[2] as is usual in Oriental societies women were also regarded as the husband's property, bearing his children and satisfying his sexual needs. It is an interesting juxtaposition that while one of the Ten Commandments enjoins the honoring of parents, another speaks of a neighbor's wife in comparable terms with his house, slaves, ox, or ass as objects not to be coveted![3] Divorce was easy, and by giving her a written bill of divorcement a husband on any pretext could send away his wife "if then she finds no favor in his eyes because he has found some indecency in her" (Deut. 24:1).[4] There were doubtless many instances of genuine love between husband and wife, and between parents and children. Love has a way of transcending law and custom. Yet there is no suggestion, either in Old Testament law or in the world to which Jesus came, of a true equality of women and children with the husband and father of the family. The assumptions of the time sanctioned monogamy rather than the polygamy found in much of the earlier Old Testament, but it was a monogamy of the thoroughly paternalistic type. So common was this view that Paul simply echoed it in a new context when he wrote, "Wives, be subject to your husbands, as to the Lord. For the husband is the head of the wife as Christ is the head of the church. . . . As the church is subject to Christ, so let wives also be subject in everything to their husbands." (Eph. 5:22-24.)

Into this male-centered world Jesus came, and with incomparable insight treated men, women, and children equally as persons. So familiar has this idea of the equality of all persons before God now become that

[2] Cf. the provision in the Deuteronomic law for levirate marriage for this purpose (25:5-10).
[3] Cf. Fosdick, op. cit., p. 103.
[4] Ibid., pp. 106, 126.

it is difficult to project one's thought back into a time when it was a new and startling experience to talk seriously with a woman about her soul (John 4:7-27), or to set a child in the midst and say, "To such belongs the kingdom of heaven" (Matt. 19:14). Such comments as "They [his disciples] marveled that he was talking with a woman" and "The disciples rebuked the people" are in the text, but they carry much more weight than we usually discern.

However, Jesus exalted the position of women less by what he said than by the tenor of his life. The record shows no trace of sex discrimination. While considerations of propriety would have made it difficult, then as now, to have had a woman among the Twelve, Jesus had as his close friends Mary and Martha at whose home in Bethany he seems often to have visited. He healed women as freely as men (Matt. 8:14-15; 9:18-25; 15:21-28), and was not afraid to accept Mary Magdalene's tribute of understanding friendship (Luke 7:36-50). He cut so sharply into the current custom of easy divorce that it is no wonder the disciples were shocked into exclaiming, "If such is the case of a man with his wife, it is not expedient to marry" (Matt. 19:3-10). On the other hand, in a passage of doubtful textual authenticity but true to his spirit, he shocked those who were stoning an adulteress with words stinging to them and merciful to her, "Let him who is without sin among you be the first to throw a stone at her. . . . Neither do I condemn you; go, and do not sin again." (John 8:7, 11.)

The primary words of Jesus about the sacredness of marriage and the home are those which link it with the order of creation:

Have you not read that he who made them from the beginning made them male and female, and said, "For this reason a man shall leave his father and mother and be joined to his wife, and the two shall become one"? So they are no longer two but one. What therefore God has joined together, let no man put asunder. (Matt. 19:4-6.)

This is the bedrock foundation of Christian marriage, and on it all that is best in Christian family life has been erected.

It is evident from this focal passage, from those cited as to his equal treatment of persons, and from all that was said in Chapter III as to the grounding of his ethical insights in a spiritual relationship to God, that Jesus' attitude toward the family was never one of expediency or mere social conformity, much less of personal indulgence. The family to Jesus was a holy relationship, marriage a holy bond not lightly to be broken. Within it there were obligations and responsibilities as well as joys; all were centered in the creative act of God and the blessing of God upon the union formed under his sight and in his name.

In a day when marriages are too easily and too selfishly entered into and soon severed, this word of Jesus stands as a beacon pointing toward security, goodness, and truth. None may disregard it save at the peril of losing his happiness and his home. We must now see what light it throws on certain vital problems of our time.

3. Is monogamy essential?

At first glance this may seem like a superfluous and altogether academic question. Are not bigamy and polygamy prohibited by law? Is not monogamy the accepted family pattern in every civilized society? One may answer Yes, and still raise the question. For at two very vital points the monogamy which is accepted theoretically and legally is challenged in practice. One is the frequency of extramarital sex intercourse. Though the Kinsey reports are to be taken "with a grain of salt" because of their restricted sampling from those who felt free to report such intimacies, there is no doubt that they reveal a startling breakdown in sexual morality. The second factor, evident to all, is the ease and frequency of divorce with subsequent repeated remarriages. When one marriage in four ends in divorce, and plural husbands or wives are acquired one after another in rapid succession, it can hardly be said that monogamy is our universal practice.

What is monogamy? It may be defined as the marriage and subsequent sexual union of one man and one woman, entered into with the expectancy of permanence and with the assumption of legal and personal responsibilities entailed by this relation. The marriage ceremony, whether civil or religious, is not simply a perfunctory form, but is the announcement to society that this relationship is being assumed. A secret marriage, however undesirable, is still monogamous if there is a legal registry which can later be made public and which forms the basis of the assumption of mutual responsibilities. A "common law" union, still less defensible, assumes in some respects the status of monogamy when the union is permanent and the family that results is faithfully supported. Sexual intercourse outside of marriage, even when love is present, is not monogamy, nor is "trial marriage." There must be, on the part of the two entering into the marriage relation, an expectation that it will be "till death us do part" or it is not true monogamy.

Monogamy can be viewed, on the one hand, from the standpoint of sociology and psychology. It is an aspect of human culture about which a scientific judgment can be made as to the most advantageous form of domestic relationship. On the other hand, it must be viewed by the Christian in a religious perspective, to discern what is the will of God as that will is revealed by Jesus. From both standpoints, monogamy is the only right form of marital relation.

To begin with psychological and social factors, monogamy appears to be the natural form of family life, in spite of the powerful drive of the sexual impulse. It is generally believed among anthropologists that monogamy, rather than promiscuity, is the characteristic form of domestic relation in primitive societies. Where polygyny and polyandry[5] are found, these are extensions of an otherwise monogamous relation through secondary causes, such as the prestige of possessing plural wives or the desire that they bear sons to perpetuate the family name. The biological fact of the numerical equality, or near equality, of the sexes favors the monogamous relation, and precipitates problems of social adjustment regarding the unmated where there is deviation from it. More serious, however, is what happens to family life as a whole on any other than a monogamous basis. Whether the alternative is a houseful of jealous, quarreling wives, or concubinage with the inferior status of all but the first and legal wife, with the procreation in either case of a bevy of children who cannot have adequate parental care, the outcome is bad. Hence as societies advance, polygamy tends to be outgrown.

To translate this into conditions of modern Western society, what happens when a man has to support two families, or when marital unions are lightly formed only to be quickly broken? The resulting in-

---

[5] Polyandry, which is the practice of having more than one husband at the same time, is much less frequent than polygyny, the practice of having more than one wife at a time, but is found in a matriarchal stage of development among some tribes.

security and unhappiness of the adults involved is driving many thousands to psychiatrists and into mental hospitals, while the toll taken upon the children by broken homes is a familiar cause of juvenile delinquency and many other problems of personality disturbance. Quite apart from the Bible, or the Church, or the teachings of Jesus, anything else but monogamy simply does not work!

There is a further psychological factor in the nature of human sexual love. As Emil Brunner puts it:

This does not mean . . . that the polygamous instinct does not exist, nor that it is not particularly strong in the male; but it certainly does mean this: that, quite apart from all ethical obligations, those who love each other do feel the intrusion of a third person to be intolerably disturbing, that a strong and genuine love—still quite apart from any idea of ethical obligation —does want the loved one wholly and solely for itself.[6]

This fact is, of course, the source of much distress and tension when the "eternal triangle" appears and breeds at times a fierce jealousy which wrecks marriages. Yet, though subject to perversion, this particularity which makes the mate within a love relationship feel that the other must be *his*, and not another's, is based on a sound instinct. Within the order of creation it is an essential foundation of monogamous marriage.

But what of the Christian view of marriage? This is clear and unequivocal.

To the Roman Catholic Church, marriage is a sacrament. Most Protestant communions do not hold it to be a sacrament in the same sense that baptism and the Lord's Supper are, yet it is a sacred act. It is rightly spoken of as "holy matrimony," and as the time-honored ritual for its solemnizing has it, marriage is

an honorable estate, instituted of God, and signifying unto us the mystical union which exists between Christ and his Church; which holy estate Christ adorned and beautified with his presence in Cana of Galilee. It is therefore not to be entered into unadvisedly, but reverently, discreetly, and in the fear of God. Into this holy estate these two persons come now to be joined.[7]

---

[6] From *The Divine Imperative* by Emil Brunner, Copyright, 1947, by W. L. Jenkins. The Westminster Press. Used by permission.

[7] The form quoted is from the Methodist *Discipline*, 1956, ¶ 1917. This is an abbreviated form of the ritual in the English *Book of Common Prayer*.

Such marriage must of necessity be monogamous, based on a holy love with vows of mutual fidelity and with the expectancy of permanence. Any other form of union between the sexes is a distortion and perversion of what God has ordained and sanctified.

The fact that marriage is an "honorable estate, instituted of God" is of itself a sufficient answer to the Roman Catholic view that celibacy is a higher state to which priests, monks, and nuns are called. In fairness, however, to this view and to voluntary celibacy among Protestants where this is found, it should be clear that the divine vocation, or calling, is not the same for all persons. It sometimes happens that one's fullest service to God and his Kingdom may be rendered outside of marriage; where this is the case, celibacy is equally a "holy estate." Neither marriage nor abstention from marriage is of itself sacred; what sanctifies either situation is God's blessing upon it and the fullness of Christian devotion within it. Whatever one's marital status, a rich and useful life of Christian service is the will of God. Whenever one is confronted with a crucial decision at this point, then celibacy equally with marriage is "not to be entered into unadvisedly, but reverently, discreetly, and in the fear of God."

Nevertheless, for most adults marriage and family life are the normal and right relationship. But to make it "right" in quality and context is not easy when the contracting parties are not angelic beings but simply human beings who are mixtures of good intentions and sin. In no area of existence does the "sin which clings so closely" stick tighter or cause more havoc. What light, therefore, is thrown upon the family by the principles of Christian ethics?

4. Foundations of Christian family life

We must look at the foundations of Christian marriage and family life. Here it is important once more to see the relations between *agape*, *eros*, and *philia*. Agape, we have seen repeatedly, means uncalculating, self-giving love. Eros means the love of what is lovable, or desirable, or for some reason desired by the one who loves. As we have had occasion to use the term in previous discussion, based on its usual Platonic connotation, it did not mean the "erotic" in a sexual sense, but any longing for what is prized. Within the relations of the sexes it connotes romantic love with the desire to possess the beloved, and has as an important, though not its sole, ingredient the desire for sexual pleasure. *Philia* suggests a love based on compatibility and kindred interests, and is more accurately rendered in English by the term "friendship" or "affection."

It is important in Christian marriage that all three types of love be present, but with *agape* as the controlling factor. No marriage is likely to be successful without strong ties of romantic love and adequate common interests. The first requires deep emotion, the second rational judgment, as the marriage is contemplated. Yet neither an emotional love based on desire for self-gratification nor a calculated balancing of tastes is sufficient to carry a couple through the stormy days which almost inevitably come. To quote again the marriage ritual, it is "for better, for worse, for richer, for poorer, in sickness and in health" that vows of faithfulness are taken. Unless one is seriously able to pledge permanent fidelity in days that are "for worse," "for poorer," and "in sickness," he ought not to marry, and it is only *agape* love that makes this possible. Otherwise, as Paul Ramsey has suggested in a neat rendering of the meaning of *eros*, " 'I love you' may simply mean, in all sorts of subtle ways, 'I love *me*, and *want* you.' " [8]

The type of fidelity, therefore, that roots in self-giving, unclaiming love is very vital to Christian marriage. It is the only foundation that will hold a marriage steadfast through a clash of dispositions over matters minor in themselves but cumulative in a multitude of daily flurries and irritations, that will forgive hurts and avoid jealousies, that will outlive fading physical charms, that will undergird "affection that hopes, and endures, and is patient." The absence of such *agape* love is the major cause of the appalling percentage of divorce in contemporary marriages, and the root of much unhappiness in legally persisting but inwardly severed marriage bonds. Much that goes under the name of "mental cruelty" is simply self-centered, erotic love turned back upon itself.

To such *agape* love, centering not in emotional attraction only but in a deep and unselfish commitment to the other through every possible situation, must be added two important forms of "respect." One of these is respect for personality. Though these words do not appear in the New Testament, the idea they connote was basic to the attitudes of

[8] *Op. cit.,* p. 330.

Jesus, and is central to the Christian outlook wherever this is spiritually sensitive and discerning. It means within the family a due sense of the importance—and equal importance—of every member of it, father, mother, and children. It does not mean that every member will have the same duties, functions, gifts, or opportunities, for these vary with maturity and circumstances; but it does mean that every member shall have such treatment as will afford to him or her the fullest dignity, the fullest possible opportunity for self-development and creative growth, the fullest happiness the circumstances permit. Put negatively it means that no member of the family shall be exploited by another for his personal enjoyment or treated simply as a means to another's gain. Put affirmatively it means that every member of the family, infinitely precious to God, shall be so regarded by those most intimately connected by ties of blood and human love. The ramifications of this principle of respect for personality are endless, for they permeate the total structure of family life. I shall mention only a few, which when neglected are among the more common sources of perversion.

It is fairly well established in our society that due care shall be given to the physical health of each member of the family; it is by no means established that mental health shall be thus safeguarded. Among the most frequent causes of disturbance is continual "nagging" with sharp words and temper tantrums. No family life can be wholesome in such an atmosphere. But this situation may in itself be effect as well as cause, the result of unalleviated strain or the denial of normal freedom or a continually smoldering sense of frustration. Few family situations are ideal or can be made wholly so, but respect for personality in the form of understanding kindness and control of the tongue could go far.

There is the ever-present problem of authority. Whose word is to be "law"? The putting of the question suggests the root of the problem, for Christian ethics cannot be legalistic within the family any more than it can be elsewhere. Yet decisions must be made. They are best made by family counsel and mutual consent. Parental authority must be exercised over the immature, or no child will learn self-discipline, but it ought not to be exercised dictatorially. And as between husband and wife, who is "the boss"? Again the question suggests perversion, for neither can dominate the other when a Christian respect for personality

133

is present. It is no accident that in most marriage services of the present the wife does not promise to "obey," but there is instead a mutual promise by each to "love . . . comfort . . . honor . . . and keep" the other. Only when this vow is faithfully maintained can a marriage be what it ought to be.

Again, there is a nest of problems with regard to money and work and the related issues of recreation and leisure time. We cannot go into them here except to say that the principle of respect for personality has a bearing on them all. In general, it may be said that every member of the family who is able, children as well as adults, ought to have some money to spend as he or she desires, some responsible work to do with reasonable freedom from interruption, some chance for freely chosen enjoyment. But this is not to sanction the selfish individualism that too often prevails in the modern family. There should be family sharing, family work projects, family fun. Paul said it for the family, as well as for every other form of human relationship, when he wrote: "Let love be genuine; hate what is evil, hold fast to what is good; love one another with brotherly affection; outdo one another in showing honor. Never flag in zeal, be aglow with the Spirit, serve the Lord." (Rom. 12:9-11.)

But we noted two basic forms of "respect" as essential to Christian family life. The second is indeed a form of respect for personality, but it is so central and specific an aspect of it that it must be looked at separately. This is respect for the sexual relation.

It is a mistake to regard sex either as something base and degrading or as something to be indulged in simply for personal pleasure. Beyond the function of the sexual act for procreation, shared with the animal world, lies the fact that on the human level it is a symbol, ordained of God, that the "two shall become one." James A. Pike has spoken wise words upon this subject which may well be quoted:

Sexual intercourse is meant to be a sacrament. A sacrament, of course, is "an outward and visible sign of an inward and spiritual grace." The inward and spiritual requisite is the total and permanent pooling of hopes and fears, of strengths and weaknesses. The outward and visible sign is, as in other sacraments, both expression of spirit and means of grace.

. . . .

Sex apart from marriage is wrong, not because sex is bad, but because it

134

is so good. . . . Indulging in relations without the total commitment which marriage represents is to use a good thing in a wrong way, and the gravity of the wrong is in direct proportion to the degree of the goodness of this relationship. Since it is very good its misuse is very bad.[9]

This has direct bearing on two problems very much in current thinking, the legitimacy of extramarital sex relations and birth control within marriage. A word therefore needs to be said upon each issue.

To the matter of sex intercourse outside of marriage a very positive No must be spoken, not only because it is condemned repeatedly in the Bible and throughout the Christian tradition, but for the reason cited above. The sex relation between a man and a woman was instituted by God for marriage and for marriage only; any other use of it is a sacrilege. But if a couple love each other and plan later to be married, does this not hallow it? It does not, for short of actual marriage there is no pledge of unending fidelity, no assumption of permanent responsibilities, no assurance that the very act thus engaged in may not cheapen the relation between the two and terminate their love. Not fear of consequences, though with the most effective contraceptives there is still ground for apprehension, but the positive spiritual aspects of the sex relation ought to be for any committed Christian an adequate deterrent.

This is not to question the power of the sexual impulse, which presents a temptation for which sympathetic understanding rather than wholesale condemnation on the part of other Christians is in order. It is fortunate that the rigid self-righteousness reflected in Hawthorne's *The Scarlet Letter* is largely a thing of the past. But this does not mean that extramarital intercourse is to be condoned, either on ethical or on psychological grounds. For a generation under the influence of Freudian psychology and other factors in the prevailing climate of hedonistic individualism, we have been hearing that sexual repression induces neurosis and that the inhibitions of an earlier day should be disregarded. However, within this freedom neurosis has increased rather than abated, and the removal of inhibitions has contributed not only to the disintegration of family life but to the disintegration of personality as well. Psychological opinion appears now to be moving toward a reinforcement of the long-range moral insights of Christianity.

[9] From: *Doing the Truth* by James A. Pike. Copyright © 1955 by James A. Pike, reprinted by permission of Doubleday & Company, Inc.

Psychoanalysis recognizes that promiscuous sexual behavior springs from a disturbed personality, though exceptions are made in the case of the exploratory adolescent phase of development, which marks the transition between infantile and mature love. But maturity demands sexual behavior that is motivated by respect for persons, even in psychoanalytic terms, a significant testimony to the purpose of sex as it is rooted in the nature of man, which is in turn grounded in the reality of creation.[10]

But what of birth control within marriage? The Roman Catholic Church condemns it because it holds that procreation is the only legitimate purpose of sexual intercourse, and continence within marriage the only legitimate mode of family limitation.[11] Most Roman Catholics and some Protestants, though probably a decreasing number, hold that family limitation by an artificial means is "against nature," and hence against the divine will. The birth or nonbirth of a child as the result of sexual intercourse is held to be an act of divine providence, and hence not to be tampered with by any human instrumentality.

However, if the act of sexual union is a sacred bond of spiritual union, it does not exist for procreation only. Though celibacy within marriage is possible, it is doubtful that this contributes often to the fullest ripening of a high devotion. And if intercourse is engaged in, can the outcome be said to be wholly a matter of divine providence? Throughout the rest of human existence, causes bring effects, and this is no exception.

In other matters, such as providing for food, clothing, shelter, health, traffic safety, employment, and the like, it is generally accepted that the will of God requires of us rational and responsible action. One who would leave these matters wholly to chance would not be thought to be accepting providence but acting in a foolish if not foolhardy manner! And if in other things care and planning are required, why not in this most important of human events, the birth of a child? The coming of

[10] William Graham Cole, *Sex in Christianity and Psychoanalysis* (New York: Oxford University Press, 1955), p. 297.

[11] However, the Roman Catholic Church is not wholly consistent at this point, for the papal *Encyclica casti connubi* gives approval to family limitation not only by abstinence when both parties consent but by intercourse at those periods when conception is least likely to take place. However "safe" or unsafe the latter procedure, it obviously vitiates the logic of the Roman Catholic position. Cf. Brunner, *op. cit.*, pp. 370, 654.

new life may indeed be regarded as the gift of God, even as is the boon of death when in old age the earthly pilgrimage ends in release from pain, but in neither instance is human responsibility abrogated.

If children are as precious to us as they were to Jesus, we shall believe that every child has the right to be wanted and to be born into a home where adequate care is possible. This is not possible where financial resources are too limited, or the mother's strength depleted from too rapid bearing of children, or for any other reason the well-being of the parents and children requires that there be no more. The principle of agape love for one another, applied within the intimate relations of the home, necessitates what might better be called, instead of birth control, "responsible parenthood." To exercise such responsible parenthood with regard to the birth as well as the rearing of children is not to thwart the ways of God but to be responsive to them.

It is therefore the judgment of a growing number of Protestant Christians that it is not only the right, but the duty, of parents to take all relevant factors into account, including as a prime factor their service to God and his Kingdom, and plan for their family in the light of the total situation. On this basis the use of contraceptives is no more to be condemned than is any other scientific means for the enhancement of life and the fulfillment of what is believed to be the will of God. However, the matter has another side. It is an ugly fact that sexual passion can be as egocentric and unspiritual within marriage as outside of it. Lust is not limited to those who engage in extramarital relations. To use contraceptives simply as a cover for unrestrained, sensual sex indulgence is no more Christian within than outside the marriage bond.

5. Divorce

A final problem must be looked at, and this too is one of much importance on which there is a difference between the Roman Catholic and the usual Protestant view of Christian ethics. Once a marriage has been contracted, is it legitimate ever to dissolve it? An obvious corollary is the question of whether it is ever right for divorced persons to remarry.

The Roman Catholic Church, holding marriage to be a sacrament, regards all divorce as sacrilege and hence as sin. However, with the adaptability which has made this church so often able to deal with practical situations without seeming to contradict a principle, the possi-

137

bility of annulment is recognized. When a marriage is annulled, it is declared in effect never to have taken place. This to the Protestant mind leaves the dubious alternative of assuming that the couple up to the time their union was declared void were living in sin, and hence falls short of a satisfactory answer to the problem.

Is there any satisfactory answer? The first thing to be said is that divorce when it takes place is always a frustration of the true intent and purpose of marriage. I have stressed that monogamous marriage involves in its very nature the pledge and intention of unending fidelity. Marriage entered into without this intention is not only a travesty of Christian marriage but a violation of the purpose of the legal contract involved.

It is easier to say when divorce is not Christian than when it is. These negatives, if conscientiously observed, would enormously cut down on the present state of easy and frequent divorce which seriously honeycombs our culture and undermines the foundations of the home.

Divorce is unjustifiable when permanence is not intended in the first place. It is not justified when the couple make of their union simply a legalizing of sexual passion or any other form of selfish personal indulgence. It is not justified before and until every effort has been made at reconciliation where there is quarreling or incompatibility. It is not justified when one simply tires of one mate and desires to marry another. It is not justified in selfish disregard of the effect of such a broken home upon the children.

But is divorce ever justified? The words recorded in Matt. 19:8 as spoken by Jesus state that "for your hardness of heart" Moses allowed divorce, though it was not so in the order of creation. Twice in Matthew, Jesus forbids divorce "except for unchastity" (5:32; 19:9); in Mark the word is stated with stark simplicity, "Whoever divorces his wife and marries another, commits adultery against her; and if she divorces her husband and marries another, she commits adultery" (10:10). It is the opinion of many biblical scholars that the form in Mark is more likely to be what Jesus really said. The question then is whether divorce may ever be justified without disregard of the express command of Jesus.

The answer is to be found in the total spirit of Jesus rather than a legalistic interpretation of his words. What Jesus is apparently here doing is setting forth the requirements of pure, unclaiming, faithful

138

love as the basis of marriage. Such love and consequent fidelity are, as we have seen, fundamental to Christian marriage. But is it never the will of God that a marriage be terminated? To say so would be to doom some persons not only to a lifetime of unhappiness but to a frustration of the "abundant life" that Jesus said he came to bring.

As for the exception "except for unchastity," it is true that adultery breaks the marriage bond at its foundations. However, it can hardly be said that this in every situation justifies divorce, or that nothing else ever does. The message of Hosea in restoring his erring wife, Gomer, to his home is a symbol of the forgiving love of God, which ought to be practiced in the human relation before there is any easy recourse to divorce. But human sinfulness and stubborn wills being what they are, there is no guarantee that the broken marriage bond can be reknit. And when, even without direct infraction of the sexual code, life becomes so intolerable that the marriage in spirit is shattered, there may be no proper alternative but to dissolve it in form.

All that has earlier been said about the legitimacy and necessity of compromise is applicable here. Divorce is always a compromise with the highest ideal of family life. It is unequivocally wrong to compromise prematurely, or for selfish, petty, and individualistic reasons. Marriage is not a game to be played or terminated at will; it is a sacred and holy relationship. Only when it is clear that its sacredness has been irrevocably shattered should divorce be contemplated.

In those circumstances where divorce is right, so is the remarriage of the "innocent" party, if such innocence can be determined. Divorce simply for the sake of remarriage to some other mate is not to be condoned, for longing for another too easily encourages infidelity. Though love cannot be commanded, it can be restrained, and the marriage vow ought decisively to narrow the circle of erotic love. Yet when the marriage has been broken in spite of one's best efforts at forgiveness and reconciliation, the victim of this situation ought not to be forbidden ever to begin again. To condemn such a second marriage as adultery is to contravene the spirit of Jesus and make of his words a legalism that is incompatible with his total message.

Little has been said in this chapter about the foundations of Christian family life in the form of faithfulness to the Church, family worship, grace at meals, the practice of individual prayer, the atmosphere of Christian devotion that pervades the home. This is not because they are unimportant, for they are all-important. It is in the home that Christian experience is most surely nourished and made vital, and where this is lacking, there is great loss.

However, all this is another story. It belongs in a discussion of the devotional life and the methodology of Christian nurture. At this point we must rest our examination of Christian ethics in marriage and family life. As the total moral outlook of Jesus centered in his relation to God, so must everything that has been said in this chapter find its foundation in the relation of the family and its members to the "God and Father of our Lord Jesus Christ." On no other foundation can Christian marriage achieve true fulfillment; on this foundation in spite of much human shortcoming the grace of God can find a way.

VIII. The Ethics of Economic Life

IF ONE WERE to draw a diagram with a point at the center to indicate the individual person and a series of concentric circles for his major relations in society, the first circle would represent the family and the second his economic life. Next to the family, it is the "order of creation" on which his life is most dependent and with which his entire earthly existence has its most intimate connection.

But what is "economic life" or the "economic order"? This is by no means so clear-cut in its meaning or so easy to define as is the family. While it is obviously not the same as man's spiritual life or moral ideals or intellectual achievement or aesthetic appreciation, it spills over into the whole of existence including these elements. It has to do with the material foundations of life—that is to say, with money, property, and "wealth." Yet it is also concerned with human problems of work and vocation. If we limit the term "economic" to the traditional trilogy of the production, distribution, and consumption of material goods, it will not do to forget that in these processes human values are very intimately at stake. It matters enormously not only *what* goods are produced, distributed, and consumed, but *how* this is done. Economic life in a competitive society raises problems of power versus insecurity —an insecurity that is psychological as well as economic. In cases of economic domination the results are seldom limited to economic circumstances, but tend to affect the entire life of an individual or people. Furthermore, when an economic system dominates the policies of a nation, as in the present clash between Communism and the democracies of the West, the line between economics and politics becomes tenuous and at points indistinguishable.

As I shall use the term, economic life means everything connected with the acquisition, possession, and use of material goods. This will necessitate a look at labor, capital, and the systems which attempt to regulate their relations. The field is enormous, and I shall make no attempt to cover all of it. After we see what the biblical foundations are, the primary matters to examine will be the Christian view of property, work and vocation, and some principles of economic justice by which a Christian may be guided amid current conflicting systems.

1. The economic ethics of the New Testament

As has been noted, Jesus had very little to say about specific social institutions of any kind. His concern was chiefly with individuals in their person-to-person, face-to-face relationships. Therefore in his recorded words there is less to be found about the structures of economic life than about the family. There is, for example, nothing comparable to Matt. 19:5-6 to undergird a particular economic system as this passage does monogamous marriage.

Throughout the letters of Paul and in other parts of the New Testament there are scattered economic references, such as the obligation to work in self-support and not become a burden to others (II Thess. 3:6-12) and the injunction to slaves to obey their masters with due docility (Col. 3:22; Eph. 6:5; Tit. 2:9). Yet there is no clear focusing on any social system as good or evil, a fact which made it possible for slavery to go unchallenged by Christians for many centuries. In the prophets there is a much more direct reference to the evils of economic exploitation with repeated, ringing denunciations of it. It is to Amos, Hosea, Isaiah, and Micah that we are most apt to turn for the biblical foundations of social and economic justice.

There are a number of reasons why the New Testament is relatively so silent at this point. First, there is the fact that the Christian message centers so largely in faith and love that justice in social relations tends to be overshadowed. In the gospel of redemption there is no overlooking of divine justice. But in the call to love one's neighbor and even one's enemy, to pray for one's persecutor and to accept injury with nonresistance, to give freely and beyond necessity to those in need, the emphasis lies on uncalculating love and not on the correction of unjust systems or the punishment of evildoers. This note in Jesus was carried on into the early Church with the further emphasis on accepting Christ and finding new life in him as all-important.

142

In the second place, eschatology permeates the ethics of the New Testament. For reasons given in Chapter IV, the expectancy of a speedy end of the existing world scene did not basically pervert the ethical insights of the early Church, and still less those of Jesus. But it did foreshorten the perspective and divert attention away from social systems to the individual soul. Since it was the Christian believer, and he alone, who would dwell with God in his eternal kingdom, it was the soul alone that mattered. This attitude survived long after the passing of apocalyptic expectations and has not yet been surrendered.

A third factor explains at least in part the keener social conscience of the prophets as contrasted with the early Christians.

No Christian writer of the New Testament, so far as our records reveal, ever faced the responsibility of applying high moral principles to preserving the institutions of society, administering governments, handling international relationships, prosecuting social reforms, or even mitigating by public measures the inequities of an economic system.[1]

Their life as an "odd sect" with the simplest of economic pursuits within occupied territory did not give occasion for such responsibility. The prophets as the challengers and advisers of kings in a State struggling for political survival and economic power were much closer to the perennial problems of social injustice and conflict than were the relatively detached early Christians.

Yet Jesus stood in the succession of the prophets, and there is danger of overstressing the fact that he said nothing about economic systems. From his words and spirit has come a challenge that has persistently affected the economic order. Not only does the love commandment have a bearing on property as well as every other social issue, but in unequivocal terms he denounced some tendencies still very prevalent in modern economic life.[2]

There is nothing clearer in the message of Jesus than his indictment of acquisitiveness, and the putting of one's trust in material rather than

[1] Fosdick, op. cit., p. 80. Used by permission of Harper & Bros.

[2] George F. Thomas in Christian Ethics and Moral Philosophy (New York: Chas. Scribner's Sons, 1955), p. 307, puts this interesting and relevant query, "May it not be, therefore, that many Christian laymen resent the 'interference' of the Church on economic issues, not because the Gospel has little to say about them, but because what it does say is so disturbing?"

spiritual goods. Again and again this note is sounded. "You cannot serve God and mammon." (Matt. 6.24.) "A man's life does not consist in the abundance of his possessions." (Luke 12:15.) "Do not lay up for yourselves treasures on earth, where moth and rust consume and where thieves break in and steal, but lay up for yourselves treasures in heaven." (Matt. 6:19.) To lay up treasures on earth without being rich toward God is to follow the foolish way of the rich man who, thinking he had goods laid up for many years, heard the inescapable decree, "Fool! This night your soul is required of you" (Luke 12:16-21).

Jesus was very forthright as to the perils of riches. He did not hesitate to condemn in stinging terms those who "cleanse the outside of the cup and of the plate, but inside they are full of extortion and rapacity." In his reference to the camel and the needle's eye, it is hardly likely that he denied all access to the Kingdom to the rich, but this arresting hyperbole states with great vividness the spiritual dangers and temptations of wealth. Yet this does not mean that he thought lightly of the material foundations of life. "Give us this day our daily bread" undoubtedly means material, not spiritual bread; and in the passage in the Sermon on the Mount in which he warns against overanxiety as to what one will eat or drink or wear, it is significant that he nowhere indicates that these are unimportant. So important, indeed, are they that "your heavenly Father knows that you need them all" (Matt. 6:32).

Such passages indicate a perspective on the part of Jesus which puts material goods in their proper place as the instrument, and not the end, of man's existence. Out of them has come an impulse within Christianity toward honesty in the acquisition and philanthropy in the use of economic goods which through the centuries has had great social influence, and which ought never to be disparaged or lost. Our chief lack has been, not in directive principles from Jesus, but in the scope of their application by Christians.

As has been noted repeatedly, it is not alone from specific words that we get our directives, but from the total spirit of Jesus in his estimate of the worth of persons to God. As a fuller awareness of this became prevalent among Christians, the scope of economic concern broadened. It was seen that economic conditions affect vitally every person and the whole man; hence they must be a Christian concern. It gradually became—or is becoming—recognized that personal integrity and Christian giving to those in need will not meet the full requirement of the Christian ethic. We have today problems more complex than those of any previous age, but we have also a fuller sense of Christian obligation in and to a "responsible society."

2. The Christian view of property

The basic note in the Christian understanding of material possessions is *stewardship*. This term is often understood too narrowly to mean personal giving, usually with an emphasis on tithing. That Christians ought to give of their material resources for the support of the Church and many worthy causes, for the extension of the gospel and the relief of human need, is indisputable. That this should be on the mathematical basis of the tithe is more open to question, not because this often indicates too much to give but because for those who are well-to-do it is too little. The amount of personal sacrifice involved in setting aside the tithe varies greatly from the one-thousand- to the ten-thousand-dollar income, and still more as incomes go up. The Pauline observation that the Christian should put something aside "as he may prosper" (I Cor. 16:2) if taken seriously might yield larger gifts, and with more Christian dedication, than the Old Testament provision.

However, stewardship is not primarily a matter of personal giving. This is secondary and derivative. Stewardship means the recognition that *all* our goods, not some portion only, belong to God and we hold them in delegated trust.

> The earth is the Lord's and the fulness thereof,
>   the world and those who dwell therein;
> for he has founded it upon the seas,
>   and established it upon the rivers. (Ps. 24:1-2.)

If this principle of God's sole ownership and our stewardship, which is stated in the creation story (Gen. 1:26) and presupposed throughout the Bible, were taken seriously we should have a less acquisitive and more just society. Before it our vast disparities of wealth and poverty, wasted natural resources, and the use of God's good gifts solely for selfish ends could not stand.

But what of private ownership in the sense of each man's individual proprietorship of a portion of economic goods? Christians have not

145

always agreed as to the answer. The main trend of thought, however, both in the Bible and in the history of the Church, reinforces the conviction that some measure of individual ownership is right and Christian. The very existence of the commandment "Thou shalt not steal" presupposes the right of ownership, and one of the offenses against which the prophets had most vigorously to protest was its infringement. While there was for a time in Jerusalem after Pentecost a communal sharing of goods (Acts 2:44-45; 5:1-5), there is no evidence that this became a general arrangement. It was apparently a product of Christian fellowship rather than a social policy. Christian monastic orders with surrender of personal possessions have existed since the sixth century, and outside of Christianity long before that, but there has been no general conviction on the part of Christians that society as a whole should be thus organized. Asceticism and voluntary poverty, where practiced, have been considered as a divine vocation rather than as a mandatory social practice.

Furthermore, quite apart from the biblical and traditional grounds, there are other reasons why private ownership is right and Christian. The most basic of these is that the fullest development of personality requires it. Economic insecurity, we noted, is very closely linked with personal insecurity. The child may find his security in his parents without personal ownership, though even a small child ought to have some things that he can call his own. No adult, unless the Church or some other institution has assumed for him a protective status, can feel secure without some ownership.[3] Contemporary Communism has attempted to make the State assume this function, but with very doubtful results, and has been led by experience to reinstate much more private ownership than was envisaged at the beginning of the Soviet regime. In our society the "lift" one gets from owning something—whether one's clothing or furniture, a car or a home—is more than an outcropping of acquisitiveness or the prestige of possession; it is a response to a deeply embedded craving for security and a measure of personal independence.

A second factor is one about which the Bible is silent but which cannot be disregarded in the modern world. This is the greater degree of

---

[3] This applies also to adults within the family. A wife needs to have not only her husband's protection, but some possessions of her own over which she can exercise personal initiative.

economic efficiency and the higher standard of living that has ensued where the right of private ownership has been recognized. This is not to say that "enlightened self-interest" or a policy of unrestrained economic individualism will make a society either just or as a whole prosperous. The contrary is evident. Nevertheless, it is hardly disputable that not only in the production of goods but in the development of human skills and in the increased availability of both goods and skills for the service of human need, the right to possess has played no minor role. Individual ownership has produced a more advanced as well as more opulent society than has been possible under feudalism or any form of communal ownership in ancient or modern times.

A third and closely related factor is the relation of property to work. Personal ownership is necessary for economic motivation. There are some kinds of work one delights to do regardless of pay, as Bliss Perry elaborated in his book with the intriguing title *And Gladly Teach*. Christian leaders do not ordinarily choose their vocations chiefly from considerations of salary, or they would choose occupations better paid. Nevertheless, society as a whole with all of its hard, monotonous, and disagreeable jobs could not run without private profit and private ownership. It is fatuous to say that throughout all society there ought to be glad, voluntary co-operation; the fact is that there is not! With the human impulse what it is, it is unlikely that it will be possible to dispense entirely with personal profit as the reward of labor.

Private ownership and private profit are so deeply embedded in both our Christian and our democratic heritage that few would wish to see them eradicated if this were possible. But this is not to say that all the results are either beneficial or Christian. It is essential that the Christian conscience remain sensitive to perversions and continue to challenge evils which thrive all too frequently within this view of property.

The most common evil is the encouragement of acquisitiveness, and with it all the perils of self-aggrandizement, self-righteousness, and a false trust in material possessions against which Jesus spoke so vigorously. It is a half-truth, which when cited to justify unrestrained individualism becomes an untruth, to say that the sin does not lie in the system but in the people. Only persons can sin, but in the complex structures of present-day economic life it is impossible to draw a clear line between willful acquisitiveness and fair profit, or between individual and group sinning. Private ownership we must have, but not the amount and range of possession-centeredness that dominates our current society.

An accompanying evil is the vast disparities of wealth and poverty that have developed within every country, and in particularly acute form between opulent America and the hungry Orient. It is this which gives Communism its primary appeal, and no informed person needs to be reminded that this disparity is one of the major sources of world tension. Such vast inequalities of possession have always existed, but as the instruments of potential destruction become more deadly and the underprivileged become more conscious of the possibilities of change, the ferment of revolution and unrest becomes inevitable. Whether this will lead to global destruction in the clash of competing systems or to a greater measure of freedom and justice through the lifting of the living standards of the underprivileged peoples of the earth, no one can predict.

How much property ought a person, or a group, to possess? There is no simple answer. Competition alone cannot ensure justice, for competition encourages not only effort and skill but shrewd manipulation and the scramble for power. Equality is not the answer, for whether income and ownership are measured by earning or by need, inequalities must inevitably be reckoned with. An equal wage for all would not be an equitable one, for great differences exist both in the quality of services rendered and in family obligations, cost of training, and many other factors.

In judging what one ought to receive or possess, two simple rules may suggest the answer as well as anything more complex: (1) every person ought to have enough income to meet his basic physical and cultural needs without anxiety and with some surplus for saving and for giving; (2) no person ought to have so much that possession breeds indifference to the needs of others or becomes a peril to the soul. Within these limits a Christian society will find some latitude to be both inevitable and desirable. If this seems somewhat lacking in equalitarian justice, a higher spiritual justice is established by the principle of responsibility announced in the words, "Every one to whom much is given, of him will much be required" (Luke 12:48).

A third major evil is the linkage of power with possession of economic goods. This is not wholly evil, for power may be constructively exercised. There are rich men who manage a business benevolently without its being a benevolent despotism, and who use their money constructively for great philanthropies. These facts ought to be neither overplayed nor overlooked. Nevertheless, the temptation to an irresponsible and selfish use of power is always near at hand, and only a few at any economic level successfully resist it.

One of the major causes of social conservatism is the fact that churches, schools, and other social institutions are so largely influenced by persons whose advantage it is to preserve the *status quo* and who are prone to regard any departure from it as an affront to Christian morality. Not all social change is good. Yet under the guise of preserving freedom (and in the present scene, of resisting Communism) unjust conditions are perpetuated, and any attempt at social criticism is viewed as subversion. When the attitude is joined, as it frequently is, with a deep Christian piety in personal matters, the power becomes the more impregnable. Since human motives usually "come mixed," only God is wise enough to judge how much of this resistance to social change is due to self-interest, how much to the pull of tradition, and how much to sincere Christian conviction.

Yet it is not this exercise of power by individuals that is the most serious aspect of current society. Widespread though it is, where it can be isolated, challenged, and changed, there is the possibility of a creative use of economic power. It is corporate social sin, *by* great groups of persons *against* great groups of persons, that causes the most serious evil consequences and is hardest to reckon with. *Persons* are involved, as both sinners and victims, or it would not be sin. Unemployment, for example, is more than an inevitable, tragic fate; it is caused by circumstances for which human beings are morally responsible. When a worldwide depression occurs, as in the early 1930's, many millions of persons are made to suffer acutely, and economists can give some reasons for its occurrence. But this is not to say that guilt can be precisely allocated. In less widespread but deeply disrupting conflicts, as in a clash between a giant corporation and a giant labor union, the fault is seldom all on one side; and while some persons are more responsible than others, it is seldom possible with justice to pin the responsibility wholly upon particular individuals.

This illustrates what was said in Chapter VI—that there is *social evil* and there is *social sin*, and the two must be neither identified nor too

149

sharply separated. The Christian view of property is that to the degree that a person is even indirectly responsible for a misuse of it which is harmful to others, his conscience must remain sensitive and he must do all in his power to turn it to just and creative ends. Not everything is within his power, but *some things are*. It is in those areas where he can act, as these are prayerfully and reasonably discerned, that his Christian duty lies.

3. *The Christian view of work*

We have been tracing some basic issues with regard to property, or "capital"; we must now look at the other side of the dual structure of economic life, namely, "labor." No attempt was made in the previous section to discuss capitalism as such, though some things said have a direct bearing upon it, nor shall I in this section attempt to defend a rival system. The purpose at this point is simply to examine the place of work in the total life of the Christian.

a) *Why work?* To this question a variety of answers may be given, and these may be put in psychological or in normative Christian terms. A look from each angle may throw light on the issue as a whole.

Why does anyone work? The simplest answer is that one works because he has to. Economic pressures overcome the natural impulse to idleness. This fact is not universal, for there are those who through immaturity, illness, old age, indigence, inherited wealth, or for some other reason live by the product of the labor of others. Nevertheless, it remains normal for the mature adult who is able to do so to work for a living, either directly for pay and profit or, as in the case of the housewife, to co-operate in providing for the family.

Yet people work for other reasons. People economically secure still work because they enjoy it, or prefer activity to an empty leisure, or because they feel a responsibility for accomplishing something, or because they wish to please and serve someone who is loved. Work is any activity entered into for the sake of an end, and it is normal for the human spirit, in contrast with animal experience, to have ends in view for which the immediate pleasures of idleness will voluntarily be surrendered. It is a cynical, and a false, view of man which regards economic forces as the sole determiners of human conduct.

Other reasons are less laudable but powerful. Some people work because of the force of social approval, letting both the nature and the amount of their work be determined by prevailing social patterns. One works as little, or as much, as those around him do. Or one works under coercion, because of fear of the disfavor of "the boss," or from fear of penalties affixed or favors withheld in the case of failure to produce results.

Work habits are not easy to acquire, for children naturally prefer play to work, and this tendency if uncorrected carries over into adult life. But a work habit, once formed, is tenacious, and some people work simply because they always have and lack the will power to stop. This is particularly true of our high-pressured age, in which people work from a mixture of motives of which necessity, habit, and a feverish desire to keep busy are large components. Brunner calls this state "work-fanaticism" and says of it:

There is a vacuum in the soul, an inner unrest from which one escapes by work. Work-fanaticism is proportional to the poverty of the soul. As nervous people cannot keep still, man with his unrestful soul cannot but work. The modern Western world is somehow possessed with this work-fanaticism as a result of inward impoverishment.

. . . .

It is a strange paradox of the present day scene that we are suffering from a work-fanaticism and work-idolatry as well as from a lack of will-to-work. . . . Both these phenomena come from the same root, the loss of the sense of the eternal meaning of life.[4]

To this current state of work-fanaticism, religion has indirectly contributed. Max Weber in his famous essay *The Protestant Ethic and the Spirit of Capitalism* overstates the contribution of Calvinism to the rise of capitalism; yet it is true that in the religious sanction given to the Puritan virtues of hard work, frugality, and thrift, an emerging capitalism found strong support.[5] Now largely divorced from its earlier moorings, a feverishly competitive society is carried along by a combination of conscience and compulsion which will not let one rest while there is

[4] *Christianity and Civilisation*, Part II: Specific Problems (New York: Chas. Scribner's Sons, 1949), p. 70. Used by permission of the publisher.
[5] For a fuller exposition and critique of this thesis, see my *John Calvin: The Man and His Ethics* (New York: Henry Holt & Co., 1931), chs. viii-x.

still work to be done. Thus by a curious inversion the drive to incessant work which formerly came from a sense of divine vocation becomes a symptom of the loss of a sense of life's meaning.

If these are the reasons why people work, which of these motives are right and which wrong? Here the Christian ethic draws no clear-cut lines, but neither does it leave us without direction. Within the complex range of motives just outlined, not all are morally and spiritually on the same level. It is right to work to support one's self and one's family, providing for future needs as well as the present. It is right to work to express a creative impulse, contributing of one's best to "the good of the whole." Explicitly and centrally, it is right to serve God through serving other persons. To the degree that this is done, every vocation becomes a divine calling.

With equal certainty it may be said that it is wrong to work solely to gratify an acquisitive impulse, amassing more and more riches as the "chief and highest end of man." Though certain social standards must be met, it is wrong to work to secure or to maintain a superficial prestige. It is wrong to fall into a state of "work-fanaticism," finding no satisfactions through other channels and seeking escape from an inner vacuum through feverish activity.

Other motives are in a more ambiguous status. To work because one enjoys doing something or because another demands it may be right or wrong according to the nature of the enjoyment or of the demands. One has to judge the total situation in the light of the relative importance of enticing occupations or of external pressures. There is always a temptation to neglect one's main job for some trifling occupation that may soothe the conscience with a sense of busyness! Acquiescence to the demands of others is disciplinary and may be needed to curb our rebellious self-will; it may also stifle initiative and breed a rankling sense of grievance.

Is there an ideal work situation? Yes, if by "ideal" is meant not some flawless perfection but a situation that is all a human being ought to aspire to for his fullest satisfaction. A work situation is right when one works voluntarily from a service motive, under a sense of divine calling, and does the most creative job his talents permit; when one finds deep enjoyment in his work and has happy relations with his associates; when it does not overtax his physical strength or his nerves, and leaves some time for interesting and productive leisure; and when one receives for this work an income adequate to meet his needs without anxiety. So blessed is this situation, if one is blest with it, that another requirement must be added—one must know when to stop!

Such a work situation is possible. Yet few attain or possess it. Its absence is one of the major evils of our society.

b) *Work as vocation.* We noted above that one's daily work ought to be viewed as a divine calling, and done as far as possible in a spirit of service. This is the expression in economic life of the demand to love God and our neighbor. But to do this is no simple and easy requirement, nor have Christians always agreed as to its meaning. A brief historical review may throw light upon it.

In the Bible it is taken for granted that work is ordained of God. To be sure, in Gen. 3:17-18 work is presented as a curse for the sin of Adam, yet in Gen. 2:15 the command to till and to keep the garden precedes sin. The explicit word of Paul, "If any one will not work, let him not eat" (II Thess. 3:10), is implicit elsewhere in the Bible, though generally on a more communal basis as it is assumed that work is the duty of the "house," or family unit.[6] There is division of labor in the Bible and there is slavery, but little suggestion of a class stratification condemning manual labor as inferior.

This was very different in Greek society, which was thoroughly aristocratic. Both Plato and Aristotle regarded the "working class" as a distinctly inferior group who must do the manual labor in order that intellectuals might have leisure for philosophy. Helots and slaves must work in order that the free man might pursue his achievements of the spirit. This stratification, along with a characteristic Hellenic dualism of body and spirit, was to have serious consequences in medieval thought.

In the Middle Ages this depreciation of manual labor was blended with the class structure of feudal society and given a religious sanction. The religious vocation of priest or monk or nun was viewed as having a higher spiritual sanctity than ordinary labor, the contemplative being ranked above the active life. Within the active life manual labor, though recognized as necessary and ordained of God, had an inferior status. In part this was due to the influence of Aristotle, in part to emphasis on the "curse" of the Fall, and in part to the ever-present tendency to give

[6] Brunner, *Justice and the Social Order* (New York: Harper & Bros., 1945), p. 148.

religious support to an existing social system. As a result, social stratification was tightened by the belief that every man must remain in the station in life where God had placed him and there perform faithfully its duties.

Martin Luther broke radically with one element of this medieval view —namely, the ethical dualism of the religious and the secular. His emphasis on the sacredness of the common life was a highly important new note in Reformation Protestantism. Said he:

> It looks like a great thing when a monk renounces everything and goes into a cloister, carries on a life of asceticism, fasts, watches, prays, etc. . . . On the other hand it looks like a small thing when a maid cooks and cleans and does other housework. But because God's command is there, even such a small work must be praised as a service to God surpassing the holiness and asceticism of all monks and nuns.[7]

Luther's doctrine of *Beruf*, or calling, gave dignity to one's daily work, however humble, and could have had a great democratizing influence. Unfortunately, however, he never surrendered the medieval idea of "my station and its duties." It was the Christian's duty and high calling to serve God in his appointed place, not to change his station in life. For this reason Luther sided against the peasants in the Peasants' War, and gave added religious sanction to a social stratification which is still much in evidence in European society.

Calvin's view of calling did not differ materially from Luther's. Yet by his advocacy of the "middle-class virtues" of industry, frugality, honesty, and sobriety; his removal of the prohibition on the taking of interest (commonly referred to as usury); and his recognition of the right to change one's calling if one remained in humble obedience to God and his employer, he reinforced the growing ferment of free enterprise. Through a complex set of forces which cannot here be traced,[8] Calvinism by way of Puritanism gave an undergirding to both political democracy and economic individualism.

Current society is both involved in, and divorced from, this legacy from the past. In America, far more than in Europe, social stratification

[7] *Works* V. 100.
[8] See R. H. Tawney, *Religion and the Rise of Capitalism* (New York: Harcourt, Brace & Co., 1947); A Mervyn Davies, *Foundation of American Freedom* (New York and Nashville: Abingdon Press, 1955); and my *John Calvin* for expositions of these connections.

has broken down, and the dignity of manual labor is recognized. The characteristic American "success" story is of the person who from the humblest beginnings by his skill and persistence has won a high place for himself in income, power, or public esteem. This climb to fame and fortune has seldom more than an incidental religious connection, if any. The advantages of democratic opportunity and free enterprise, in connection with pluck, shrewdness, and persistence under difficulties, are made focal in the telling, though there is an occasional reference to being sustained by prayer and religious faith. Seldom is there a conscious sense of divine calling in one's work, and the Reformation concept of the sacredness of the common life has virtually disappeared under the pressures of a highly competitive society.

The World Council of Churches, the National Council, and some denominational agencies are attempting to restore a sense of Christian vocation with regard to daily work. A section was explicitly devoted to this study at the Second Assembly of the World Council in Evanston in 1954.[9] Vocational conferences of laymen to consider the implications of the Christian faith to their occupations are held with increasing frequency in Europe, and occasionally in America. It is well that this problem is coming into attention, for the frustration and loss of a sense of Christian calling in occupations other than those ostensibly religious is a serious aberration of our time. That Christian ethics demands honesty in business dealings is still recognized in principle, however much flouted in practice, but beyond this it may be doubted that laymen often think of their religion as having a connection with their daily occupations.[10] Yet it is in one's work and in one's family that most of one's life is spent, and it is here that both the most acute problems and the most creative opportunities of service to God and other persons are to be found.

What must be done to restore and vitalize this sense of divine calling? The principles are not difficult to state, though their application con-

[9] *The Evanston Report*, ed. W. A. Visser 't Hooft, pp. 160-73. See also the report of the North American Lay Conference on *The Christian and His Daily Work*, held at Buffalo, New York, February 21-24, 1952.

[10] A research study made by Murray H. Leiffer and reported in *The Christian Advocate* of March 1, 1956, p. 7, reveals that "not a single person who characterized himself as a laborer or domestic servant felt 'called' to his work." The percentage of those reporting affirmatively is highest among professional people, like teachers and doctors, and among housewives.

stantly confronts opposition in a secular society. There is need of a recognition not only of possessions but of the ability to work as the gift of God to be held in stewardship. Work should be chosen, where choices are open, with regard to the greatest possible service in it. If what is required affronts the Christian conscience of the worker, or if what is being produced in it is clearly not useful but harmful to society, one ought to look elsewhere for employment.

This is not to say that there is anything evil about working, as most persons must, to make a living for themselves and their families. To do this is a Christian duty, and a direct bearing on Christian service is not always easy to discover. There are dull, distasteful, routine jobs to be done, in which references to the "glory of the commonplace" are bound to seem a mockery. Yet to a greater degree than is commonly done, it is possible to look beyond the immediate task and find satisfactions in the work through its usefulness to society as a whole. One who is fortunate enough to have an ideal work situation ought to view with sympathy and understanding the plight of the many who do not; one who must earn his living under unpleasant conditions ought to try to see in his job something more than its irksome necessities.

So long as one's job is an honest, serviceable one in which one is doing the best he can, it is a divine calling, and one should endeavor like Brother Lawrence to "practice . . . the presence of God" within it. There are high opportunities in vocations of Christian leadership such as the ministry, the mission field, and Christian education, and many more young people should be entering them; there are also rich opportunities for Christian service and witness in an endless number of occupations to which God calls the layman.[11]

4. What is economic justice?

We come now to an issue with which many discussions of economic ethics begin—namely, the nature of a just economic order and the principles by which such justice is to be judged. We have left it to this point, not because it is unimportant, but because the two great con-

[11] For a fuller elaboration of these principles, see the chapter on "Christian Faith and the Day's Work" in my The Modern Rival of Christian Faith. Excellent brief treatments are to be found in God and the Day's Work by Robert L. Calhoun (New York: Association Press, 1943), and Christian Faith and My Job by Alexander Miller (New York: Association Press, 1946).

stituents of an economic society—property and work—must be seen in relation to God before any true perspective is possible upon their relationships.

Two cautions are in order as we move into this moot area. The first is the need to recognize that in the tangled complexity of modern society—in which not only the divergent interests of capital and labor but the pull of tradition, the uncertainties precipitated by a flood of new scientific discoveries, and the interlocking nature of the modern world are ever-present factors—perfect justice is not to be expected. This can be said without mention of sin, but when the forces of acquisitive self-interest, insistent determination to dominate others, and a deadly moral dullness are added to these other complicating factors, the result is a mixture of social evil and social sin in which no Utopia, either now or later, is attainable. A realistic economic justice is to be found in the best possible adjustment of life to life within the actual situation, not some imaginary perfection.

The second necessary caution is the need to recognize that no situation is hopeless. No situation—however impregnated with meanness and "man's inhumanity to man"—is so bad that Christian effort to correct it is irrelevant. As the increase of love among persons is always a Christian obligation, so is the increase of justice. Furthermore, in individual circumstances, though not in society as a whole, there are situations so free from injustice that one may well "thank God and take courage." There are persons who have money enough but not too much for their personal well-being, who have earned it honestly in work serviceable to God and humanity, and who not only acquire but use it with a Christian conscience in sensitiveness to human need. This recognition ought never to induce complacency, but it needs to be made in answer to a pessimistic view of the total injustice of human society.

The most authoritative compendiums of the principles of Christian ethics in relation to the problems of economic justice are to be found in the reports of Section III of the Oxford, Amsterdam, and Evanston Conferences of the World Council of Churches, and in a statement on *Christian Principles and Assumptions for Economic Life* adopted by the General Board of the National Council of the Churches of Christ in the U.S.A. on September 15, 1954. These statements represent a surprising degree of unanimity of Christian thought in an area where precise unanimity is impossible, and where an authoritarian word even if obtainable would to the Protestant mind be undesirable. What follows is consistent with these statements, though necessarily in briefer form than even these relatively brief affirmations.

a) *Misconceptions.* Certain misconceptions must be guarded against. Though no man living is wise enough to give a complete blueprint of the "next steps" to economic justice in every concrete situation, certain widely held errors stand in the way of these steps, and their discernment is essential to moving in the right direction.

In the first place, no economic system ought to be identified with the kingdom of God. In the past feudalism and slavery have been thus identified with the will and favor of God, and it was assumed that any change in the economic *status quo* was an affront to biblical teaching and to Christian morality. Not a little blood was shed to preserve these institutions with appeals to divine sanction in the process, but they had to yield to changing circumstances and a more enlightened conscience. Most American Christians now recognize the error in these particular forms of "absolutizing the relative," but new forms of idolatry have replaced them.

The most common of these identifications is the assumption that "the American way of life," meaning American capitalism and the free enterprise system, is ordained of God and any challenge to it a form of both political and religious subversion. Whether or not explicitly stated, this is the implicit assumption of many who inveigh against the "welfare state" and view with suspicion any criticism of economic individualism. On the other hand, there are those who espouse state socialism and a large measure of government ownership and control as *the* Christian answer. This view has had wide acceptance among religious liberals who saw in socialism an expression of the prophetic demand for social justice, but in recent years the evils in this system also have become apparent. Socialism ought not to be confused with Communism, which is clearly unchristian in its foundations and methods; yet two decades ago some Christians thought they discerned in Communism the way to economic justice.

In response to such identifications the Christian needs to be clear on two points: (1) that no system devised by man is completely Christian, or can be as long as human error and sin persist, and (2) that some systems are better fitted than others to be carriers of economic justice. Communism with its suppression of human freedom and ruthless violation of personal integrity cannot bring justice, though it can challenge injustice and possibly ameliorate some forms of it.[12] The answer, as far as we can see it, lies in a blend of free enterprise and state control in accordance with certain positive Christian principles.

A second misconception is that benevolent intentions justify paternalistic domination by those who have superior status or power. To be sure, there can be no justice without love, for in its absence self-interest prompts to unscrupulous domination. Yet its presence in the form of attitudes of kindness is no guarantee of justice, and is too often a cloak for injustice. "Benevolent intentions have been used with sincerity at one time or another to justify slavery, to give religious sanction to white supremacy and the continuance of imperialism, to prevent the poor from having education or the suffrage, or to discourage land reform or the organization of labor." [13] Such attitudes perpetuate injustice more often unconsciously than consciously, but are a particularly insidious form of the moral dullness to which reference was made earlier. They injure personality both in the holders of such power and its victims, for as the passage above quoted goes on to say, "It is quite as true of irresponsible economic power as of irresponsible political power, that such power tends to corrupt those who exercise it."

A third misconception, implicit in the two preceding, is that personal evangelism will automatically take care of the economic evils of society by generating Christian character. It is to the credit of the social gospel movement in American liberal Christianity that the need of changing social structures has been persistently stressed, and however far it may be necessary to go beyond it to a deeper emphasis on human sin, this must never be lost sight of. Not even John Wesley, most socially-minded of all the great religious leaders of an earlier day, fully grasped this necessity.

One looks in vain in Luther, Calvin, Baxter, Wesley, Edwards, and all the major figures of three centuries of Protestant writing, for any more than incidental treatment of the problems of the economic, political and legal

---

[12] Further discussion of both capitalism and Communism is found in my *The Modern Rival of Christian Faith*, ch. 10.
[13] *Christian Principles and Assumptions for Economic Life*, p. 3.

structures of life. The realisation of the fluidity of social structures and the capacity of man to alter his political and economic environment is a nineteenth century insight, which became the inheritance of liberalism and neo-Protestantism as well.[14]

b) *Positive principles.* Let us now note some general principles of which the serious and determined application by Christians could, without creating a Utopia, remake society. Obviously, Christians are not the only persons who affect economic structures. Yet without waiting for all of society to become Christian—a "far-off divine event" certainly not to be anticipated in the near future—even a devoted minority of Christians could make a vast difference in the economic scene.

First, *the welfare of persons should be paramount over all other interests.* This applies to all the conditions regarding property and work which were examined in the early part of this chapter. It means that Christians should attempt by education, persuasion, and where necessary by legal action to secure a minimum standard of income for all, commensurate with the cost of living. Conditions of employment should be such that work can be done in physical and mental health and without undue anxiety for sickness, old age, or other forms of enforced unemployment. Young people should have equal opportunities to develop their capacities and to find the employment best suited to them. Enough economic security should be provided to permit marriage and the rearing of children in adequate housing and educational facilities, without undue luxury and without slums.

The ramifications of this primary principle are endless, but some because of frequent violation need special mention. There must be no racial discrimination in employment or housing, or in opportunities for education and for medical care. This alone, if taken seriously, would bring about a vast reconstruction in American life! And while racial prejudice creates the most obvious form of discrimination, a Christian conscience must be on guard also against economic injustices caused or perpetuated by family status, social stratification, political "pull," or

[14] Waldo Beach and John C. Bennett in "Christian Ethics" in the symposium *Protestant Thought in the Twentieth Century,* ed. Arnold S. Nash (New York: The Macmillan Co., 1951), p. 138.

even by church connections. Much as we stress democracy, democracy is affronted on every hand by factors such as these.

Second, *due consideration must be given to the realities of economic life*. It is customary to stress "hard facts" as canceling out the considerations put forward by a Christian conscience. "One must live," and to live one must compete, and to compete one must do what others do. There are both rationalization and reason in this plea, and where to draw the line is an exceedingly difficult but basic need. To repeat what has been said earlier upon compromise, sin appears at the point of disparity between the actual and the best possible. To discern the highest possibility of Christian justice in a very complex world, not only a Christian conscience but technical knowledge is required. This the gospel cannot supply, though it may well provide the dynamic for acquiring and using it in a Christian frame of reference. Laymen who live close to economic realities, if they are informed and spiritually sensitive Christians, are often better equipped than ministers to judge the concrete next steps to be taken toward economic justice.

Third, *a proper balance must be maintained between individual freedom and social control*. Just what is "proper" has, of course, no easy answer. Much of the task of "Christianizing the social order"—to cite the title of an important book by Walter Rauschenbusch—lies at the point of determining this balance and putting it into effect. Some principles, however, may serve as norms of judgment. Every adult individual should have freedom to choose an occupation, exercise some creativity and initiative within it, earn an income sufficient for his personal and family needs, and determine within limits how he shall spend his money. Totalitarian control by the state is neither democratic nor Christian. On the other hand, unrestrained individualism leads neither to democracy nor to Christian social justice, but to the enhancement of acquisitiveness, an irresponsible use of power, exploitation of the weak, and to disregard of basic social obligations. It is right that by taxation and by legal restraints the grosser aspects of individualism should be curbed, and provision made for security against the hazards of illness, unemployment, and old age. A "welfare state" or a "planned economy" can be a great step toward justice, provided an informed and conscientious citizenry insists that the welfare of all be taken into account.

Fourth, *economic justice must be viewed in a world setting.* There is a persistent provincialism which makes men tend to see political and economic issues from the standpoint of their own class or culture or nation. Few Christians fully divest themselves of it. Yet it is rooted in the Christian gospel that *all men* are of supreme and equal worth in the sight of God. Inequality of personal endowment or of social contribution or of economic need does not cancel out this basic equality. To the degree that we are fully Christian, we shall do our utmost to see that all men, all women and children of all races and in all lands are provided with the material foundations of healthful, wholesome living and the good life. How basic this is, we must observe in later chapters.

This chapter is, and is not, finished, for economic conditions ramify throughout the whole of the world's social fabric. These principles of economic justice must be applied in the personal relations of the community and the market place, in corporations and labor unions, in national affairs and in the world scene. If they are disregarded anywhere, evil consequences occur there and elsewhere, so interdependent is our world. And if they are persistently disregarded, there may before long be no world to talk about.

IX. Christianity and the Race Problem

WE COME NOW to one of the most baffling and difficult of all contemporary problems. In the world scene, questions of race and color mingle with those of national status and of economic abundance and poverty to create great restlessness and tension. In our own land, the violent reactions evoked by the Supreme Court's decision of May 17, 1954, that segregation in the public schools is unconstitutional have revealed how deep are the differences that divide us. Though integration in the schools is accepted more readily in northern states, there is scarcely a community anywhere, North or South, that does not show the marks of racial cleavage in segregated housing, employment, and social attitudes.

Even in churches this virus is widely prevalent. It was not a theological, but a racial, issue that split the Methodist Church in 1844 and kept it in sectional units for almost a hundred years, with the breach only partially healed by the formula of union in 1939. The northern and southern Presbyterians and Baptists are still separated with race in the background, though with important theological differences in addition to the racial attitudes that have prevailed in Methodism. Yet it is the existence not of separate denominations, but of segregation within virtually every denomination, that is the most telling evidence of the depth of the problem. This separateness, whether or not required by organizational structures, is everywhere present. One has but to enter almost any church and look around to discover it.

Paradoxically, it is this issue among all our major social problems on which there is the greatest agreement *in principle*. Representative church bodies have again and again called for a "nonsegregated church in a nonsegregated society." The Federal Council of Churches in 1946 declared:

163

The Federal Council of Churches of Christ in America renounces the pattern of segregation in race relations as unnecessary and undesirable and a violation of the gospel of love and brotherhood. Having taken this action the Federal Council requests its constituent communions to do likewise.[1]

Similar resolutions, including endorsement of the Supreme Court decision, have been passed by the churches again and again. One of the most significant of these is the affirmation of the Southern Baptist Convention in 1956 in view of the fact that this is the largest southern denomination and its members are widely involved in current tensions:

We recognize the fact that this Supreme Court decision is in harmony with the constitutional guarantee of equal freedom to all citizens and with the Christian principles of equal justice and love for all men. . . . [We urge our] people and all Christians to conduct themselves in this period of adjustment in the spirit of Christ.[2]

Comparable declarations have been made by other churches even in those areas where racial tensions are most acute. "Denominational conference statements of the mainline Protestant churches in the South have almost uniformly affirmed the incompatibility of segregation with Christian principles and the need for revision of local practice." [3]

To cite one more statement from an inclusive perspective, the World Council of Churches at Evanston in 1954 issued an extraordinarily forward-looking statement on race relations which contains these words:

When we are given Christian insight the whole pattern of racial discrimination is seen as an unutterable offence against God, to be endured no longer, so that the very stones cry out. In such moments we understand more fully the meaning of the gospel, and the duty of both Church and Christian.

The skeptic is prone to say that the churches make these "ringing resolutions," yet hypocritically disregard them. That there is wide disregard is evident, but it cannot be charged simply to hypocrisy. The

---

[1] Quoted by John C. Bennett in *Christian Ethics and Social Policy* (New York: Chas. Scribner's Sons, 1946), p. 10 n.

[2] *The Christian Century*, June 23, 1954, p. 759.

[3] Waldo Beach in "Storm Warnings from the South," *Christianity and Crisis*, March 19, 1956, p. 30.

issues are complex, and we must attempt to sort out some of the inter-woven strands that constitute the ugly net of race prejudice.

1. Biblical foundations

As has been done in other chapters, let us take a look at the biblical foundations of the Christian view. This can be brief, for the directives are unequivocal.

In the first chapter of Genesis it is written,

Then God said, "Let us make man in our image, after our likeness; and let them have dominion over the fish of the sea, and over the birds of the air, and over the cattle, and over all the earth, and over every creeping thing that creeps upon the earth." So God created man in his own image, in the image of God he created him; male and female he created them. (1:26-27.)

There is no suggestion here of a white God, or even of a Semitic God. Nor is there any intimation that some who are thus to "have dominion" are to constitute a dominant race while others do the menial tasks of mankind. Even though Negroes be assumed to be the descendants of Ham, the Jews of Shem, and the Aryans of Japheth—a view which anthropologists discredit—all are equally the sons of Adam and made in the divine image. There is not a little *religious* exclusiveness in the history of the Hebrews as it is recorded in the Old Testament, and this gave rise to a Jewish particularism which the greater prophets had to condemn as they stressed the love of God for all men.[4] Yet the doctrine of creation that is the common heritage of Jewish and Christian faith asserts unequivocally the unity of mankind and leaves no standing ground for *racial* exclusiveness.

In the New Testament this becomes unmistakable. The equality of all persons before God was basic to the outlook of Jesus. The parable of the good Samaritan is the most dramatic challenge to racial exclusiveness, but it appears again and again in Jesus' own service to human need regardless of racial or national backgrounds and in his portrayal of the conditions of entrance into the Kingdom. In the last judgment scene, it is not one's Jewish ancestry but care for the hungry and thirsty, for the naked, sick, and imprisoned, that will determine one's place (Matt.

[4] As in Amos 9:7 and the "servant songs" of Isaiah. Cf. Isa. 49:6; 51:4; 52:10; 56:3, 6-8.

25:31-46). In the great consummation, "men will come from east and west, and from north and south, and sit at table in the kingdom of God" (Luke 13:29). Jesus did not hesitate to condemn the shallow self-confidence of those who trusted in their Jewish prerogatives, or to commend the faith of a Roman centurion as being superior to theirs (Matt. 23; 8:10-13). Had Jesus been willing to be neutral toward Jewish exclusiveness for fear of causing trouble, he might have escaped crucifixion but he would not have been our Lord.

In the early Church, the contest between Jewish exclusiveness and Christian universalism was at first sharp, but the latter won out to become the settled policy. The decision recorded in Acts 15:19-21 thereby becomes a watershed in the history of the Church. Peter's vision (Acts 10) and its bearing on the acceptance of the Roman centurion Cornelius into Christian fellowship bears directly on the issue of segregated churches today, and the truth could hardly be more forcefully put than in Peter's words that clinch the matter, "Truly I perceive that God shows no partiality" (v. 34). Paul repeatedly declared that "all men, both Jews and Greeks, are under the power of sin" (Rom. 3:9), but that Christ died for the redemption of all, and has reconciled us to God and to one another. "There is neither Jew nor Greek, there is neither slave nor free, there is neither male nor female; for you are all one in Christ Jesus." (Gal. 3:28.) No greater charter of race equality need be cited than that found in Ephesians, "For he is our peace, who has made us both one, and has broken down the dividing wall of hostility" (2:14).

But why multiply citations? The record is so clear that almost any Christian will admit that in principle race prejudice is wrong. But what of our practice?

2. The causes of race prejudice

Race prejudice is a pervasive human phenomenon. Yet clearly it is not inborn. Colored and white children will play together when permitted to do so with full friendliness. On the street where I live there is also a Negro physician and his fine family, and it is an attractive sight to see these children playing with the white children of the neighborhood. Little Gentiles get along very well with the little Jews, or at least, as well as with other little Gentiles. It is when frightened parents erect prohibitions that the seeds of prejudice are planted. These in most cases are planted early and grow luxuriously.

By the time of adolescence, unless positive steps are taken to counteract it, segregation has emerged as a dominant pattern. So powerful are the drives toward conformity in high school and college years that it is not uncommon to find an intense and irrational cruelty toward those of other races. On the other hand, young people are more apt than their elders to break through the patterns of racial discrimination if there are democratic and Christian influences upon their thinking and friendly group contacts are possible with those of another race. Where segregation is removed in practice, its justification in principle rapidly subsides.

Confront an adult with the fact of his race prejudice, and he will do one of three things. He will deny it, he will admit it but admit also that it is irrational, or he will begin to rationalize his attitudes. The rationalizations will usually take the form of words about being different from "our kind of people"; about inferior and superior races; about dirt and smells, or dishonesty and treachery and the "yellow peril"; about the danger of intermarriage; about how those of other races are "creeping up on us" and "don't know their place." When sifted out these rationalizations indicate that psychological, cultural, social, nationalistic, and economic factors have been superimposed upon and confused with biological facts. As a result, we have a "color caste" of which the roots are not primarily to be found in biological differences, but with its evil effects irrationally transferred to great groups loosely designated as racial.

Race is a most ambiguous term, in which many national, geographical, cultural, and linguistic elements are mixed. Though race is sometimes correctly designated by basic biological types as Caucasian, Mongolian, or Negroid, in practice it is more often indicated by color, as black, white, red, yellow, or brown; or by nationality, as Japanese, Chinese, Filipino, Mexican; or by geographical origin, as Oriental, Asiatic, European, African; or by a combination of ethnic, national, and geographical factors, as Nordic, Teutonic, Slavic, Latin American, French Canadian. A particular problem is posed by an attempt to classify the Jews, for while they are a Semitic people who have had relatively little racial intermixture through the centuries, it is an ever-present problem as to whether the terms "Jew" and "Jewish" refer mainly to a race or to a religion.

Such adjectives give evidence that the race problem is never wholly a matter of biological distinction and stratification. Racial intermixtures have produced some very white-skinned Negroes with blue eyes and fair hair, yet the product of such a union remains a Negro.[5] Race as the term is commonly used designates very nearly what the Germans call *Volk*—a group sharing a common cultural tradition, whether of achievement or servitude, with some measure of national, geographical, and biological affinity. Our language being what it is, we must use the term "race" in spite of its looseness.

Racial prejudice is, first of all, a *psychological* factor, rooting in collective egotism and pride and the pervasive human tendency to dislike the different. Though an ancient evil, it began to receive intellectual defense more recently than most evils, for it was only a century ago that Count Gobineau published in French his four-volume *Essay on the Inequality of the Human Races*, in which he contended that color of skin determines mental and spiritual differences, and that mixture of blood produces degeneracy and the fall of civilizations. There was little, if any, racial discrimination in the early or medieval Church, the conditions of membership and fellowship being determined by faith in Jesus Christ and fidelity to the ordinances of his church. "Race and color did not count in the early existence of the Protestant church. It was when modern Western imperialism began to explore and exploit the colored peoples of Africa, Asia and America that the beginning of segregation and discrimination based on color and race was initiated."[6] Nevertheless, the *roots* of race prejudice are as old as the human race in the tendency to like those who are like oneself and to dislike those who for any reason, biological or cultural, are different.

Sometimes this psychological dislike of the different is intensified by proximity, again by separation. For example, it is not uncommon for American Christians to be quite concerned to send missionaries to the Negroes of Africa, and to admire greatly Albert Schweitzer's service to them, and yet to stand rigidly for segregation in one's own community or church. It is easy for persons in New England to be more "broad-

[5] For very telling evidence of this fact, read *A Man Called White* (New York: Viking Press, 1948), the life story of a very light-skinned Negro, Walter White, who was long the general secretary of the National Association for the Advancement of Colored People and one of the outstanding leaders of his race.

[6] From an address by Dr. Benjamin Mays at the Second Assembly of the World Council of Churches in Evanston, Ill., August 21, 1954.

minded" on the matter of racial integration than they would be if they lived in Mississippi. Nevertheless, proximity need not breed tension; it can create fellowship. As we shall observe in noting what the Church can do about racial tension, one of the first steps in overcoming it is to bring people together, both physically and spiritually, so that what seems to be difference can be discovered to be kinship. This calls for a mingling of the races wherever this can be done without fresh outbreaks of animosity, and a sharing of the best in every cultural tradition.

Another form of rationalization, we noted, was the claim of "superior" and "inferior" races. Count Gobineau's contentions were widely believed until quite recently, and are still bandied about by those who never heard his name. Yet for the past two decades they have been scientifically exploded, and no reputable psychologist or anthropologist now accepts them. In 1938 the American Psychological Association went on record as declaring that there are no innate mental differences among races. In the same year the American Anthropological Association asserted that there is no scientific basis for the biological inheritance of cultural traits, or of any traits implying racial inferiority.[7] These judgments have been corroborated by medical science in reference to the Negro blood bank by declaring that there is no difference in the blood of colored and white persons, thus reinforcing the biblical word that God "hath made of one blood all nations of men" (K.J.V.) to dwell together.

There are, of course, primitive and advanced groups even as there are stupid and highly capable individuals within every group. These discernible differences have lent support to the myth of natural inequality. Informed opinion, however, agrees with Gunnar Myrdal in An American Dilemma that there is a vicious circle at this point.[8] Denied the cultural, educational, and economic advantages held by others, underprivileged groups tend to remain in this status, as in America the restriction of Negroes to unskilled labor and meager educational facilities has prevented their advancement to positions of leadership comparable with the more privileged. Increasingly in the world scene, as in America, it becomes evident that there arc persons of extraordinary ability in every racial group, and the flowering of such talent awaits only the opportunity.

[7] H. A. Wallace, et al., Christian Bases of World Order (New York and Nashville: Abingdon-Cokesbury Press, 1943), pp. 104, 107.
[8] Ch. 3, sec. 7.

Cultural aversion to those of other races, whether in the form of depreciating their ability or in more offensive matters of name calling and the attaching of uncomplimentary labels, eventuates from the common tendency to commit the fallacy of hasty generalization. Some Negroes have grown up in circumstances where they have not learned to bathe; hence it is assumed that all are dirty. Under economic pressure for many centuries, some Jews have developed a tendency to drive a sharp bargain; hence it is assumed that this is a universal racial trait. Japan attacked Pearl Harbor, and China is held by the Communists; hence nobody from the Orient is to be trusted! The internment and relocation of 110,000 Japanese on the Pacific Coast during the Second World War, not for any acts of disloyalty but simply through a suspicion based on racial identification, was less virulent in its effect than the Nazi destruction of the Jews but equally irrational. The outbreak of violence, intimidation, and the formation of "white citizens' councils" that has come with the effort to desegregate the schools is a carry-over both from the Negro's former status as a slave and from the assumption by white persons of the Negro's general inferiority.

Such hasty generalization cannot be dealt with simply by demonstrating its irrationality. That it is irrational to judge whole peoples by mass standards of approval or disapproval rather than by individual status is certainly true, and needs to be constantly kept in mind. But since this type of judgment is basically a matter of feeling rather than reason, only a change of feeling can correct it. This is why the Christian faith, when it is made vital in terms of the equal worth of all persons to God, is a more effective solvent of ill feeling than argument, even as a sense of sin about race prejudice is a necessary prelude to repentance and change.

This cultural aversion appears in its most potent form in the *fear of intermarriage*. This is cited again and again as the all-sufficient reason why there must be no social intermingling of the different racial groups, and in particular why the young people must be kept apart not only in schools but in churches. About this two judgments must be passed. The first is that miscegenation ought not to be encouraged. Not because any biological inferiority results from a mixing of racial stocks, but because in the present state of society tensions are more often increased than abated by it, intermarriage is on the whole a step away from the solution of the race problem rather than toward it.

The second judgment is that there is no law of God against such intermarriage, and there ought to be none of the State. The World Council of Churches took a bold and true step when it declared:

While it can find in the Bible no clear justification or condemnation of intermarriage, but only a discussion of the duties of the faithful in marriage with partners of other religions, it cannot approve any law against racial or ethnic intermarriage, for Christian marriage involves primarily a union of two individuals before God which goes beyond the jurisdiction of the state or of culture.

Some intermarriages have produced happy and effective Christian homes; others have not. Here as elsewhere, hasty generalization must be avoided. What can be said with certainty is that the fear of intermarriage, erected as a barrier to social fellowship, does harm and thwarts constructive effort far in excess of the actual justification of such a fear.

Ramifying through all these factors are *economic rivalry* and a fear of the loss of prestige or power through the influx or advancement of those of other racial stocks. This is evidenced by the fact that in industry, schools, and many other aspects of community life, a racial minority will be tolerated as long as it is a *very minor* minority. Let the numbers increase, or the positions other than those of unskilled manual labor be taken by those of another race, and there is an outbreak of objection which is easily stirred into violence.

Paradoxically, labor unions have gone further than any other group in America, not excepting the churches, to witness against racial injustice and try to secure equality of treatment. This is probably due chiefly to a certain sense of solidarity in injustice in protest against the dominant white, bourgeois, employing classes. Yet in both labor unions and churches, the official group pronouncements are on a higher level of insight than the actual practices of great numbers of their membership. While the unions exercise a coercive power that the churches cannot, psychological reaction to economic rivalry follows a consistent pattern. Wherever status is touched or income is jeopardized, the liberality of attitudes tends to shrink and rationalizations of discrimination to emerge.

Racial and cultural are mixed with *national* factors to make the term "foreigner" one of opprobrium. This is evident in the tendency to speak of the Italians, Mexicans, French Canadians, or Irish as a separate racial stock, the degree of acceptance even in the "melting pot" of democratic

171

America being by no means certain. In the Old Testament the Jews drew tight lines between themselves as the chosen people of God and their neighbors, in the New Testament the "Jews have no dealings with Samaritans," and in every culture from the beginning of recorded history to the present there are evidences of antipathy between the "in-group" and the "out-group." Robert P. Tristram Coffin in a whimsical but nevertheless serious poem has represented the men of Ur and Akkad as telling why they do not like each other:

The Man of Akkad:

> The men of Ur have heads too round.
> They have to build themselves a mound
> > To reach their god. Their toes turn in,
> > They have no hair upon their chin.
> They are not men. Their women wear
> The finer wool and build their hair
> > High as towers in their pride,
> > The men go meekly dressed in hide.
> They eat the fat part of their goats,
> Their speech is low down in their throats.
> > To them the only proper word
> > Is the thin edge of a sword.

The Man of Ur:

> The men of Akkad have no faces.
> Their curled beards are the nesting places
> > Of the vermin and the flea.
> > They turn their toes out wantonly.
> Their heads are squeezed too long for brains,
> They have to ask their gods for rains.
> > They beat their wives, they wear soft clothes,
> > Their speech is high and through the nose,
> Their noses are as great as plows,
> They eat the udders of their cows.
> > The language that will suit them best
> > Is the arrow through the breast.

> Ur and Akkad are dead sands,
> But they have sons in living lands.[9]

[9] Used by permission of the author's estate.

Thus far we have been noting the merging of race prejudice with cultural, economic, and political antipathies in the domestic scene. Yet no informed person needs to be told that racism is a world-wide phenomenon and that in our interdependent world, racial antipathies anywhere endanger the security and welfare of persons everywhere.

Let us look, therefore, somewhat more briefly at the effects of race prejudice.

3. Effects of race prejudice

Racism imperils the peace of the world. Not race, which in the order of nature has been established by God that there may be variety among his children, but racism. Racism is the perversion of this variety, the injection of attitudes of domination, superiority, and enmity where there ought to be fellowship within this diversity. Since this is a moral universe, racism cannot continue without injury and peril to all—to those who dominate as well as to those who suffer from the domination of others.

In the past the major wars have been fought between those of Caucasian stock. The colored peoples of the earth, though outnumbering the white peoples two to one, have lacked not only the incentive of hope of victory, but the economic resources and the technical skills by which massive conflicts could be waged. In the past two decades this situation has changed radically. Many millions of persons formerly in colonial status have come to a new nationhood since the Second World War—India, Pakistan, Burma, Ceylon, the Philippines, Indonesia, South Korea, and South Viet-Nam, with at least nominal freedom also in North Korea and Viet Minh. Others feel the ferment of the possibility of both political freedom and release from hunger, and will no longer accept domination complacently. In two of the most troubled areas of the earth, South Africa and the Middle East, racial conflict and tension are at an all-time high, with no hope of any immediate abatement.

There is no evidence that any of the peoples just mentioned desire, or will press for, world conquest. There is, however, another power in Eastern Europe that apparently does desire world domination and with great skill manipulates the longings of these people for racial equality, economic subsistence, and political freedom. If they do not receive support from the West in these legitimate aspirations, they will look to the East to get it. The result could be a third world war and global destruction.

It cannot be said that there is complete racial equality within Communism, for Jews have been discriminated against in Soviet Russia as elsewhere. Yet there is little doubt that race equality is practiced further under Communism than is general in the democracies of the West, and it is certain that our racial inequalities, though exaggerated, are a chief weapon in the psychological war against us.

I make no claim to being a prophet. Yet in 1944, when Russia was still generally viewed as a faithful ally, I wrote these words:

Let us rejoice heartily that there is race equality anywhere, whether under a Christian or Communist ideology. But let us beware. When the time comes to make the peace, the suppressed longings of the colored and racially under-privileged peoples of the world, if they do not see freedom in prospect elsewhere, will turn to Russia to get it. The color question cannot fail to be a powerful leverage to enhance the authority of Russia after the war. One may doubt whether Russia is altruistic enough to use this authority to increase the welfare of the world; one cannot doubt that the union of capitalism with race discrimination puts a weapon of incalculable power in the hands of Mr. Stalin.[10]

Since that time Stalin has passed from the scene and his authority as well, but what he set in motion has not passed away. Since that time also, the emergence of the atomic and hydrogen bombs has vastly increased the peril to the total world that racial conflict might fan to hideously destructive power.

But what of the effects of race discrimination in the immediate, domestic setting?

The effects upon its recipients are so manifold in the form of hurts, frustrations, denials of opportunity, and the continuance of a rankling sense of injustice that I shall make no attempt to catalogue them.

In our own country millions of people especially American Negroes are subjected to discrimination and unequal treatment in educational opportunities, in employment, wages and conditions of work, in access to professional

[10] *Ibid.*, pp. 196-97.

and business opportunities, in housing, in transportation, in the administration of justice and even in the right to vote.[11]

In recent years some advance steps have been made, as in the opening of Pullman cars and diners to Negroes, elimination of segregation in the armed forces, and the admission of Negroes to some southern state universities. Yet the attempts made to nullify the Supreme Court decision even at the cost of eliminating the public schools and passing acts of open defiance in state legislatures, to say nothing of rioting and violence and the nonviolent but intimidating acts of white citizens' councils, indicate how long a road there is yet to travel. Not since the Civil War has the internal harmony of the United States been so seriously disturbed.

Not only does race discrimination hurt those who are its recipients, but those who practice it become also its victims. As Benjamin Mays, himself an eminent Negro college president, stated eloquently before the World Council of Churches in Evanston,

Usually the question is: What does discrimination or segregation do to the person segregated, to the disadvantaged person? . . . But we seldom realize what discrimination does to the person who practices it. It scars not only the soul of the segregated but the soul of the segregator as well. When we build fences to keep others out, erect barriers to keep others down, deny to them freedom which we ourselves enjoy and cherish most, we keep ourselves in, hold ourselves down, and the barriers we erect against others become prison bars to our own souls.

A major effect in the domestic scene is what racism does to public respect for the principles of democracy and of Christianity. In both connections there are endless reverberations, which can be touched upon only in barest mention. When one becomes accustomed to perversions of justice with reference to those of another race, these are likely before long not to seem perversions, and the democratic conscience that should be demanding "liberty and justice for all" is dulled into acquiescence. Those on the receiving end of the injustice can scarcely avoid the feeling that democracy is being flouted, and the temptation to flout it in return is

[11] From the report of the Delaware Conference of the Federal Council of Churches, March, 1942. This statement, though old, puts the issues as succinctly as they can be put.

175

strong. Both of these reactions together are responsible for not a little of the domestic unrest and incidence of crime in our society.

In the Church also there is a sheaf of bad effects. The most obvious one, by the continuance of segregation, is to negate the principle of the equality of all men before God, which even the most casual secularist recognizes to be Christian, and thus to bring the Church into disfavor. More subtle effects, however, are found in the thwarting of the growth of Christian personality by denials of opportunity and fellowship that should be open to all, and in the deepening of the sin of moral dullness through all the forms of rationalization that have been outlined.

Only God can judge fully the range and depth of these evil effects. In an issue so complex and so serious, claims of human omniscience are very inappropriate. There is need to be tolerant and understanding, to "judge not, that you be not judged." Yet there is need also to be clear-sighted and to be firm. To be neutral or acquiescent in conditions so clearly at variance with the Christian gospel is to deny our faith.

4. Proposals for Christian action[12]

The Church cannot let these conditions continue without action. The security of the world calls for the mitigation of racial tensions through justice. Yet deeper than the demand for security is the obligation of the Christian gospel to increase love in human relations.

In the first place, the Church must understand and proclaim its gospel. Vague generalities about the fatherhood of God and the brotherhood of man have often been spoken which do not cut down through our crust of convention to where the race problem is. We need to recover the insights of Jesus on this question. And one of the most amazing things about Jesus is how he met the racism of his day. Reared in a Jewish tradition that prided itself on being the chosen people of God, living in occupied territory where Roman superiority and Jewish superiority were always in uneasy tension, he lived on a plane that made a Roman centurion say of him, "Truly this was a son of God!" (Matt. 27:54). Jew, Roman, Samaritan, Syrophoenician, were to him equally

[12] The remainder of this chapter is reprinted with some changes and additions from my article on "The Racial Issue and the Christian Church" in The Church and the New World Mind. Used by permission of the Bethany Press.

the children of God. In the presence of human need, his healing knew no bounds.

If we examine the democracy of Jesus—a democracy which he never talked about but always practiced—we discover in it both the fountainhead of our democracy and certain radical challenges. We talk much about the dignity of man. This he did not deny; in fact, he assumed it, but always in the framework of man's dependence upon God and the obligation to obey God and love one another. His emphasis was not on the claim of personal rights, as so much of ours is, but on the doing of duties. This may well lead to the claiming of rights *for others*, but such a demand must first be expressed in the acts and attitudes of daily life. These four—divine dependence, mutual obligation stemming from love, sound judgment of human nature, and the practice of brotherhood in daily experience—are the basis of any true democracy. Not until the Church both preaches and practices such Christian democracy will it touch the fringe of the race question.

Second, the Church must put its own house in order. This means the welcome presence of colored Christians in the membership, the worship services, church schools, discussion groups, and social gatherings of the Church. It means the presence of colored persons in the conferences and policy-making bodies of the Church. It means the refusal to permit segregation in the living arrangements connected with church meetings. It means the sharing of the recreational, educational, and hospital facilities of the Church with all who need them. It means the interchange of pulpits between colored and white ministers, and much further advance in what has already been here and there undertaken, an interracial ministry. As qualified persons can be found or trained, there must be interracial teaching, medical, and administrative staffs in the institutions of the Church. In such arrangements there must be equal and nonsegregated living and working conditions, equal pay, equal opportunities of promotion, regardless of color. Differentiation on grounds of contribution and fitness does not justify differentiation on grounds of race. If such a program arouses opposition, as it is likely to, this calls for the tactful but courageous insistence that the house of God is a place of prayer and service for all peoples and the Church of God cannot sanction discrimination at any point.

I am aware that the relatively mild proposals of the preceding sentences, if acted upon, would be revolutionary. Already I hear someone say, "You couldn't do that in my church!" Have you tried? The ideal of race equality will not arrive all at once. But it will not arrive at all until we stop conforming to prevailing attitudes and practices and give the Church an opportunity to lead in the shaping of community standards. Even conflict, if dealt with in love, can prove a creative experience.

In bringing about such changes, there is particular need to avoid incrimination and self-righteousness and to act upon the basis of true facts and principles, not upon emotional impulse. Race prejudice, we have seen, is basically a matter of emotion, and there can be no effective challenge of it without right counter-emotions. Such depth of concern does not justify unloving attitudes toward or name calling of one's opponents. "Speaking the truth in love" is a supreme need.

It is easy for one to say this who has not personally felt the sting of race discrimination. Yet the need becomes far more eloquent when it comes from the lips of one who bears the brunt of it, yet without hatred. It was put in words that ought to become classic by the Rev. Martin Luther King, Jr., a few hours after his arrest as a leader of passive resistance against segregation in the Montgomery, Alabama, bus lines:

If we are arrested every day, if we are exploited every day, if we are trampled over every day, don't ever let anyone pull you so low as to hate them. We must use the weapon of love. We must have compassion and understanding for those who hate us. We must realize so many people are taught to hate us that they are not totally responsible for their hate. But we stand in life at midnight; we are always on the threshold of a new dawn.[13]

The race problem must, for the most part, be met by person to person contacts which create understanding. This calls for more intervisitation and social fellowship, both locally and nationally, and as occasion permits, in the world community. It is hard to remain hostile toward a people whose individuals one has come to know and love. Such fellowship has been one of the major contributions of the ecumenical movement.

In cases of racial discrimination by public agencies within the com-

[13] *The New York Times*, February 24, 1956.

munity, the Church must be willing to stand up and be counted on the side of equality. It must act in co-operation with other community forces if possible, but in any case it must act. Not alone prophetic indictment, but patient mediation, is the function of Christian leaders.

From time to time, political aspects of the question call for action. Among these are the steps to be taken toward desegregation in the schools and universities, the poll-tax issue, the passage of guarantees of fair employment practices, the removal of restrictions in housing and the use of public facilities. Segregation cannot be justified on the ground of "separate but equal" facilities, for what is separate is discriminatory and hence not equal. Though the right next steps to take are not always clear, the principle is, and Christian citizens who take their gospel seriously should lead the way.

Since the race question is a world issue, and not simply a local or national one, education and action as to its world implications are necessary. Support by citizens of such action as will lift the living standards and the human dignity of the millions of underprivileged, nonwhite peoples of the earth is imperative. Congressmen must be made to feel that their constituencies insist upon it.

Finally, the total problem must be lifted into the realm of prayer and worship. We must pray for those of other races; we must be responsive to the awareness that they are praying for us. When one enters truly into the mood of intercession, bitterness departs and fellowship takes its place. It has been the contention of this chapter that the removal of race prejudice is a duty laid upon us by God, and if it is God's business we are engaged in, we must give God an opening in our souls.

Since it is God's business, let us not despair. The solution will not come tomorrow, but it will come. In the midst of the walls of opposition erected by men stands Christ, who breaks down the "dividing wall of hostility" that separates us. It is the business of Christians to give him a chance to act.

X. The Christian Conscience and the State

WE ARE TO EXAMINE in this chapter some of the most difficult and complex aspects of Christian decision. The relations of Christian ethics to political power have had to be anticipated somewhat in preceding discussions; but though the Christian acts within a system of law in reference to his family, his job, and his relations with those of other races, these are essentially matters of personal contact and adjustment. We come now to his relations with what is by its very nature an all-encompassing, impersonal framework of his life.

Almost every Christian is at the same time a citizen of a national state, and those few who are not citizens in the official sense of having explicit political rights and duties are still required to obey laws. Ever since Augustine early in the fifth century drew a distinction between the *civitas dei* and the *civitas terrena*, the interrelatedness and at points the conflict between the demands of the "city of God" on the one hand and the earthly power on the other have been crucial issues in Christian ethics. Long before this time, Christians who faced martyrdom under the persecutions of the Roman emperors rather than deny Christ met this problem in practice, even as many of our contemporaries have been forced to in our own day.

Let us begin with a brief statement of what is meant by the State, followed by a look at the biblical foundations for Christian decision. The greater part of the chapter will then be devoted to certain major problems such as the interplay of justice with love, the legitimacy and limits of coercive power, the application of the principles of liberty and equality in a democracy.

1. What is a State?

A State is a sovereign political unit to which its citizens as members of a national community owe allegiance. It offers protection to its people and in turn demands obedience to its laws. Though in strict accuracy the term "nation" refers to the people and "State" to the political authority exercised upon and through them, in practice the two words are generally used interchangeably. Unless there is occasion to do otherwise, we shall use the term to refer not to a single state within the State, such as New York or California, but to the government that has jurisdiction over the nation as a whole.

There are certain inherent difficulties in considering the ethical dilemmas of citizens in relation to the State. The first of these is suggested above in the difference yet convergence of nation and State—that is, of people and political authority. Even in the most totalitarian regime the State is never wholly an impersonal thing. What it demands, persons demand; what it does, whether for good or ill, persons do. Government "of the people, by the people, for the people," is the explicit aim of democracy, but there is no government of any kind unless some persons govern. Thus it comes about that no State, even the most autocratic, is morally neutral, for those who exercise authority within it are morally responsible beings. On the other hand, a State always contains elements not directly subject to change by acts of will—accumulations from the past in the form of tradition, law, or constitution that can be changed but slowly if at all, competing interests within its membership, interlocking relations with other states in which the interests of justice and of security at times conflict. For these reasons it is a mistake to assume either that states are solely impersonal mechanisms of coercive power or that they are responsive to the moral demands of love and justice to the same degree that individual persons can be expected to be.

A second inherent dilemma appears at the point of the definition of a State as a "sovereign" political unit. It is here that many difficulties regarding world government in principle, and the United Nations in practice, are focused. No nation can be a State unless it can exercise authority over its own people; if it loses that authority, it is either absorbed by some other sovereign State or becomes a constituent, federated part of a more inclusive State, such as are the various states in the United States. The perennial clash between states' rights and the federal government, brought to fresh virulence in the American scene by differences of opinion over the desegregation issue, shows what an uneasy tension there is even within long-established sovereign authority. The United Nations makes no claim to being a super-State, but the bounds between domestic and international issues are so hard to fix that opposition to its jurisdiction at some points is inevitable.

These difficulties and dilemmas are present even before one says anything about the claims of Christianity in reference to the State. But at four points there is bound to be a difference in the demands made upon the Christian citizen by the two "worlds" in which he has membership. These are: (1) The State tends to regard its power and authority as supreme; the Christian owes his ultimate loyalty to God alone. (2) The chief concern of the State is with its own national community; the Christian sees all men as beloved of God and hence envisions a world community. (3) The State has as its primary moral demands the maintenance of justice and security; the Christian finds his highest obligation in love to God and his fellow men. (4) The State must use coercive power to enforce its authority; the Christian can accept some forms of coercion as right and necessary, but at others his conscience is bound to rebel. How to act as a Christian should within this tension is a matter on which directives are discernible in the gospel, yet no arbitrary authoritative word can be found. But let us see what help we get from the Bible and from the assured convictions of Christian faith.

2. Our biblical and theological base

We must look first at the Old Testament, for there we find, particularly in the messages of the prophets, a more explicit reckoning with social problems than is reflected in the New Testament. Israel, unlike the early Christian community, was a political State, and during much of its history its leaders had civil as well as religious authority. This dual relationship, as we saw in Chapter II, gave a particular turn to the significance of the covenant, the Law, and the prophets. It is both asset and barrier as we try to apply the moral insights of the prophets to our own times.

No literature of any people reflects a keener concern for social righteousness than is found in the writings of Amos, Hosea, Isaiah, and Micah, and in a different setting in Jeremiah and Ezekiel. The prophets did not hesitate to rebuke kings, as well as people, who disobeyed the commands of God. The evils reflected in their words, and indeed portrayed throughout the Old Testament—avarice, exploitation, bribery, chicanery, and attempts at seizure of power for personal gain—are perennial human tendencies which appear in every State. Both the situation and its remedy are timeless. In the message of the prophets there is a call to personal and social righteousness which stems from the sovereign rule of a righteous God. They spoke to the conditions of their times from the standpoint of both the judgment and the proffered deliverance of Yahweh, and proclaimed their faith in a divine Ruler who moves within political events as in all other events of human history. Dark as their messages appear to be with indictment and doom, hope through the mercy and faithfulness of Yahweh was never withdrawn. Both their discernment of human affairs and their insight into the moral nature of God make their messages of incalculable and permanent worth.

Yet when we are confronted with the need to apply the social teachings of the prophets to a particular measure before Congress in our time—for example, to expenditures for military defense, or a farm bill, or fair employment practices—the directives are less clear. Aside from the obvious disparities in the general social situation, there are major differences between Israel's political structure and our own. Israel was a theocracy, owing its very existence to the intermingling of political with religious destiny, while we are committed to the principle of separation of Church and State. Israel was not a democracy, as we are, and while the prophets pleaded eloquently for personal righteousness in social relations, there was no expectancy of or challenge to the individual civic responsibilities basic to a democracy. Thus even the highest moral insights of the Old Testament leave us with a large gap.

Is the New Testament a more specific guide? It is, and it is not. The most direct political reference in the words of Jesus is the familiar "Render to Caesar the things that are Caesar's, and to God the things that are God's" (Mark 12:17). This is ambiguous because it does not tell us how to distinguish between what is Caesar's and what is God's. As we have noted repeatedly, Jesus was concerned to set up a spiritual, not a political, kingdom, and it is unlikely that he gave much thought to the structure of the political state in which his followers were to find themselves. He did foresee that they would endure persecution as he sent them out "as sheep in the midst of wolves," but his call was to fidelity in witness rather than to assumption of the wolves' prerogatives and power.

Nevertheless this passage through the centuries has had very great value, and it is so today. For one thing, it recognizes the right of duly constituted civil authority to exercise control—and this at a point before which human nature is chronically reluctant, the payment of taxes! More significantly still, it recognizes that God has claims upon the citizen that cannot be wholly subsumed within the claims of the State. On the strength of this declaration, Christians from the first century to the twentieth have refused to let the State have their total allegiance, and not a few in our own time have died in Nazi concentration camps and Communist purges rather than render to Caesar the things that are God's.

When further directives are sought within the experience of the early Church, the principle enunciated by Jesus stands, but the ambiguity is not removed. Peter's "we must obey God rather than men" (Acts 5:29) carried the first Christians boldly through persecution to victory or death. Yet there is a sharp contrast between Paul's conservative and on the whole conciliatory attitude toward the ruling powers and what is portrayed in the book of Revelation. Paul could say in words destined to have great influence, "Let every person be subject to the governing authorities. For there is no authority except from God, and those that exist have been instituted by God." (Rom. 13:1.) Similarly in I Pet. 2:17 we read, "Honor all men. Love the brotherhood. Fear God. Honor the emperor." These injunctions seem to have equal status, and there is no suggestion that only the good emperor is to be thus honored. Nevertheless, the book of Revelation emerging out of the persecutions under the emperor Domitian does not hesitate to refer to Rome in cryptic but pointed terms as "Babylon the great, mother of harlots and of earth's abominations . . . , drunk with the blood of the saints and the blood of the martyrs of Jesus" (Rev. 17:5-6).

In general the Church has followed the lead of Paul in enjoining obedience to the ruling powers. This has been more true of the Lutheran than of the Calvinist tradition. It led Luther to side with the princes against the peasants in the Peasants' Revolt, and modern Lutheranism in Germany to defer revolt against Nazi tyranny until it became clear that Hitler was usurping the place that belonged only to Christ. Calvin established a theocracy in Geneva in which the Church dominated the State, though not without a long struggle to establish this control, and this temporarily resolved the tension between the two. However, he did not hesitate to sanction resistance to rulers who defied God and commanded abominations, saying that "when they rise against God they must be put down, and held of no more account than worn-out shoes." [1] Both the Puritan and the American Revolutions drew largely from Calvinism for their spiritual undergirding.

With this ambiguity as to the degree of allegiance owed to the State embedded in the Bible and in the history of the Church, we cannot expect to be wholly extricated from it. Yet two other aspects of Christian faith throw light upon it and must not be left out of consideration. These are the sovereignty of God and the Christian view of man.

Reference has been made to the claim of every State to sovereign political authority. Yet to the Christian there is a higher sovereignty, that of "God the Father Almighty, Maker of heaven and earth." Since the State like the family is an "order of creation," it owes its very existence to God. God has ordained that men should live together in communities and that such communities, larger or smaller, should be structured into forms of government. But God has not ordained that any existing national State should be exactly as it is. As we saw regarding economic systems, none is perfect enough to be equated with the kingdom of God—or can be while human sin exists. Some are better, some worse, carriers of divine justice; democracy is better fitted than either fascism or Communism to bring about the kind of human society willed by God. Yet before the sovereign Ruler of the world, every political State must be judged defective, and all Christian citizens must seek to bring their State more nearly into harmony with what is believed to be God's will for human life. This we noted was the major concern of the prophets of Israel, and in this they gave us a permanent legacy that must never be surrendered. Taken seriously, recognition of the ultimate and final sovereignty of God could transform the structure of human society.

The second principle stems more directly from the New Testament. It is the recognition of the supreme and equal worth of all persons to

[1] *Calvini Opera*, xli, 415-16. See my *John Calvin: The Man and His Ethics*, ch. xi, for more extended citations.

God. It is here that democracy is grounded. It is apparent that "equal worth" cannot mean equal endowment or ability; certainly to us and presumably to God it does not mean equal usefulness to society or equality in the attainment of personal character. Yet the equal and impartial love of God for all men, both saints and sinners, both high and low in the world's esteem, is the indisputable deduction to be drawn from the words and acts of Jesus. Here is a guiding principle for both personal and political action which is bedrock.

Thus it comes about that to say that every soul everywhere is "a person for whom Christ died" is more than pious verbiage; it is an affirmation of the duty to treat every person as a being of supreme and infinite worth. One may speak in some contexts more formally of the "dignity of human personality," but in a Christian context this stems from the conviction of the immeasurable love of God for every man. A religious insight has profound political significance when it makes the difference between a fragmentary adherence to democracy and its practice in human relations.

3. Love and justice

This brings us to a crucial matter, the interplay of love with justice in Christian moral decision. To the brief statement at the end of Chapter IV must now be added more specific analysis.

Love has been repeatedly defined here, and it has been said that the Christian's love commandment is to *agape* love and not of necessity to *eros* or *philia*, though these may often be subsumed within it. But what is justice?

The time-honored and seldom disputed definition of justice is "giving to every man his due." It goes back to classical Greek thought, was accepted both by the Roman Catholic Church and by the Reformers, and is generally cited today when a definition is called for.[2] With such a weight of evidence behind it, it requires temerity to dispute it.

The positive note in this definition need not be disputed. In every

---

[2] Emil Brunner, who makes it basic to his discussion in *Justice and the Social Order*, says of it: "According to Plato, *Republic*, 1, 331, the *suum cuique*, though not in this clear and definite form, goes back to Simonides. It is explicitly formulated by Aristotle, *Rhet.* 1, 9. That it was, however, the principle of justice, not only in the Catholic law of nature, but also for the Reformers, is proved by hundreds of texts in Luther, Zwingli and Calvin." P. 263.

issue of justice or injustice some element of "belonging" or possession is involved—whether of material goods, status and prestige, power over another, personal opportunity, or any other of life's many intangibles. A situation is *just* when a person, or a group of persons, has what he (or they) ought to have; a situation is unjust when for some reason this is denied.

To say this is to affirm that there are certain rights which cannot be set aside or infringed upon without injustice. From the playground, where even young children sense the difference between fair play and its opposite, to the relations of governments to their own citizens and to other states, justice involves the preservation or the securing of basic rights. What these rights are may be a matter of differing opinion; that there are such rights is inherent in any consideration of justice.

Yet when this has been said, it must also be pointed out that the definition is seriously defective at the point of its ambiguity. When does a man have "his due"? Aristotle, who gave the definition its classic formulation, regarded slaves as instruments for the use of free men, held that barbarians had no rights that the free-born Greek was obligated to respect, and regarded women as an inferior group existing only for the bearing and rearing of children. This was corrected somewhat within the Christian Church, though Aristotle's scorn of manual labor was carried over into it. Christian history shows progress toward an equalitarian conception of justice, but the Church has never fully divested itself of aristocratic assumptions. Even with the present democratic and Christian emphasis on the dignity of personality and concern for "liberty and justice for all," we are still far from agreement as to what constitutes for every man "his due." Every clash over racial status, labor and wages, or the legitimacy of some particular form of power gives evidence of the ambiguity of this principle.

Can justice be rescued from ambiguity by equality? In one respect Yes, and in another No. Where basic human rights are at stake, they ought not to be denied to anybody because of "class, color, creed or previous condition of servitude." Brunner is right that there is a certain impersonality about a system of justice, a definiteness and a structured quality which is not dependent on attitudes of personal like or dislike.[3] Yet justice within a family requires adaptation to individual need, and

[3] *Ibid.*, pp. 19-20. As noted presently, I do not in general accept his position.

justice within an economic order requires some variation in income according to contribution as well as need. Even in those structures of justice aiming to be completely impartial—the apprehension of law-breakers and the affixing of penalties for crime—the best jurisprudence takes into account the maturity and the motive of the offender and the possibilities of remedial as well as of punitive treatment. Hence it appears that no rigid equalitarianism, but only equality of opportunity according to individual circumstance, will give to every man his due.

What is just can never be determined apart from a social context. A young child is not treated justly if responsibilities are placed upon him beyond his years, or a mature adult if treated like a child. A just system of grading in school, or of compensation in work, must take into account the legitimate expectancy of performance of the individual within his group. The Oxford Conference on Church, Community, and State redeemed the classical definition of justice somewhat from ambiguity when it stated that justice is the "ideal of a harmonious relation of life to life." [4] This has its own ambiguity in that it states no criterion of harmonious relationship, but it rightly stresses that justice can never be an abstract or static thing. A person's right is not something fixed by a "primal order" of creation;[5] it must be determined impartially but not impersonally by adjustment of life to life within every concrete situation.

What, then, is the relation of justice to love ? According to Brunner there is a radical difference between them, with love belonging to the sphere of personal relations and justice, because of its fixity and impersonality, to institutions and systems. Justice then must precede love to give to society an ordered structure; the Christian must seek to ensure it as a foundation for the exercise of love, but justice and not love is the principle of the social order. Reinhold Niebuhr is less dualistic in that he stresses the relevance of love as an "impossible possibility" to every human situation, but he warns so continually against a sentimental substitution of love for the requirements of justice that the major impact of his thought is a dichotomy in which again justice, and not love, is the

[4] *The Oxford Conference* (Official Report), Section III, 1.

[5] Brunner's term, *Justice and the Social Order*, pp. 18-19. Though he recognizes that what justice requires changes with changing circumstances, his thought about justice is so dominated by a "sense of things fixed" that little if any place is left for personal adaptation in its exercise.

determining principle of social ethics. Hence, both Brunner and Niebuhr make much of the need to use coercive power to secure even an approximate justice in human relations.

If what I have said as to the meaning of justice is true, no such separation of justice from love or substitution of justice for love is consistent with it. The difference appears sharply at the point where Brunner says, "If I treat a man justly, and only justly, I regard him as fitting his place in the structure. . . . I do not see him himself. I see his 'claim,' his right, we might even say his 'share' in the whole structure. As contrasted with love, justice has this statutory quality, this sense of things fixed." [6] In between this inflexible and impersonal view of justice and one which blurs the distinction between justice and love is an intermediate view which I hold to be the true one.

Justice is the "harmonious relation of life to life" as this harmonious relation is determined by concern for other persons in *agape* love. Where it is felt toward persons who are not known in face-to-face relations, it takes the form of good will, respect for personality, eagerness to serve, willingness to be helpful at personal cost. It is not the sole prerogative of Christians, but Christians who do not have this attitude can scarcely be said to be either loving or just.

To illustrate, there are millions of Negroes in America and of Africans in South Africa who are denied their rights as persons and hence are unjustly treated. My duty to act in love to try to secure for them justice, insofar as my voice or vote or influence extends, is not limited by the fact that my personal acquaintance extends to only a small fraction of this number. Wherever there are victims of Communist tyranny, of prostitution, of underworld gangsterism, of the traffic in narcotics, of injury to children, of economic exploitation, of any denial of basic human rights, I am obligated by love to do my utmost on the side of justice even though my influence may be slight and my connection with these victims of injustice very indirect. Responsibility for action increases with opportunity; I am more responsible for the race situation in America than in South Africa. Yet at no point will Christian love, if I am sensitive to it, permit me to be acquiescent before injustice.

Furthermore, justice actuated by love requires concern for the perpetrators as well as for the victims of injustice. Understanding and

[6] *Ibid.*, p. 19.

sympathy must temper condemnation. Remedial action is called for which may take the form of expressions of understanding, indictment given in love, forcible deterrence or punishment, but which so long as it is Christian can never be actuated by vindictiveness or the simple desire to "get even." The latter, which often poses as justice, is far more often its antithesis. Structures of justice must be embodied in laws. We are in fact the present recipients of centuries of concern for justice in the laws that govern a civilized society. Some of these are bad laws that require change; most of them have stood the test of time, and ought not to be disobeyed by a Christian unless his conscience convinces him of a higher law in the will of God. In many areas of life more laws, or modifications in those we have, are required for a just society, and Christian *agape* should stir us to work for their enactment.

Thus it appears that there is no basic antithesis between Christian love and justice. Neither is a substitute for the other, but neither can do without the other. Love for persons gives justice its structure and marks it off from vindictiveness on the one hand and indifference on the other. Justice in social relations, to be embodied in just laws and their enforcement, is one of the primary pursuits to which we are called by neighbor love.

The practical programs and political strategies available in the attempt to secure justice at the call of love will, of course, vary with circumstances. It is seldom that in a complex issue, such as the race question or the international order, the immediate next steps that are open will embody everything that love prompts us to desire. Progress comes slowly, and often by compromises, but it is essential that Christian goals should always point the way forward.

For this process J. H. Oldham has coined the phrase "middle axioms," and the term is effectively used by John C. Bennett in *Christian Ethics and Social Policy*. A middle axiom is not something of permanent validity, as the love commandment is, nor is it a specific legislative policy, but an intermediate guidepost derived from Christian ethics as to what must be done next. Says Oldham of the meaning of middle axioms, "They are an attempt to define the directions in which, in a particular state of society, Christian faith must express itself. They are not binding for all time, but are provisional definitions of the type of behavior re-

quired of Christians at a given period and in given circumstances." [7]
Bennett gives as examples of middle axioms for our time the need of
international collaboration in the United Nations, the maintenance of
balance between free enterprise and government control of economic
power, the removal of racial segregation in the churches and its progressive elimination in society.[8] Provided such middle axioms are taken for
what they are, as Christian "next steps" and not as a watered-down
version of the full implications of the love commandment, they can be
extremely helpful in the quest of a fuller justice as this is actuated by
Christian love.

4. Love and coercion

The foregoing may be accepted, and still a deep problem will remain. Justice ought to be actuated by love, with concern for persons
even in the most impartial, and in this sense impersonal, structures of
law and its enforcement. But can justice be maintained—or an approxi-
mation of justice—without coercive force? The answer is clearly No.

Even within the intimate relations of the family where love ought to
be most regnant, there can be no justice without the exercise of authority, and authority sometimes necessitates coercion. Children have
their "just rights" within a family, and excessive domination by their
parents is neither good psychology nor good religion; yet the undisci-
plined child suffers severely from his lack of restraint, and without some
coercion there can be no "harmonious relation of life to life." This is
clearly evident within the State, which would not be a State at all unless it could exercise coercive force upon recalcitrants and thereby
ensure a measure of security and order for all its members.

Coercion is necessitated by sin. All men are sinners; all are in some
respects self-seeking. For "law-abiding citizens" this does not generally require the penalties of the law to be invoked, though one need only to
ask himself how far his driving is affected by known traffic regulations,
or his income-tax filing by fear of penalties, to realize the degree to
which the law is in the background as a restraint to his self-centeredness.

[7] W. A. Visser 't Hooft and J. H. Oldham, *The Church and Its Function in Society*
(Chicago: Willett, Clark & Co., 1937), p. 194.
[8] *Op. cit.*, pp. 77-83.

In some, a sinful and selfish defiance of the rights of others leads to crime, and coercion must be invoked for restraint and punishment.

The need for coercion does not stem from sin only. As in the family immaturity necessitates coercive authority, there are immature adults in every State. Coercion is required also by the sheer complexity of human existence, where even mature and law-abiding adults "tread on each other's toes" unless their proper bounds are marked out and these enforced.

Granted that coercive power is necessary if a State, or even a harmonious lesser order of society, is to exist, several very basic questions remain. Is Christian love compatible with the use of physical force? What of competing coercive groups within a State and their relation to law? When, if ever, is revolution justified? Is it ever right for one State to use coercive force upon another? The very asking of the questions suggests the enormity of the problems involved. I shall attempt only to point the direction of the answers.

Physical force must always be available; it should be used as little as possible, and always under restraint. No State can get along without police protection for its citizens. Though this fact should not be used illicitly to justify vast military establishments and their use in international war, there is justification for an international as well as a domestic police force, provided this is used with due restraint. These restraints, to look at the domestic scene, require the avoidance of brutality and excessive cruelty in the use of physical force, its use under impartial and established processes of law, and the preservation of personal freedoms up to the point where these freedoms infringe on the rights of others. To illustrate, a citizen ought not to be arrested for expressing an unpopular opinion; he can properly be arrested for inciting or engaging in acts of violence, but the physical force with which he is restrained ought not in turn to become counterviolence. The customary regard for policemen as trusted protectors in a democratic state and the terror with which the police are regarded in a totalitarian regime, as in Nazi Germany, give evidence of the difference.

But what of competing centers of power within a State? This issue becomes vividly evident in the contest between "big business" and "organized labor," and the effort of both to secure government backing for their interests. A "middle axiom" at this point is that *a government* ought not to become the tool of either interest, and laws must be enacted and enforced to restrain the aggression of one group upon the other. The processes of a democracy, as contrasted with economic feudalism or a Communist society, are favorable to the exercise of such restraints, but injustices are bound to exist in the struggle for power. It is a particular imperative of the Christian conscience to have enough concern for persons to work for the correction of injustices by both personal and political means whenever these are perpetrated by any group upon another.

It is not true that "the best governed people is the least governed." The Old Testament reflects a situation in the period of the judges when "every man did what was right in his own eyes" (Judg. 21:25), and the result was anarchy restrained only by family and tribal custom. Governments exist to exercise control, not only upon individual persons, but upon great groups of persons. The Christian Church, with its membership in all economic strata and among persons of virtually all occupations representing all sectional interests, has a special opportunity and obligation to develop in its members political attitudes transcending narrow group interests. This is true in spite of the fact that secular alignments in the contest for power are often tragically evident in the practices of the churches.

A particular problem which stems from the two preceding is the right of revolution when a ruling group dominates another against its will and sense of justice. Here some definition is imperative, for while revolutions seldom occur without some bloodshed, there is a difference between violent revolutions like the French Revolution or the American War of Independence, and the relatively peaceful Industrial Revolution or the Gandhian revolution by which India secured her independence. The problem is particularly pertinent now in the Orient, where many subject or recently subject peoples are in the processes of revolutionary change.

It is characteristic that every people thinks its own revolution justified and tends to decry uprisings elsewhere. Edmund Burke wrote scorching invectives against the French Revolution and John Wesley against the American, but neither man doubted the rightness of the English Revolution of 1688. What, then, can be the position of the Christian conscience?

Without minimizing the great complexity of issues in most concrete cases, which make snap judgments out of order, some principles can be affirmed. Among these are:

1. That violent revolution wherever possible should be averted by any honorable means, since it not only induces hate and bloodshed but often destroys more than it builds;
2. That objection to revolution should never take the form of complacent acquiescence in injustice;
3. That Christians should seek to be a reconciling and mediating force to remove the causes prompting revolution, to avert its outbreak, and to preserve justice and good will within it if it occurs;
4. That if it is adopted on apparently just grounds to overthrow tyranny, it must never be regarded as more than a preparatory step to positive structures of law and justice.

The issue is not whether the American Revolution ought to have occurred. It did occur, and a great nation has come out of it. But what of the present? If Communism could be overthrown by internal revolt, most Americans would rejoice, and few Christians would condemn flatly all forms of revolution. But the positive note needs always to be sounded. The aspirations of subject peoples today for political and spiritual freedom should be viewed with understanding and sympathy by those who prize their own liberties, bought by the effort of their fathers. In particular in the Orient, where the impact toward revolutionary change is so largely the product of the Christian emphasis on the dignity and worth of the individual, Christians are obliged to see the issues through by sharing their spiritual, moral, and economic resources.

The final question, as to the Christian conscience and the coercive use of military power by one State upon another, we shall defer to the next chapter which will be devoted centrally to this issue. This one will conclude with some observations upon liberty and equality and their meeting point in a Christian democracy.

5. Liberty, equality, and democracy

Democracy is both an ethical ideal and a form of political government. As an ideal it stresses the worth and dignity of every man, and hence the need of securing for every man his basic human rights and his highest attainable self-development. This has Christian roots in the New Testament, though its roots are also to be found in Platonic eros and in a natural law of morality which has come down to us from Stoic philosophy.[9] As a political system democracy stresses not only the "rights of man," but the opportunity and obligation of every mature citizen to have a part in shaping the direction his government will take. However far from the ethical ideal it may be in practice, it is always in a measure guided by it and responsive to it. Where democracy prevails, men are never perfect, but their worst impulses are held in check both by the inner discipline of responsible citizenship and by external coercion upon the irresponsible. Reinhold Niebuhr's epigram is relevant: "Man's capacity for justice makes democracy possible; but man's inclination to injustice makes democracy necessary." [10]

Basic to the principles of democracy are equality and liberty. Both are ambiguous terms requiring definition to avoid distortion.[11]

Democracy as an ideal is not to be identified with *equality*, although it is closely related to it. Equality may mean (1) equality of intrinsic personal worth (that is, spiritual equality before God), (2) equality of endowment, (3) equality of opportunity, or (4) identity of function. A democratic ideal presupposes equality in the first and third senses, but not in the second or fourth. It is obvious that not all persons are created "free and equal" from the standpoint of either biological or cultural inheritance and therefore ought not all to do the same things or enjoy the same experiences. Yet within a framework of disparate biological inheritance fixed by nature and of disparate social inheritance which is the result of both biological and human forces, the democratic ideal requires that every person be given an opportunity to experience the "abundant life" and do the work for which he is best fitted.

Democracy as a form of social organization clashes at some points with democracy as an equalitarian ideal. This happens when persons of inferior intelligence or ethical sensitivity are able by force of numbers

[9] Greek philosophy, other than Stoicism, was strongly tinged with an aristocratic note. Greek political practice, though never fully democratic, was in advance of the insights of Plato and Aristotle as to human equality.

[10] *The Children of Light and the Children of Darkness* (New York: Chas. Scribner's Sons, 1944), p. xi.

[11] The next three paragraphs are restated from the chapter entitled "Christian Faith and Democracy" in my *The Modern Rival of Christian Faith*, pp. 87-88.

to exercise coercion upon other persons in such a manner as to thwart their fullest self-realization. It happens also when for the real good of the greater number, legislation is enacted the enforcement of which works injustice to a minority. The former situation presents a problem to be dealt with through education, particularly moral education. The latter is embedded in the metaphysical problem of evil. Neither can be wholly eliminated in a complex social order.

The democratic ideal is a principle of *liberty* as well as equality, but again it is necessary to distinguish among types of liberty. Liberty may mean (1) freedom to do as one pleases without social restraint, (2) freedom of thought, worship, or expression of opinion, or (3) freedom to act in social relations within limits set by the group. All three are types of individualism but with quite different social consequences. The first conforms to the democratic ideal of respect for personality only in small, highly moralized groups. Ordinarily it coincides with egoistic hedonism, anarchy, and "rugged" (that is, ruthless) individualism. The second, which is a major presupposition of both secular and religious liberalism, is not only consistent with but essential to the maintenance of the democratic ideal, and is formally guaranteed in all democratic societies but often violated in practice. The third is both an indispensable prerequisite to the democratic ideal and a primary source of its corruption. Rightly used it grants "liberty under law," uniting freedom with order; misused it unduly restricts freedom for the sake of order or upsets order for the sake of freedom. A large part of the problem of social and political ethics lies in distinguishing between its use and misuse.

So essential is liberty to democracy that any setting aside of civil liberties, or attempts to stifle freedom of thought and honest, peaceable expression of it, must be viewed with much apprehension. Under the hysteria caused by some degree of actual Communist infiltration, fear of subversion has grown out of all proportion to the actual danger, and prophetic Christian utterance has fallen under the same condemnation as Communist distortions of truth and democracy. It is a basic Christian duty and an obligation of responsible citizenship to preserve the right of minorities to challenge the *status quo* and of individuals to express unpopular views, provided this is done without violence and without subterfuge within the law.

On rare occasions, a Christian may even feel called upon to defy the civil law for the sake of the higher law of God. This ought never to be done without much soul scarching, and with full willingness to take the consequences. It is more safely done for others than for one's self, and there is no general basis on which it can wisely be encouraged. It is one of the truly great things about democracy that it provides so extensively for conscientious dissent and upholds the right of minorities to differ with prevailing opinion.

A democratic political system makes possible both more equality and more liberty in the right sense, and hence more justice, than any other alternative system. Under it the values the Christian ethic exalts can thrive and grow as in no other. Hence, not only from its roots but its fruits there is a valid sense in which it is possible to speak of Christian democracy. But always this needs to be spoken with caution. Democracy ought not by any superficial synthesis to be identified with Christianity simply because in the democratic West the majority of the citizens profess to be Christians. Political power and spiritual power are not identical, and no actual democracy has been—or while sin remains will be—the city of God.

Both the possibilities and the perils in the issues discussed in this chapter come to focus in the matter of international order and conflict. They assume their gravest significance at the point of recourse to war when this is waged in defense of democratic ideals. These issues are so complex, yet so overwhelmingly vital, that a full chapter will now be devoted to them.

XI. War, Peace, and International Order

WE COME NOW to the most basic issue that confronts mankind. With atomic and hydrogen bombs now stock-piled by both the United States and Russia in sufficient quantity and potency to destroy all human life upon the planet and with guided missiles to deliver them quickly to their targets, the annihilation not only of great cities but of entire nations in a matter of minutes has now become a staggering possibility. The phrase "coexistence or no existence" has become more than a neat play on words; it is a clear putting of the only two alternatives before us.

At this juncture there are great agreements and also great differences among Christians. All agree that war is a terrible evil, fraught today with possibilities of destruction undreamed of in an earlier day, and to be avoided by any honorable means. At this point, however, opinions diverge. Many Christians, and at present the majority, believe that there are occasions when war cannot be honorably averted and therefore must be participated in as a Christian duty, while Christian pacifists hold all war and moral support of war to be contrary to the teachings of Jesus, and hence to be rejected by the Christian conscience.

The case for and against each of these positions must be stated later in this chapter. More important, however, is what Christians as both pacifists and nonpacifists can together do to remove the causes and avert the outbreak of war. We must combine our efforts for lasting peace,[1] not only with one another but with "men of good will" outside the Christian Church, or there will be no peace and no survival. But first let

[1] The symposium *"To Combine Our Efforts"*—*For Lasting Peace* is an excellent study book issued by the Methodist Woman's Division of Christian Service. It may be procured from the Literature Headquarters, 7820 Reading Road, Cincinnati 37, Ohio.

us look at the biblical and theological foundations of our mission as peacemakers.

1. Basic Christian foundations

The Old Testament has in it much of carnage and strife, with Yahweh in not a few instances represented as calling his people to battle and contending for them against the enemy. The statement, "For many fell slain, because the war was of God" (I Chr. 5:22), is made once but implied often. Yet few would question that Isaiah's vision of a warless world, restated by Micah in nearly identical words, reflects a higher insight. For many centuries these words have been a rallying cry, not to battle, but to the ways of peace:

> and many nations shall come, and say:
> "Come, let us go up to the mountain of the Lord,
>   to the house of the God of Jacob;
> that he may teach us his ways
>   and we may walk in his paths."
> For out of Zion shall go forth the law,
>   and the word of the Lord from Jerusalem.
> He shall judge between many peoples,
>   and shall decide for strong nations afar off;
> and they shall beat their swords into plowshares,
>   and their spears into pruning hooks;
> nation shall not lift up sword against nation,
>   neither shall they learn war any more;
> but they shall sit every man under his vine and under his fig tree,
>   and none shall make them afraid;
>   for the mouth of the Lord of hosts has spoken. (Mic. 4:2-4.)[2]

In the New Testament, Jesus stands revealed not only as the Son of God but as the Prince of Peace, proclaiming the love of God, forgiving his enemies even at the point of death on the cross, calling all men to a type of neighbor love which if put into practice would abolish wars. His words, "Blessed are the peacemakers, for they shall be called sons of God," are fully consistent with all that he was and did as he set before men the nature and will of God.

[2] See also Isa. 2:3-4. Micah adds to Isaiah's words the note of security at the end.

It is impossible by quoting texts to justify either a pacifist or a non-pacifist position. The often quoted, "I have not come to bring peace, but a sword" (Matt. 10:34), is certainly in its context not a justification of the use of military force, but a warning that fidelity to the Christian cause would precipitate peril and persecution. Similarly the word spoken by Jesus in the Garden to restrain his disciples from violence, "Put your sword back into its place; for all who take the sword will perish by the sword" (Matt. 26:52), is no final pronouncement on the matter. True as this statement has proved repeatedly to be, Jesus was probably speaking not of international but of personal conflict.

What we derive from Jesus is a spirit and an outreach to persons that is the antithesis of war. Just as he spoke no specific word on slavery or slums, but gave an impulse that can let no sensitive Christian be at ease while they exist, so he injected into human history a spirit that must eventually lead to war's abolition. That mankind has been so slow about it is due in part to human sin, in part to the immense complexities of the international situation.

When Christian faith is viewed as a whole, there are certain basic convictions which bear upon war and the tasks of peacemaking. Let us briefly review them.

First, there is the fact that *God is the creator and ruler of our world*. However dark may be the mysteries of his ways and however theoretically insoluble the problem of evil, the Christian knows that God made the world for good and not for evil. He knows that war's wanton destruction of human lives and property and its long aftermath of physical and social evils cannot be God's will. The passions that arouse war, the tragic events that occur within it in ever-mounting proportions, and the consequences that flow from it are almost wholly antithetical to what we know of the love of God as we see this love revealed in Jesus. Thus we are called to labor with all our powers for war's abolition.

Derivative from the Christian doctrine of creation is our stewardship. Stewardship means far more than direct giving to good causes, though it includes that; it means the holding of all that we have as a trust from God to be used responsibly in ways that advance his kingdom. Thus, it means that the total resources of the earth, our technological skills and scientific achievements, our sources of power including atomic

200

energy, belong to God and should be used at his call for the increase of human good. Only as such possessions are used for the alleviation and not for the production of human misery can we be true stewards of the Creator and Giver of all.

Second, *God is a God of judgment.* It is not enough to stress only the love of God. God is also a God of judgment who does not treat sin lightly. Any individual or any people who flouts his righteous will stands under condemnation, though his judgment is always linked with love. The result in practice is that sin always brings evil consequences in its wake. The world has been so made with a pervasive moral order that we cannot sin with impunity. When a society or a nation tries to direct its course on the basis of aggressive self-interest, denial of the rights and liberties of others, economic greed, lust for power, race prejudice, vindictiveness, and deception, situations are created which if unchecked lead to war. In this sense, then, war can be said to be a form of divine judgment, though we cannot assume that God deliberately sends wars to smite sinners with the wrath of his displeasure.[3]

In this connection a question always arises in time of war: "What is God doing? Why does he not stop it?" The answer is far more complex than to say simply that war is God's judgment upon human sin, for the suffering and disaster of war fall with terrible force upon the innocent as upon the guilty. Without presuming to give a final answer, the direction an answer must take can be found in our Christian faith. God is maintaining a physical order within which it is possible to live in happiness and peace, but within which also fire burns, bombs destroy, and bodies starve and die. He is maintaining a social order in which we are meant to help one another, but within which the innocent suffer with and for the guilty. He is maintaining a moral order within which our goodness helps and our evil harms our neighbor. God's gift of human freedom, which makes possible the sin, error, and terrible folly of war, is also that which makes us morally responsible beings. We could not surrender it and remain human, and we would not surrender it if we could. Our task is to use it in obedience to his righteous will.

[3] This paragraph and several which appear later in this chapter are reprinted from my contribution to the symposium *"To Combine Our Efforts"—For Lasting Peace.* Used by permission of the Woman's Division of Christian Service of The Methodist Church, 150 Fifth Ave., New York 11, N.Y.

During the Second World War, this truth was expressed by the Calhoun Commission of the Federal Council of Churches in words that are worth preserving:

In this war, then, He is not neutral, and not helpless. He is maintaining invincibly an order that men cannot overthrow. . . . God is not a combatant, nor a neutral onlooker, nor a helpless victim. First of all, He is, in war as in peace, the Creator and Sovereign whose power sustains and governs, but does not annul, the activities of nature and of men.[4]

Third, *God alone is sovereign.* This is implied in the doctrines both of creation and of judgment. As was noted in the previous chapter, every State claims absolute sovereignty over its people. The Christian faith affirms that God alone is man's supreme Ruler, and in his will alone is man's final authority. This is why Christians have again and again felt impelled by conscience to defy their political rulers and to say with Peter, "We must obey God rather than men" (Acts 5:29).

If God alone is sovereign, this has a bearing on international co-operation. It means not only that "above all nations is humanity," [5] but that above all humanity is God. International order, first through the United Nations and eventually through a more inclusive world federation of nations, is the only sure road to peace. We are not apt to have more than an uneasy tension, with open hostilities held in abeyance, until some surrender of absolute sovereignty among competing national States is brought into being. This development in turn is not likely to occur until we have moved closer to an acknowledgment of common moral principles implicit in the spiritual insights of mankind.

Finally and supremely, *God is Redeemer and Father.* Neither creativity nor judgment nor sovereignty is the attribute of God by which we know him best. It is as redeeming love that he comes closest to us. This means that in his creation of the world with an invincible order he is never indifferent to human need; in his judgment he is never merely punitive; in his sovereignty he is never arbitrary or despotic. God

[4] *The Relation of the Church to the War in the Light of the Christian Faith,* p. 33. Report of a Commission of Christian Scholars Appointed by the Federal Council of the Churches of Christ in America, 1944.

[5] This inscription, carved over the entrance of Goldwin Smith Hall of Humanities at Cornell University, impressed me deeply as a student and has remained with me.

is seeking always to win individuals, societies, and nations to ways of righteousness, justice, good will, and peace.

If it is our faith that this is the way God rules his world, it has all-important consequences. Though it does not settle the pacifist issue, it does mean that all we do must be done in love and with supreme regard for the persons whom God loves. It means, furthermore, that in spite of our weakness and unwisdom, God can use in the making of peace any gift that is brought in love for the service of human need. He is working always, even in the darkest of human situations, through redemptive love, and in this he summons us to be his co-workers.

Taken seriously, this Christian judgment regarding God's nature and activity calls for a re-evaluation of widely prevalent opinion, and the holding of attitudes by Christians which are different from those commonly held by the secular world. Every soul that God has created, whatever his race or nation, his political or economic views, his class or culture, is precious in God's sight. Those whom we tend to dislike or to call enemies are, like ourselves, mixtures of good and evil, persons whom God loves. We are all made in God's image; we have all in some measure marred it. All are persons whom God sent his Son to save, and for whom Christ died.

This means that a very basic even though difficult distinction must be drawn. We must never identify evil systems, of which Communism is certainly one, with the Russian or Chinese people who live under this system. Some misguidedly support Communism; many acquiesce in it because they see no way to do otherwise. But all are still our brothers, for whom we ought to pray and toward whom we ought to feel pity rather than ill will. Many millions of Russians and many thousands of Chinese are Christians who pray to God and read the Bible as we do. Yet those who are atheists are still beloved of God, whose love is broad enough to take in all mankind. The New Testament gives no blueprint as to what to do about war, but it does not lack directives:

Love your enemies.—If your enemy is hungry, feed him.—Judge not, that you be not judged.—As you did it to one of the least of these my brethren, you did it to me.—And he [God] made from one every nation of men to live on all the face of the earth.—Do not be conformed to this world but be transformed by the renewal of your mind.—Do not be overcome by evil, but overcome evil with good.

Such passages as these, which are unquestionably in the spirit of Jesus, show us the direction in which our spirits and our deeds must move.

Holding in abeyance for the present the matter of decision regarding the pacifist issue, let us assume that thoughtful Christians will for the most part agree in what has been said thus far. On the basis of such Christian convictions, what can we agree upon further as to necessary steps to take for the conquest of war?

2. Points of convergence in Christian opinion

There are elements of very great importance, not only as to the theology of war and peace but as to analysis of the existing situation and procedures for acting within it, on which Christians can agree. Without necessarily reaching unanimity at every point, this consensus has been reached and stated again and again in pronouncements of the World Council of Churches, the Federal and National councils, and the various denominational bodies. Although only the historic peace churches—the Friends, Mennonites, and Church of the Brethren—are avowedly pacifist, there is a deep and thoughtful concern for peace among many groups, and the agreements far outweigh the differences. Let us enumerate some of them, with a look at their relevance to the task of peacemaking.

a) *The frightful character of modern war.* Opinions differ as to whether any war under present circumstances can be just; there is no disagreement as to the magnitude of potential destructiveness. The power of modern weapons to incinerate vast civilian populations with no available civil defense must now be reckoned with. A third world war would spell the doom of civilization, if not of total human existence, upon this planet. There is difference of opinion as to whether such a war is likely to be launched; there is no doubt among informed persons of its awful consequences if this occurs. War itself has therefore become the chief enemy to be overcome.

b) *The rejection of "preventive" war.* It is now generally agreed that to launch a war with the idea of a quick victory would be ghastly folly. Earlier in the cold war this was advocated by some, though never by the churches, as a way of seizing the advantage and ending the tensions between East and West. Virtually no one believes any longer that this would do more than to precipitate the carnage and destruction that all sane men dread and seek to avoid.

c) *No war of aggression can be justified.* There is, of course, great difficulty of interpretation at this point, for in the complexities of the international scene the line is not easy to draw between aggression and defense, and every country regards its own cause as just. Nevertheless, it is significant that the World Council of Churches at Evanston stated as the first of the constructive steps out of the present impasse the following:

We first of all call upon the nations to pledge that they will refrain from the threat or the use of hydrogen, atomic, and all other weapons of mass destruction as well as any other means of force against the territorial integrity or political independence of any state.[6]

A resolution was also adopted and widely communicated to both churches and governments calling for the "certain assurance that no country will engage in or support aggressive or subversive acts in other countries." [7]

d) *War is not inevitable.* This is very important, for a fatalistic belief that war is bound to occur breeds a defeatist attitude that militates against positive peace action. Furthermore, it is a reflection on the spiritual power for peace that God stands ready to impart through the gospel of reconciliation. Again the World Council spoke forcefully at this point:

Because of their belief in this gospel of reconciliation and their experience of its power, Christians can never accept, as the only kind of existence open to nations, a state of perpetual tension leading to "inevitable" war. On the contrary, it is the Christian conviction that war is not inevitable, because God wills peace.[8]

Theology is reinforced by history at this point. The Dun Commission of Christian scholars in 1950 in their report on *The Christian Con-*

---

[6] *The Evanston Report*, Sec. IV, 15, p. 133. Used by permission of Harper & Bros.
[7] *Ibid.*, p. 146.
[8] *Ibid.*, Sec. IV, 20, p. 134.

science and Weapons of Mass Destruction stated that "to accept general war as inevitable is to treat ourselves as helpless objects carried by a fated tide of events rather than as responsible men," and went on to say, "One reason why fascism and naziism gained their dread power over great nations was because otherwise decent people bowed before what they regarded as 'inevitable' and allowed a 'wave of the future' to inundate them." [9]

e) *War itself cannot be creative or curative.* Caution is needed at this point, for to affirm this is not to say that no war has ever been just, or that no good has ever come out of any war. There is, of course, wide disagreement on these issues, some holding that war is sometimes necessary for the restraint of evil and the winning of time for positive steps toward peace, others holding that war itself erects such barriers to these steps that it is completely futile as well as unchristian. The point, rather, is that any positive, creative, curative processes for the improvement of mankind must rest on other grounds.

There is large agreement among Christian leaders, and increasingly among statesmen, that if war is either to be averted or made to serve any good purpose, constructive service to human need must be our chief reliance. Without moral and spiritual power, military power may restrain aggression, but it cannot build international order. This conviction actuates the effort to remove poverty, hunger, ignorance, and disease by economic aid. It also undergirds negotiation looking toward disarmament and the effort to alleviate world tensions by conference rather than the threat or the use of military force. "Without the development of peaceful alternatives, collective military effort may win a temporary victory, only to plunge the victors into new conflict.[10]

f) *International co-operation through the United Nations must be supported.* Christians generally regard the U.N. as our best political hope of peace and an indispensable organ of law and order among the nations, though none would say that it has functioned perfectly. There

[9] P. 16. Sponsored by the Federal Council of the Churches of Christ in America.

[10] *Christian Faith and International Responsibility*, p. 16. Report of the Fourth National Study Conference on the Churches and World Order, Cleveland, Ohio, 1953. Published for the Department of International Justice and Goodwill by the Department of Publication and Distribution of the National Council of Churches. Used with permission.

are some few who regard international organization as being opposed to national interest, and some pacifists are unable to sanction the U.N.'s use of military force for collective security. Nevertheless, there is a wide consensus among Christian leaders that the formation of the U.N. was a long step in advance toward international order, that in spite of difficulties it has functioned helpfully along both political and social lines, and that it merits the active moral support of peace-minded and world-minded citizens.

The U.N. has provided a world forum for the discussion of controversial issues and by its mediation has almost certainly averted wars. By its program of technical assistance, World Health Organization, Food and Agriculture Organization, UNESCO, various relief agencies, and care of refugees it has proved both a symbol and a channel of international co-operation. In its Universal Declaration of Human Rights it has given the world its first considered and inclusive statement of the rights of man.

Collective security involves much more than the use of military measures, such as were invoked in the conflict in Korea. The Fourth National Study Conference on the Churches and World Order had this to say about it:

We now live in the age of the hydrogen bomb. Therefore, we must explore every possible means of ensuring collective security, apart from the use of military power.

We urge our government, therefore, to press for the largest practicable degree of disarmament through the UN, as we seek the goal of universal enforceable disarmament. We urge also that the functions of the UN in developing moral judgment as to conditions causing tensions and threatening war be magnified. We ask our own government to take the lead in emphasizing all those activities of the UN which aim at the substitution of good offices, mediation, conciliation, arbitration and the counsel of the world community for armed force as a means of settling disputes.[11]

One of the hopeful factors in the present scene is that American Christians, in general, have come to see that our destiny, both politically and morally, is bound up with that of the rest of the world. Isolationism is not past, but waning. It was only a little over a half century ago, in

[11] *Ibid.*

1899, that the first Hague Peace Conference was held. Since then there has occurred the formation, not only of the U.N., but also of more than a thousand international organizations, some unofficial, some intergovernmental. Future historians may regard the twentieth century not only as the atomic age and the technological era, but also as the first great period of international co-operation.

g) *The armaments race must be curtailed.* At this point sharp divergences appear, for while church bodies have repeatedly opposed universal military training, some Christians favor it, and while many deplore the size of our military budget as compared with other peacetime services, there are those who would think it folly to lessen it. Christian opinion converges, however, with the best political thought in the desire to discover processes of securing universal enforceable disarmament. This cannot be brought about simply by new pacts without mutual trust and without safeguards for inspection and control. Yet the terrific economic drain of military expenditures, pre-empting about three fourths of all money paid for taxes, the psychological strains of conscription of youth for military service, and the perils to democracy of a militarized public mind require unremitting effort to lift the armaments burden.

On this point also the World Council of Churches has spoken. In the resolutions adopted by the Evanston Assembly there is stated as one of the "two conditions of crucial importance which must be met, if catastrophe is to be averted": "The prohibition of all weapons of mass destruction; including atomic and hydrogen bombs, with provision for international inspection and control, such as would safeguard the security of all nations, together with the drastic reduction of all other armaments." [12]

h) *The living standards of underprivileged peoples must be lifted.* Economic factors are not the only causes of war, but they are large contributors. In the present crisis, the hungry peoples of the Orient, long acquiescent in poverty and disease because they saw no escape, are filled with a new hope, and the Communists are feeding these hopes. On the

[12] *The Evanston Report,* p. 146. The other of the two conditions mentioned is the renunciation of aggressive war.

basis of simple expediency, economic aid is a better preventive of war than atomic or hydrogen bombs. If it is not given in amounts more nearly comparable with our vast military expenditures, Communism will win the allegiance of the now neutral Asiatic nations.

America's loss of prestige and friendship in the Orient is a matter of grave concern. In part this is due to false propaganda, but it is also the result of contrast between America's fabulous opulence and the poverty of chronically hungry peoples. Demonstration of willingness to share is realistic political strategy.

Yet the Christian cannot be actuated by expediency alone. It is because these persons are *persons*, precious to God and in need of help, that we are called by the obligations of neighbor love to share what God has blessed us with.

This sharing must be done through many channels. The giving of technical assistance, through both the U.S. Point Four Program and the United Nations, has values out of all proportion to the amount of funds thus far appropriated. Church bodies have again and again endorsed such effort and summoned their people to support it. Its inauguration is one of the most significant developments of our time as a channel of service, as a means of creating friendship, and as a foundation of peace.

Relief of suffering needs also to be undertaken through nongovernmental channels. In such effort the churches are in their native province. Much has been done, and much more needs to be done, to care for the victims of war and other forms of disaster, for millions of refugees, and for those who have never known comfort or material sufficiency. Americans on the whole are a generous people, and in the aggregate have given many millions of dollars and many tons of food and clothing to those in need. This relief has included ministry to former enemies, as to Germany after both the First and Second World wars. What has been done needs greatly to be extended, both as a ministry of helpfulness to human beings and as one of the surest bulwarks against Communism and the outbreak of war.

i) *Racial injustices and tensions must be eliminated.* Unfortunately we cannot say that the churches are themselves free of racial tension and discrimination. The opposite is altogether too evident. Nevertheless, in principle race prejudice is seldom defended by Christians, and there is a growing ferment in the Church to abolish in practice what is condemned in principle.

That racial equality has a direct bearing on world peace is evident to anyone who views the world scene as a whole, though it is often forgotten in the local setting. Communism's strategy is to persuade the colored peoples of the Orient that along with the economic exploitation of so-called "Western imperialism" there has been race discrimination of the most evil sort. Communism, it is claimed, will liberate the colored of the earth from bondage and set them on an equality with the now dominant white groups. Both the charges and the claims are exaggerated, but there is enough truth in both to make of the race situation a very powerful appeal.

An immediate next step toward both peace and justice is to correct the racial inequalities that exist in America and around the world. In part this can be done by law. Basically it must be done by changes in attitudes, and in the effecting of such changes Christians have a vital role to play.

j) Communism must be curbed and civil liberties preserved. I place the two together because they must be kept together, or the correction of one evil will precipitate the other.

There is no danger of any general acceptance of Communism in the United States, or by many Christians elsewhere who are free to choose. Its economic and political philosophy is distasteful, its atheistic materialism, cruelty, deceitfulness, and disregard of human personality revolting. There is, however, danger of Communist infiltration by subtle means. This must be guarded against both by informed citizens who detect the signs and refuse to be duped and by government agencies such as the F.B.I. that are skilled in detecting illicit practices.

The double jeopardy in which we are placed is the danger that in the attempt to preserve democracy, democracy may be lost. This happens when freedom of thought, speech, and expression of honest conviction are stifled under charges of subversion. Both by the methods used in some Congressional committees and through public hysteria, accusation, and spread of evil rumors, this has happened to an appalling degree. Such censorship has tended to curtail the freedom to teach in the public schools and universities and to stifle prophetic utterance in pulpits. It is one of the gravest dangers of our time affecting both security and peace, for when a people have become acquiescent through fear, they are the more easily swayed by dictators, as Germany discovered to her undoing.

Here as in other points noted, the churches in practice have not always been wise or courageous. Yet in principle, there has been a clearer discernment of the need to preserve civil liberties than has been found in most of the structures of society. Loyalty to conscience and the duty before God to discern and speak the truth have not been abrogated. By insisting on the right of conscientious dissent, the churches have helped to preserve our democratic freedoms. This is no small asset in laying the foundations of peace.

In these ten areas Christians, even without complete unanimity, have been able to a high degree to work together. These convictions give no complete formula for the making and preserving of peace, but as they are pursued earnestly, both security and justice are enhanced. Christians who believe in procedures based upon them have done much to stabilize our world. These same steps must be carried much further, and they can be advanced to the degree that Christian citizens are informed and motivated to action. It is one of the blessings of democracy that this is so, for in part these procedures depend on individual attitudes, and in other matters on political action in which representatives in government must eventually be responsive to the people's demands. So let no Christian anywhere say that there is nothing he can do!

3. Pacifism and nonpacifism

We come now to the crucial issue that divides Christians into two groups of differing judgment. Fortunately, this division is less accented and less acrimonious than was formerly the case, but its presence is inescapable. Only the person who drifts along with prevailing opinion— and such drifting tends of itself to put one into the nonpacifist majority —can escape decision when he is faced concretely with the alternatives of military service and conscientious objection to war. Others may manage to "sit on the fence," but every Christian ought thoughtfully to decide where he stands, and why.

I shall not attempt here to decide the issue for anyone, but to present

211

the considerations that bear upon each side. That there are powerful, and in some measure true, considerations on each side is what makes the issue so difficult. It is a natural impulse to want to find an answer that can be said to be *the* Christian answer. This is not possible in any absolute sense. One can and ought to find what is the Christian answer for himself, but just because there is so much of vital importance that points in either direction, he has no right superficially or dogmatically to impose it on another.

Let us begin by clearing away some false approaches. In the first place, there ought to be no name calling or imputing of bad motives to conscientious fellow Christians. To charge a pacifist with lack of patriotism or with cowardice, or to call a nonpacifist Christian a militarist or a warmonger, accomplishes nothing except to reveal one's ignorance and arouse bad feeling.

The issue cannot be settled simply on the basis of accepting or rejecting coercive force. Every State must have coercive power of law enforcement and the protection of its citizens from evildoers. Although there are a few "Tolstoyan" pacifists who view all such use of force as negating the Christian ethic, this is not typical Christian pacifism. Most pacifists recognize the legitimate functions of the police and of civil law enforcement when these are administered justly. It is a common caricature of pacifism to ask the question, "Would you stand aside and let gangsters murder your wife?"

Nor is the matter to be settled on the basis of the presence or absence of compromise. To be sure, a crucial decision must be made as to the type of compromise one accepts and the level on which one accepts it. Yet it is self-deceptive to assume that compromise can be avoided. Simply by living as a citizen of a State that maintains gigantic armaments, to say nothing of paying taxes to that State, one makes concessions to the use of military force.

Neither is the question basically a matter of resistance to evil. *Modes* of resistance are central to the issue. Yet every pacifist who seeks to be actuated by the spirit of Jesus knows that evil must be resisted, even as Jesus resisted it in his total ministry. Citation of the passage, "Do not resist one who is evil. But if any one strikes you on the right cheek, turn to him the other also" (Matt. 5:39), is not irrelevant, and neither is it definitive. This passage was undoubtedly spoken with reference to

212

personal relations rather than national conflict, but in its context the emphasis on *agape* love is clear. Because Jesus did resist evil, not by the sword but by deeds of love and mercy, the Christian pacifist believes that the followers of Jesus are called to resistance by the same methods.

Again, acknowledgment of the reality and heinousness of human sin is not a basic point of division. Pacifists are sometimes charged with being naïve at this point, and too trustful of human nature. However, pacifists as well as others know that "man's a tough rascal," [13] and believe that all the potential evil of the human spirit comes to expression in the barbarous cruelty and deceptiveness of war. On the other hand, fair-minded Christians in either camp are willing to recognize the heights of courage, dignity, and sacrifice to which the human spirit can rise.

If the crux of the difference does not lie in coercive force, or compromise, or resistance to evil, or the actuality of human sin, where does it lie? The points of divergence lie chiefly in differing views of the relations of love and justice, of the need of choosing the lesser of two evils, and of the relation of the State to the will of God in human society. At none of these points is there an absolute difference, but there is a difference in emphasis which tips the scale of decision to one side or the other.

With reference to the relations of love and justice, the nonpacifist is more likely than the pacifist to draw a line of division between them and make love the supreme obligation of the Christian in personal relations, justice the supreme function of the State. This we noted is what Brunner does and Reinhold Niebuhr tends to do, and their nonpacifist views are a consistent derivative. To the degree that one believes the State exists, not to make men love one another or even to express the neighbor love of its citizens, but to preserve justice and to maintain for its citizens order and security, one is likely to believe that in some circumstances this can be done only through military force and at the risk of war.

Says Brunner:

---

[13] Quoted from the great liberal theologian Adolf Harnack by his son Ernst von Harnack as the latter was facing death for resisting Nazi tyranny. In *Dying We Live*, eds. Helmut Gollwitzer, Reinhold Schneider, and Käthe Kuhn (New York: Pantheon Books, Inc., 1956), p. 166.

The distinction between justice and love is clear. Love means going out to others, justice means the delimitation of spheres of power, and the protection of these boundaries. Love is concrete and personal, non-deliberate, non-general. Justice, on the other hand, is general, lawful, deliberate, impersonal and objective, abstract and rational.

.   .   .   .

The possibility of imposing law by force is based upon the superior power of the State. . . . In the last resort, owing to the fact that there must never be any doubt about its absolute character, this power is the power to kill.[14]

This power to kill, the nonpacifist believes, applies not only to the domestic jurisdiction of the State but to the citizens of other States which affront the principles of justice or endanger the security of those for whom justice requires protection. This is the strongest of the non-pacifist arguments, and very persuasive to many minds.

The pacifist puts the primary stress on love, but does not ordinarily make this disjunction between love and justice. He holds that love, not in the intimate sense of interpersonal relations, but as good will, eagerness to serve, concern for the welfare of persons as persons, is a necessary ingredient of justice. Without it, justice turns into vindictiveness or retribution, or at best into an impersonal structure of power which loses sight of the human values for which such power ought to be exercised. Both in the domestic and in the world scene, the pacifist Christian believes that only the power of love and the type of justice actuated by it is either Christian or effective for the restraint of evil. In view of the evils that always accompany and follow in the wake of war he does not lack historical evidence to justify his position. The bonds of friendship cemented by relief of suffering and other forms of service speak as loudly as does the negative evidence for the political realism of his position.

There is a type of pragmatic pacifism which rests its case chiefly on the folly of war and the empirical values of international friendship. This, however, is less likely to be resolute under strain than that which admits freely that love does not always "work," but holds that it is right and Christian regardless of the outcome. A pacifist of the latter type, if he is sincere, does not withdraw from conflict but gives himself to the

[14] From *The Divine Imperative* by Emil Brunner, Copyright, 1947, by W. L. Jenkins. The Westminster Press. Used by permission.

limit of his power in deeds of love and ministry to human need. The relief work of the Quakers and Church of the Brethren is an outstanding example, but such effort is found outside of the historic peace churches wherever there are pacifists of deep conviction.

The argument from the lesser of two evils rests usually on a comparison of the relative values of war and of tyranny. Neither war nor tyranny is viewed as good. Both are seen as terribly destructive of human values. War, however, can be viewed as relatively temporary, while tyranny may precipitate long-range bondage and the suppression of those freedoms basic to human dignity and welfare. Faced by these grim alternatives, the nonpacifist believes that less is to be lost by war, and hopes that by military strength and the threat of its use the final dread decision to use it can be forestalled.

The pacifist answer is not to say simply that tyranny is better than war, though some pacifists do believe that to live under Communism is less of an affront to human dignity and less of a lien on the future than to reduce a nation to a shambles in the attempt to "liberate" it, as was done in Korea. The turn the answer more cogently takes is to deny that war and tyranny exhaust the possibilities. Granting that while nations glare at each other in hostility and suspicion the possibilities are limited, the pacifist believes that there are constructive channels of negotiation, friendly intercourse, and service that could both reduce the danger of war and alleviate the evils of tyranny. No discerning Christian pacifist sanctions Communism or its methods, but he believes there are better ways of dealing with it than imitating its methods or courting mutual destruction.

As to the relation of duty to the State and to the will of God, this is the crux of the problem. But at this point great caution is needed, or it will be falsely assumed that the nonpacifist puts the State first and the pacifist exalts God above the State. This may indeed happen, and often does where the call of the State is viewed as inexorable and paramount to all else. Nevertheless, conscientious Christian citizens of both views acknowledge the duty of patriotic loyalty to the State, yet find in God their supreme object of loyalty and devotion.

The difference lies mainly in the way in which it is believed that God works through the State for the enactment of his will and the advancement of his kingdom. The nonpacifist is more likely than the pacifist to believe that God participates in human conflict, using stern measures and even if necessary the awful destructiveness of war, to protect a State against its enemies and to enable a State to protect the helpless against aggression. He believes that in spite of the evil present in every war, there are just wars that ought to be waged and supported because God demands it. The State to him then becomes the instrument of divine justice.

The pacifist Christian does not deny the presence of God in human history or even in the midst of conflict. Nor does he deny that there is often more justice on one side of the conflict than on the other. He desires as eagerly as any to see aggression halted, the helpless protected, and justice established. Nevertheless, he believes that only by healing and building for the increase of justice and human good, and not by destruction, can the State be the instrument of God. He is therefore more apt than the nonpacifist to feel a sharp disparity between the State's recourse to military power and the love commandment. The word of Jesus, "Love your enemies and pray for those who persecute you" (Matt. 5:44), is not the sole prerogative of either, but to the pacifist it makes participation in war an act of disobedience to the call of God.

The dilemma of the nonpacifist Christian is how to continue to love one's enemies and those of his nation even while he seeks to destroy their lives, property, and power. The dilemma of the pacifist is how to act for constructive building while aggression and tyranny are rampant and those about him believe that military force is the only mode of restraint. It is not strange that some of each opinion lose sight of their high goals, and succumb to hate, cynicism, or passivity. But let us rejoice that enough do not to keep these high goals before us.

So here the matter rests. "Faced by the dilemma of participation in war, he [the individual Christian] must decide prayerfully before God what is to be his course of action in relation thereto." [15] There is no other way.

---

[15] Methodist *Discipline*, 1956, ¶ 2024.

XII. Christian Ethics and Culture

WE COME NOW in this concluding chapter to some observations about the relations of the Christian ethic to our total environing society. Had our approach been essentially empirical rather than theological and biblical, this chapter should have stood first in the book. However, it may help to draw together various threads, as well as to state some things not heretofore discussed, if we consider this theme last.

The procedure will be first to define the term, for culture is an unusually slippery and ambiguous term, and to outline the nature of the problems. Then we must look, as we have done in other chapters, at the biblical and theological foundations for their solution. The chapter will conclude with a look at some of the concrete contemporary issues involved in the fields of science, art, and education.

1. What is culture?

The word "culture" has two meanings, not sharply separated but not identical, and we shall have to consider both of them. Both present difficulties and opportunities for the Christian approach to life.

In the broader meaning of the term, culture is synonymous with civilization. Every people has its culture, whether primitive or advanced, and this culture is discerned in the folkways and moral standards, forms of family life, economic enterprises, laws and modes of dealing with lawbreakers, forms of recreation, religion, art, education, science, and philosophy that constitute the social aspects of human existence as contrasted with the bare biological fact of living.

There is, however, a narrower use of the term which is related to but not identical with this inclusive meaning. In ordinary speech, who is a cultured person? By what canons does one judge another to be un-

217

cultured? Superficially but with widespread potency, one's degree of culture is judged by his manners and conformity to correct social usage, good taste in dress and appearance, cleanliness and freedom from offensive odors or habits, ability to converse agreeably and to fit smoothly into any social situation. If a person is cultured, he is not a boor! On a deeper level, one's degree of culture is to be judged by the extent of his education, the breadth of his interests, and his knowledge and appreciation of such "cultural" pursuits as good art, literature, and music.

Culture in this second sense has many manifestations, but all converge to constitute the secularism of the modern world. Social conformity plays a major part in it, even though at the point of education and the arts the right of individual differentiation is recognized. Culture in this more limited sense, as defined by the attributes of a cultured person, is an important formative factor in the total culture of a people but cannot be identified with it. For example, the prophet Amos was an uncultured person by the standards of either his time or ours, yet an important contributor to Hebrew culture. Abraham Lincoln is lauded in the American tradition because from such a lowly and uncultured background he rose to such heights of greatness.

In whichever sense the word "culture" is used, it is a distinctly *human* phenomenon. There is nothing like it in the instinctual organization of the anthill or beehive or in the gregarious impulses of animal life. Though its roots may indeed be traced to defensive, acquisitive, or reproductive traits which the human shares with the subhuman world, its manifestations are very different. Only men form civilizations, and only men insist on adaptation to the patterns of the cultural community.

It is always a *social* phenomenon. This is self-evident from the definitions given. Individuals may conform to or reject the prevailing social patterns, and thereby shape the direction a culture takes. But this never happens except in response to a social situation.

It is, furthermore, always in some measure a *spiritual* phenomenon. This does not mean that it is always a direct outgrowth of religion, though religions are always to be found in interplay with culture. Rather, every culture is the product of the human spirit, as the spirit of man wrestles with its total environment and seeks to work out a satisfactory adjustment to the material world, to other men, and to such invisible powers as are believed to control its destiny.

218

It is always rooted in a *concern for values*. That is, every culture pre-supposes in some sense a "kingdom of ends." These ends may be high or low by other standards, but to the people who live within a given culture, prize it and seek to preserve and exalt it, they are always high. There may be room for differences of individual opinion, as democracy preserves the right of minority dissent, but no culture can endure without general support by its people of the values central to it. This is why patriotism and group loyalty, though subject to perversion, not only are but ought to be regarded as virtues of great worth.

Is culture an "order of creation"? The existence of culture as a whole may be so regarded. The framework within which cultures develop is God-given, as are the foundations of family, economic, and national life which constitute so large a part of any civilization. It is apparently the will of God that men live together in civilized societies. Yet this is far from saying that any particular society or cultural group is as God would have it, or wholly the product of divine activity. The particular form a culture takes is the product of many forces, in which geographical location, economic resources, historical contingency, the pull of tradition, and voluntary human effort all play a part. This fact, with the resulting intermixtures of good and evil, is clearly illustrated by differing attitudes toward racial segregation in the North and South of the United States, or the presence of nontheological social factors in the creation of the various denominations of the Christian Church.

A culture, even one of long duration, is modifiable by human effort under the impact of a new ideology—witness the radical transformation of China under Communist influence or the other revolutionary changes now taking place in the Orient from an emergent nationalism. This malleability is what makes both advance and decline in civilizations possible. Yet there is always a "raw material" of culture which no amount of human effort can erase. The eternal human problem, as man seeks to change his status and that of his group, is how to deal with the intransigence of nature and the inviolability of the divine order in that interlocking structure of natural, human, and divine forces which constitutes a given culture.

The Christian faith must come to terms with culture in both the senses in which I have defined it, and with full regard for all these considerations as to the nature of culture. Because there is so much in

Western civilization that is good,[1] and that can be and ought to be made better, it would be fatal to withdraw in isolation from it or condemn it as wholly evil. Nevertheless, the perennial problem of the Christian is how to be a Christian within "the world," that is, within one's total environing society. When this surrounding culture is at the same time "worldly"—cultured in the narrower sense, demanding conformity at the peril of loss of social status—the problem is intensified. The American Christian of today lives in a nominally Christian but largely worldly culture. What shall he do with it?

2. Biblical and theological foundations

The Bible as a whole is the record of man's effort to conform to, and to transform, his culture under the impact of spiritual insights conceived to be God-given. That these were in so large measure actually God-inspired is what gives the Bible its "holy" character as the bearer of universal and timeless truth. Yet at every point it must be read in reference to the culture within which it emerged, so that its "situation-conditioned" and temporal elements may be seen in their true perspective. To disregard this surrounding culture is to nullify much of the Bible's spiritual meaning by reading into it what is not there but is imputed to it from the thought patterns of a different day.

We cannot at this point go into the whole matter of the relation of the Bible to its cultural setting. This was attempted in its main elements in Chapters II, III, and IV. But a further word is needed as to the relations of Jesus both to his own culture and to culture in general.

It has often been charged that by focusing attention away from "the world" to God, the kingdom of heaven, and eternal life, Jesus introduced an ascetic and otherworldly element that nullifies human culture. The Jewish scholar Joseph Klausner, for example, holds that the Pharisees and Sadducees were justified in their attacks on Jesus because he imperiled Jewish culture at its foundations, and that by ignoring everything that belongs to wholesome social life he undercut the work of centuries.[2] Others within the Christian tradition have felt con-

[1] For a survey of these elements see my The Modern Rival of Christian Faith, ch. 6, which is entitled "What Is Right with Modern Life?"
[2] Jesus of Nazareth (New York: The Macmillan Co., 1929), pp. 369-76.

siderable uneasiness lest the words of Jesus about nonresistance imperil the civil power of the State, or his words about having no anxiety for food or drink or other material possessions curtail an economic motivation essential to society. Sometimes in direct attack, as in the Roman persecutions of early centuries and the Nazi and Communist movements of our time, sometimes through sneers and the opposition of hostile public opinion, Christianity has had to defend itself against those who believed the false or utopian ideas of its founder to be dangerous. This opposition has been most overtly urged on political but often on intellectual grounds, and Schleiermacher's defense of Christian faith against its "cultured despisers" is a procedure that has again and again proved necessary.[3]

This struggle to co-ordinate Christian faith with culture is not temporary but has lasted through twenty centuries of Christian history. The fullest and most accurate analysis of it is found in H. Richard Niebuhr's *Christ and Culture*, which any reader will do well to consult. There he points out that the answers given have taken five main directions: Christ in opposition to culture, Christ in accommodation to culture, Christ as transcending culture but with some elements of synthesis, Christ in paradoxical relation to culture, and Christ as the transformer of culture. He also says wisely that "when one returns from the hypothetical scheme to the rich complexity of individual events, it is evident at once that no person or group ever conforms completely to a type." [4] I shall attempt to outline a view which follows most closely the third and fifth of these types, but adopts none of them in entirety.

It is true that Jesus said little about "the world" except to warn against letting its claims usurp the place of first loyalty to God, and had almost nothing to say about particular features of contemporary Jewish or Roman culture. Nevertheless, the message of Jesus has vital relevance, in elements which have been pointed out in all the preceding chapters. It bears upon the world to challenge culture at some points, to encourage it at others, to transform it at many. This is so for these reasons:

In the first place, Jesus' supreme concern was with persons, not in any humanistic sense of man's self-sufficiency, but because persons are

[3] *Addresses on Religion to Its Cultured Despisers.*
[4] P. 43.

221

of supreme worth as the recipients of God's love. Moreover, he cared about persons in their total bodily-spiritual unity, and with their life on earth as well as in heaven. Both his deeds of healing and his words repeatedly attest this fact. Whatever impulse his followers have had to labor for the amelioration of human life in ministering to the sick, the weak and helpless, the ignorant, the poverty-stricken, the imprisoned by any kind of chains, owes its primary origin to the love of God for persons as this was manifest in Jesus.

Cultures are of many types, and some have much and others little concern for the individual person. Yet as we noted, every culture is a human, social, and spiritual thing in which the values precious to the persons comprising it are exalted. Those cultures which approximate the view of Jesus as to the worth of every person are high cultures, democratic in political organization, peace-minded in international outlook, altruistic toward those in need, person-centered in education and a wide range of social services. These are the goals of a Christian civilization, imperfectly realized, to be sure, in any society but sufficiently manifest in Europe and America to make it evident that a Christian democracy is not merely a utopian dream.

Second, Jesus called his followers to faith, hope, and love. This particular conjunction of terms is Paul's, but what they signify abounds everywhere in the message of Jesus. And these are very important foundations for the stabilization or the progress of any culture. With faith in God people can endure dark days, even the jeopardy of their nation or personal martyrdom, and know that all is not lost and their cause is not in vain. With hope for the future, not in any illusory "progress of mankind onward and upward forever," but in the confidence that the issues for time and eternity are in the hands of God, remarkable staying power is generated even in the midst of what appears to be social retrogression. With love as a basic conviction, not even the awful carnage of war can wholly erase human sensitivity, and foundations remain for building in love beyond it. Every age has had need of these qualities, but ours more than most has cried out for them as indispensable. "In God we trust" has taken on new relevance in the darkness of our times.

Third, Jesus called his followers to challenge evil and to transform the world. It is impossible to say precisely what Western civilization would

222

have been like without the influence of Jesus, but it most certainly would have taken a very different course. Few would question the judgment of H. G. Wells, "His is easily the dominant figure of history. . . . A historian . . . without any theological bias whatever, should find that he simply cannot portray the progress of humanity honestly without giving a foremost place to a penniless teacher from Nazareth." [5]

Cultures, even with all their values which their people do well to prize, need to be challenged and transformed through the influence of Jesus as this is mediated through his followers in every age. More than once this has happened through the work of a devoted and persistent minority when the Church as a whole, enmeshed as a social institution in its surrounding culture, lagged behind. This happened with reference to the abolition of human slavery, and it is happening now in regard to race discrimination and war. Often this comes about in conjunction with other agencies, as in the factory legislation which has made obsolete the twelve-hour day and the seven-day week,[6] established minimum wage levels, and eliminated the grosser forms of economic exploitation.

New evils emerge, and these too must be challenged with wisdom and patience. New forms of work, of recreation, and of social organization bring both opportunities and perils to the human spirit. Both intelligence and persistence are required to cope with these problems, and the use of the best types of secular knowledge in a Christian framework, as in the growing convergence of Christian faith with psychotherapy in pastoral counseling. Christians in many matters must act with others outside the Christian fellowship. Where political action is required, it is not often that Christians alone bring it to pass. Yet Christians who keep witnessing to their convictions and thereby molding opinion contribute vitally to the fashioning of a better society.

In view of these facts, it cannot justly be said that either the message of Jesus or the Christian ethic derived primarily from Jesus is irrelevant to culture. In fact, nothing else is so relevant to the preservation and growth of right social attitudes, and from these attitudes the establishment of the "good society."

[5] Bruce Barton, "H. G. Wells Picks Out the Six Greatest Men in History," *The American Magazine*, July, 1922.
[6] When the Methodist Social Creed was revised in 1956, it deleted, as a vestige of an earlier day now obsolete, the words: "We stand for all workers' having at least one day of rest in seven."

3. Science, art, and education

At the beginning of this chapter I defined culture first as synonymous with civilization, and then in a narrower context. What has been said so far applies chiefly to its broader meaning.

Previous chapters in the book have dealt with the relations of Christian ethics to the culture of our times in reference to family life, economic relations, race relations, political structures, and the problems of war and peace in the international scene. These issues cover a large part of the terrain of culture in the inclusive meaning of the term. Certain other issues, however, need to be looked at both to round out this picture and to point up some special aspects of culture in the narrower connotation.

It is not necessary to say much about culture in the sense of "polish" or good manners, except that this is an important asset to Christian character and a dangerous substitute for it. Nobody ought to suppose that conformity to the accepted canons of good taste is inconsequential, for disregard of such niceties limits seriously one's acceptability to others and hence the persuasiveness of one's witness. But neither ought one to suppose that suavity and a superficial politeness are all that is needed. True politeness comes from the heart, in sensitivity to the feelings of others and adaptability to their need. The more vital one's own Christian experience and love of people, the more naturally will he reach out to them with a tact and gentleness no superficial good breeding can generate. No veneer of soft and pleasing words can ever take the place of Christian depth of character.

The major issues with regard to the cultured person are at a higher level, and are epitomized in his attitudes toward science, art, and education. At each of these we must look briefly as the book is brought to a close.

a) *Science.* It is most unfortunate, though not surprising, that there has been such a long battle between science and the Christian faith. It is unfortunate because the exponents of each have had to expend energy needed for other things in defending their position against the assaults of the opposing group. In this process neither has lost the battle, as is evident from the vigor of both at the present time. Nevertheless, at specific points such as the time and manner of creation and the expectancy of divine intervention in an established order, the defenders of traditional Christian belief have had to make more adjustments than have the exponents of the scientific spirit. This is not to say that science has remained unchanged—it obviously has not—but only that its course has been affected less by Christian belief than the reverse.

This is natural, and not to be deplored if these two great interests of the human spirit are kept in proper co-ordination. Both are modes of the pursuit of truth about one world, God's world, and therefore to the degree that their affirmations are true, they cannot contradict each other. Science, however, is a partial, objective attempt to discover facts about the empirical aspects of existence; Christian faith is an inclusive, committed approach to the totality of life's meaning as this comes to us through the revelation of God in Jesus Christ. The modifications in Christian belief above referred to in no sense discredit this revelation; they are modifications only in man's interpretation of it, and in particular, they arise from new ways of looking at the Bible as this is seen in its historical, prescientific setting. Though science has reached phenomenal heights in our time, it has at no point invalidated anything basic to Christian faith, and at no time in human history has the revelation of God in Christ shone upon the human scene with greater clarity and power. There have been more obviously religious eras, as in the medieval "age of faith" or the periods of the great revivals under Jonathan Edwards or Dwight L. Moody; it is doubtful that there has ever been a period of such general high Christian intelligence or deep commitment to Christian social ethics as in our own time.

This can be said in spite of the fact that it must also be said that secularism is a very widespread phenomenon of our culture, and secularism means conformity to the world, the organization of life as if God did not exist. How, then, shall we sort out the strands with reference to science and the Christian faith?

Science is the pursuit of truth in any particular field of observable reality, and the attempt to discover facts and formulate the laws of structure and behavior within this area. This pursuit, when an adjective is needed, is designated as pure science or descriptive science. There is, however, another use of the term to cover the application of scientific discovery to the satisfaction of human wants. This is applied science, with a meeting point in the research laboratories of most of the great industries. Applied science is sometimes called technics, but since it covers also a vast range of studies affecting human life, as in nutrititon and dietetics, medicine and surgery, psychiatry, pedagogy, geriatrics, social casework, penology, and the like, it is hardly accurate to classify all of these under the heading of technology. Whatever terminology is used, science cannot be fruitfully discussed unless we know whether we are talking about the quest for knowledge in objective detachment from personal interest, or an attempt to make hydrogen bombs, bigger and better automobiles, wonder drugs, or a million gadgets because men desire them to satisfy some real or fancied need.

Both types of science have their relations to Christian faith within our culture, but these are not the same relations.

Science as the quest for knowledge, for reasons suggested above, cannot contradict the Christian faith if it keeps to its own field of inquiry about the visible, tangible, experienced world. What it does is simply to shed new light upon the world created by God, and upon the orderly processes by which God works within his world. The evidence for biological evolution can contradict belief in a six-day creation, but not in God the Creator; astronomy can put an end to belief in a heaven "up in the sky," but not to eternal life; knowledge of the regularities of nature can recast interpretation of some of the biblical miracles, but it cannot eliminate belief in divine Providence or discredit grateful reverence before God's wonderful works.

It is only when descriptive science grows arrogant, and, not content with describing what lies within its province, makes naturalistic pronouncements which eliminate or belittle God and the human spirit, that Christian faith is affronted. When science claims that its methods and its knowledge are the only methods and knowledge to be trusted, it becomes not science but "scientism." Scientism and its usual accompaniment, scientific humanism, are serious rivals of Christian faith in the modern world. This point of view flourishes on many university campuses, and not infrequently sucks the vigor out of Christian experience by undercutting its foundations. Where this happens, the culture accompanying it may be kindly, law-abiding, and even altruistic, but it is not Christian culture.

It is at the point of the applied sciences that the more widespread and the more formidable attack on Christian ethics and culture can be found.

This is true in spite of the fact that the products of applied science have been instruments of great good in physical healing, improvement of living conditions, and social services of many types, in which the Christian believes that it is the will of God for persons to be helped. Furthermore, from the invention of the printing press to the wide use of radio and television, from sailing schooner to ever-faster airplanes, the applied sciences have been essential instruments in the spread of Christian witness. Some things viewed formerly as luxuries, such as telephones, automobiles, electric lighting, and refrigeration, are now so common in the Western world as to seem virtually necessities, and none would wish to do without them.

Yet, it is just at this point that idolatry becomes dominant in our culture. Partly because of a real need for what technology supplies, more because of artificial wants aroused through a constant, competitive barrage of advertising, modern man's attention is inevitably focused on the things science produces and money can buy. To live simply, unconcerned for the "cares of the world and the delight in riches," which Jesus said so often choke the word (Matt. 13:22; Mark 4:19), has become a possibility only for the stanchest soul. Most men feel that they must "lay up . . . treasures on earth," or they and their families cannot have the things other people have and all want. As a consequence, the word is choked, and Christian witness persuasive to a thing-centered and hence idolatrous generation becomes very difficult.

Here, then, is the real point at issue between science and Christian ethics within our culture. There are other points of great seriousness, as in the widespread production and advertising of alcoholic beverages and hence the encouragement given to their consumption, and in the doubtful validity of the production of implements of atomic destruction. The Christian conscience needs to be aroused and active upon these points, and because the issues are concrete, people are apt to take sides upon them. We are prone, however, to be far more lethargic at the point of our gadget-minded culture, not even recognizing that a moral issue is involved. It is here perhaps that our greatest difficulties lie, for we cannot revert to the pattern of the penniless teacher of Nazareth, and we cannot follow him in opulence without major temptations to the soul.

b) Art. A second sphere in which the claims of Christ and of culture both converge and diverge is art. This is a broad term, but we shall use it to designate the expression of the human aesthetic impulse, in both the creation of works of beauty and a love for and appreciation of beauty. Only the genius creates true art, and there are few geniuses in any generation, but many can enjoy and be lifted in spirit by their work.

There is a secondary sense in which we must speak of art also as craftsmanship, the work of a skilled artisan, to satisfy a desire for that harmonious blending of line and color and texture that makes a commercial product attractive, or gives one pride in the ability to construct something. This is related to art in the deeper aesthetic sense much as applied science is related to pure science, as based upon its principles but produced for another reason and with a different kind of creativity. Just where to draw the line between the artist and the craftsman is not easy, but it must be drawn. So, as we speak of the relations of art to Christian culture, we must again speak in two categories.

There is a natural kinship between art in the first sense and religion, yet each has its own autonomous sphere. Both come out of the inner spirit of man and speak to that spirit for release, reinforcement, and challenge. In both there are "new eyes for invisibles," [7] and the "vision of something which stands beyond, behind, and within the passing flux of immediate things." [8] Whether or not divine inspiration is claimed by the artist, in his work he surrenders to something beyond his ordinary self and produces some expression of inner meaning capable of evoking purer feelings in those to whom he communicates. "In any case, whether it be in poetry, painting or music, the work of art is the expression of something inward, passing on that inwardness to the one who enjoys it. Art, therefore, in all its branches, is expression capable of impressing." [9]

The artist need not of necessity be a religious person, or the religious person an artist. Yet so similar are the sources in the human spirit that through all ages, and not in Christianity alone, the worship of God has found natural expression in music and song, poetry and the graphic arts, the drama of sacrificial rites, and where not inhibited by convention, the

[7] The title of a book by Rufus M. Jones dealing with spiritual insight.

[8] A. N. Whitehead, *Science and the Modern World* (New York: The Macmillan Co., 1925), p. 275.

[9] Brunner, *Christianity and Civilization*, Part II, p. 73. Used by permission of Chas. Scribner's Sons.

dance. Man has always given to his deity, not only gifts laid upon the altar, but the gift of his soul in temples of great beauty and rituals of soul-stirring depth. What Christianity would have been like without its great hymns and oratorios, the poetry of the Bible, the time-transcending liturgies of the sacraments, and the distinctive beauty of Christian houses of worship is hard to contemplate.

Yet at this point two aberrations appear from opposite directions. One is the suspicion of art at some periods because of the prohibition of "graven images," and the rejection not only of painting and sculpture but of instrumental music as worldly and idolatrous. Fortunately, this has never been a dominant note in Christian practice, and is seldom encountered today. There are vestiges of it in the rejection by some of liturgies and any formal patterns of worship as inhibiting the work of the Holy Spirit, but the rejection is seldom made on the basis of the Second Commandment.

The other, very widely prevalent, aberration is the substitution of beauty for holiness. Again and again the quality of a service of worship is judged by the kind of music the choir renders, the aesthetic fitness of the minister's voice or vestments or manner, the beauty or ugliness of the sanctuary, the general decorum with which everything is done. That at all of these points there ought to be "comely praise" is indisputable, but that any or all of them is a guarantee of or a substitute for the presence of the Spirit of God must be questioned.

Ours is in general a beauty-loving age. Music appreciation is taught in the public schools; much good music and other forms of art are readily available. This is as it should be, but when it is carried so far in our culture that beauty becomes a substitute for righteousness and churches are bypassed unless they appeal to the aesthetic, this accent on beauty is not wholly gain.

A word needs to be said about art in the second sense, which like the products of applied science to which it is closely related, is a dominant note in our culture. It is well that the things we possess, from automobiles to kitchen equipment, are made for beauty as well as efficiency. No people in any age ever had so much that was good-looking as well as useful.

Yet this too has another side, for there is much that is raucous and blatant. There is a bizarre element in contemporary taste which corresponds to, and probably at bottom is derived from, the nervous, jittery temper of our times. One has only to turn on his radio or television—our best indexes of "what the people like"—to discover how much is directed to the amusing or lulling or startling of jaded nerves, as the commercials that accompany such presentations pull at our purses and entice us to buy what we do not need.

It will not do for Christians simply to inveigh against this state of affairs. Not all of it is bad, and what is bad cannot be cured simply by complaint. But until tastes as well as moral acts are subject to the spirit of Christ, we shall not make our best use of the high potentialities for beauty in the modern age.

c) *Education.* Education is so vast and many-sided an enterprise that it will obviously be impossible at this point to make more than a few observations upon it. It is fundamental to any culture, for the form a culture takes is shaped mainly by the way in which the people are molded in the educative process.

The processes of education are, of course, much broader than the specific instruction given in the public or private schools or the universities. It is a truism that the home is the first, and often the most potent, educative influence. From early childhood to senility, the play group, the work group, and many other types of informal group association are molding attitudes. What one reads, hears, sees, or otherwise experiences leaves in varying degrees its stamp upon both consciousness and conscience. Not all of this is educative in the sense of constructive growth; some of it promotes miseducation or retrogression. Yet in the broad sense in which education means the shaping of ideas and ideals, it never ends as long as any mental flexibility remains.

The institution devoted essentially to education is the school. What, then, are basic points at issue between the schools and Christian ethics?

That Christian education must be given in the churches and through church schools,[10] if the Christian heritage is adequately to be transmitted, can be taken for granted without argument. Whether under the name of church school or Sunday school, this is indispensable. In general, the quality of both curriculum and instruction is much better than in

___
[10] By church school I do not mean the parochial school. These have their place, if they do not invade the public treasury or displace public instruction.

former years. Three observations only I shall make in passing. First, that the time available on Sunday morning is totally inadequate for transmitting all that is vital to knowledge of the Bible and Christian faith. Second, that what is taught must not conflict with the accepted facts of science, or the pupil is bound to be in trouble as he senses the disparity. Third, that much more theology can and should be taught at every level as the undergirding foundation of Christianity.

This last point, in particular, requires far more attention than it has generally received. To teach the Bible as factual knowledge is better than not to teach it at all, but without attention to both its historical setting and its theological implications, its richness for Christian experience can be missed. Too frequently the attempt is made to teach Christian morality without foundations other than the ordinary assumptions of our culture. When a person does not know what he believes as a Christian or why he believes it—and this is true of many adults as well as of young people—he is likely to act on the assumptions of this secular culture and not on the principles of Christian faith.[11]

But what of religion in the public schools? Can we teach the Bible there? Or must we as in the past go on permitting an intellectual vacuum to exist at the point of the Judeo-Christian heritage which has done more than anything else to shape our culture? Shall we teach our children Homer and Vergil, Shakespeare and Milton, but not the words of Amos, Isaiah, Jesus, or Paul?

It is apparent that sectarian instruction cannot be given in the public schools, and that no proselyting activities can be permitted. Since it is not easy to draw the line between proselyting and evangelism, it may also be asserted that no teacher ought to evangelize for his faith in the classroom except through the silent witness of what he (or she) as a Christian is. But this does not necessitate the alternative of the religious and biblical vacuum.

It is commonly assumed that our Constitution guarantees the separation of Church and State, and this has been invoked repeatedly to ban all forms of religious instruction from the public schools. Yet this is not just what the Constitution says. The relevant article is the First Amend-

[11] I have developed this theme at greater length in *The Gospel and Our World* (New York and Nashville: Abingdon Press, 1949), especially in chs. 5 and 6 dealing with "The Layman and the Gospel" and "Christian Faith and Ethical Action."

ment, which reads: "Article I. Congress shall make no law respecting an establishment of religion, or prohibiting the free exercise thereof. . . ."

The Constitution prohibits the establishment of a State church and guarantees religious freedom in the exercise of one's faith. Yet it does not prohibit the tax exemption of churches, or the employment by the federal government of chaplains for the armed forces. It does not prohibit the giving of nonsectarian courses in religion for academic credit in the state universities, and this is widely and increasingly being done.[12] America is not a Godless nation. We place upon our coins "In God we trust," and by an official act of Congress the words "under God" have been placed in the salute to the American flag. Those who framed the Constitution apparently intended, rightly, to preserve freedom of religion. But that this should be interpreted as freedom *from* religion, and used as a means of sealing our culture against the imparting of religious knowledge, has no justification in fact.

What must be done is to keep insisting on the right to teach the Bible as history and as literature in the public schools until this not only is permitted but becomes as widely practiced there as in the state universities. Presumably, as in higher education, this needs to be on an elective basis to avoid infringement of religious freedom. However, the real issues lie (1) in the opportunity to teach religion at all, and (2) in the provision of persons properly qualified to teach it on a nonsectarian basis. For the present, the Supreme Court decision in the McCollum case of 1948 interposes barriers, but this need not be final.[13] In the meantime, the churches should seize every opportunity to give weekday religious instruction on released time outside the public schools.

Ought public funds to be used to aid parochial schools? Ought public money to go to a church to pay for the services of its nuns as public-school teachers? The answer is No, though this need not be pushed to the lengths of denying such services to the children in parochial schools

[12] Merrimon Cuninggim in *The College Seeks Religion* (New Haven, Conn.: Yale University Press, 1947), pp. 298-300, reports on a careful study of seventy state-supported institutions and finds that 80 per cent have departments of religion or courses in religion offered in other departments of the curriculum. More recent studies indicate an increase in this percentage.

[13] It should be noted that a corresponding decision in the Zorack case affirms the legality of released time for weekday religious instruction, provided this is not given in the school buildings.

as rides in school buses or access to school lunches. Services to children or their parents are not identical in principle with grants to churches as ecclesiastical institutions. About the former, opinions differ; the latter must not be tolerated.

To return to the public schools, a less controversial but still a focal matter is the teaching of moral and spiritual values. This obviously needs to be done, but it is no substitute for more specific instruction in the Hebrew-Christian moral and spiritual heritage. It is essential that teachers who take seriously their obligations in character building should be protected from attack from those who cannot distinguish between democracy and subversion. Charges of indoctrination are too often leveled at those who try to lift the sights of their pupils above prevailing culture patterns, and thus the mediocrity born of fear stifles creativity and progress.

There is remaining space in this chapter only for a brief look at the relations of Christian culture to higher education. Here the same opportunities for moral and spiritual building and the same dangers to academic freedom are found as are suggested in the preceding paragraph. Yet the situation as a whole differs both in the general recognition of the right of religion to a place in the curriculum and in the existence of many church-supported and independent as well as state institutions.

The first observation to be made is that the church-related colleges, of which many were founded in the early days of the frontier, can justify their existence only by being distinctively Christian. Through their departments of religion, in the selection of Christian faculty members, and by their general atmosphere they have an important contribution to make. When a church college seeking prestige or financial support simply imitates its secular neighbors, it has lost its birthright. Standards of scholarship ought not to be lowered, but scholarship is not all that makes a training ground for the leaders of the future.

Second, much can be done on campuses not church-related. As it is the total environment that educates, so it is the total personality of a faculty member, not his presentation of specialized subject matter only, that determines the degree of Christian influence he exerts. It is a hopeful sign that responsibility in these matters by faculty persons outside the departments of religion is being increasingly recognized. The Hazen and the Danforth Foundations have done much to encourage such interest, and the Faculty Christian Fellowship[14] merits warm support.

Third, the student must be kept in touch with the church during his college years. The student foundations, like the Wesley, the Westminster, and those of other denominations, are valuable links in keeping alive both church contacts and Christian service at a time when preoccupation with the multitude of other interests pressing for attention might leave the church far in the rear.

And finally, Christian theology—first, last, and always—is important. Moral standards rest on basic beliefs, and the moral standards prevalent in the culture of the future will rest in no small degree on those implicitly accepted or consciously formed during the college years. The intellectual climate of institutions of higher learning is apparently less naturalistic and humanistic than a decade or two ago, but where this mood still is found, the counterclaims of Christian faith must be persuasively though never dogmatically set forth. As both the numbers and the influence of college-trained persons within our culture increase, so does the vital need of having the right foundations laid within those years in which not only life attitudes, but vocational and family relations, are so often determined.

Here we must stop. The unknown author of the Epistle to Diognetus, writing in the second century A.D., said of the Christians of his time,

They spend their existence upon earth, but their citizenship is in heaven. They obey the established laws, but in their own lives they surpass the laws. . . . In a word, what the soul is in the body Christians are in the world. . . . The soul is enclosed in the body, and itself holds the body together; so too Christians are held fast in the world as in a prison, yet it is they who hold the world together.

So it is today. To the degree there are vital Christians in any culture that culture is strong in inner fabric and high in possibilities for human good. Christians who really follow Christ "hold the world together"!

[14] An autonomous group of teachers in many fields, affiliated with the Department of Campus Christian Life which is a part of the Commission on Christian Higher Education of the National Council of Churches. The official organ of the commission serving the interests of this fellowship is The Christian Scholar, with offices at 257 Fourth Ave., New York 10, N. Y.

Index